Male Alienation at the Crossroads of Identity, Culture and Cyberspace

M000267489

"I'm broken." When a boy or man says this, he is expressing deep alienation from himself and the world. Something's wrong, and he usually cannot begin to explain why. What brings boys and men into psychotherapy or analysis?

Many of them struggle with access to their inner worlds. Experiences of alienation can lead to destructive and self-destructive behaviors, including addiction and violence. This book explores the reasons for this and considers why boys and men seek professional help. How do psychotherapists and analysts engage them when they often protest that they want to be left alone?

Looking at the male psyche from boyhood through adolescence and into adulthood, *Male Alienation at the Crossroads of Identity, Culture and Cyberspace* provides examples from clinical practice, current events, art, and literature that show what happens when alienation is severe and leads boys and men to discharge their emotional problems in the outside world. The book examines compulsive internet use, flawed concepts of masculinity, difficulties with mutually intimate relationships, trouble showing emotions, and identity issues, as well as the role of fathers, with a focus on the types of fathers that many boys and men describe as being difficult. Tyminski provides various practical ideas about working with boys and men to encourage them to be open to their inner worlds, and emphasizes the contrast between having meaningful contacts or having a merely transactional approach to relating.

Male Alienation at the Crossroads of Identity, Culture and Cyberspace will be essential reading for Jungian analysts, psychotherapists, and psychoanalysts as well as a wide range of other professionals who work with men and boys.

Robert Tyminski is a psychologist and Jungian analyst in San Francisco, USA. Past president of the C. G. Jung Institute of San Francisco, he is a Clinical Professor in the Department of Psychiatry at the University of California, San Francisco. He is the author of *The Psychology of Theft and Loss: Stolen and Fleeced* (Routledge).

Male Alienation at the Crossroads of Identity, Culture and Cyberspace

Robert Tyminski

Routledge
Taylor & Francis Group

LONDON AND NEW YORK

First published 2019
by Routledge
2 Park Square, Milton Park, Abingdon, Oxon OX14 4RN

and by Routledge
52 Vanderbilt Avenue, New York, NY 10017

Routledge is an imprint of the Taylor & Francis Group, an informa business

© 2019 Robert Tyminski

British Library Cataloguing-in-Publication Data
A catalogue record for this book is available from the British Library

Library of Congress Cataloging-in-Publication Data
Names: Tyminski, Robert, author.
Title: Male alienation at the crossroads of identity, culture and cyberspace / Robert Tyminski.
Description: New York, NY : Routledge, 2018.
Identifiers: LCCN 2018013025 (print) | LCCN 2018026192 (ebook) | ISBN 9781315159751 (Master e-book) | ISBN 9781138065390 (hardback) | ISBN 9781138065406 (pbk.)
Subjects: LCSH: Men—Psychology. | Identity (Psychology) | Alienation (Social psychology) | Developmental psychology. | Father and child.
Classification: LCC HQ1090 (ebook) | LCC HQ1090 .T96 2018 (print) | DDC 155.3/32—dc23
LC record available at https://lccn.loc.gov/2018013025

ISBN: 978-1-138-06539-0 (hbk)
ISBN: 978-1-138-06540-6 (pbk)
ISBN: 978-1-315-15975-1 (ebk)

Typeset in Times New Roman
by Apex CoVantage, LLC

For Gady, and in memory of my father, Frank

Contents

Foreword

As awareness of how abusive men can be increases, more and more young men are growing up alienated from the concept of masculinity. Estranged from this part of themselves, they are rather easily caught up in social roles that are only increasing their sense of isolation from something vital but taboo. In the pages of this book, Robert Tyminski offers compelling clinical evidence that many of the psychological problems contemporary men exhibit have emerged, not because they have acted out, but because they have cut themselves off from their masculine potential. The toll of psychopathology becomes especially evident, Tyminski shows, when boys enter puberty and their output of testosterone increases thirty-fold. One of the cases he describes, a sixteen-year-old boy who had not yet gone into puberty and began compulsively to lock the doors and windows of his family's house against intruders, is particularly poignant. Tyminski believes that the feared intruders are the hormones that will eventually get the upper hand in this boy's embodied psyche and turn him into a man.

In this book, which is replete with telling case examples, this boy is hardly alone in finding the prospect of becoming a man so daunting as to be overwhelming. His story, however, reveals how little he and we really know about the masculine nature he fears – how much masculinity lies in shadow and emerges only in shadowy ways. The healing interventions described in this book come from a dynamic psychotherapy practice that has been both broadly informed by research and steeped in the realities of practical psychotherapy. Its author is well-qualified to deploy a vision of what it can mean to move from boy to man, to man who has not forgotten boy, that is as redemptive as it is compassionate.

Dr. Tyminski's post-Jungian conclusion, that masculinity is not the enemy but a form of soul, is convincing, not least because he in no way glosses over the dangers he has seen abound when masculine nature is driven into hiding and can only return in deformed and destructive guises. I am so appreciative that Dr. Tyminski has found a way outside of a binary conception that opposes masculine and feminine, men and women, and animus and anima, to speak up, as a Jungian analyst, for what remains distinctive about having to individuate in a masculine body. With a pluralism that reflects his debt to the pragmatic empiricism of William James, he manages to outline the varieties of early masculine experience as the background against which the contemporary alienation from becoming a man is taking place.

In showing us what the many adolescent personalities he describes are running away from, whether they are literal immigrants ashamed of their original roots, or psychological migrants seeking to eliminate traces of any transmission of identity from their fathers, or pseudonymous Internet users ironizing their budding identities through a soulless identification with the only remaining socially acceptable binary in the virtual world, that between winners and losers, Tyminski develops, like a photographic negative in the darkroom, an uncanny glimpse of the masculine soul. To read this book is to project into that potential space one's own intuitions, and I would like to share here what I believe I notice about the healthy masculine in these pages that record how often that is lost.

The healthy masculine, these days, is not hung up on being free of the feminine and so is not afraid to learn something about masculinity from mothers. This masculinity does not define itself as not gay, even when it has been stung in the locker room by that very accusation. Rather, it rejoices in its masculine ability, to define, in a positive way, its own orientation to sexuality itself. Further, it looks to fathers and father figures not to provide role models for persona attributes that others will easily regard as manly, but instead seeks the engaged participation of a father's soul to share the perennial struggle of each new man, which is to decide for himself what being a man means to him, whether father's soul turns out to be an anima that can be shared, a spirit that has not forgotten the child within, or someone who has learned to tolerate the failure to get it all together where being a man is concerned. In putting together an image of personal effectiveness, the masculine that is healthy is also willing to distinguish, as one of Tyminski's patients puts it, between psychological "creativity," which would require individual discrimination, judgment, and insight (Jung's tripartite *Logos* of masculine consciousness),[1] and the "curating" of other people's content from online sources. (These often celebrate the Dark Triad of Machiavellianism, Narcissism, and Psychopathy that Tyminski has located within contemporary research on masculinity gone wrong.)

Tyminski himself rethinks, in a Jungian way, some of the wrong turns that masculinity takes, looking for the aim in the self-destructive alienations that turn out, as he examines them, to be a rageful flight from impotent masculine conceptions in a frantic search to uncover fruitful ones. Taking his cue from the apocalyptic vision of the supreme Northern Renaissance engraver Albrecht Dürer, a man who was no stranger to millennial times like our own, when End of Days is being sounded not just for humanity, in general, but for masculine solutions to human problems, in particular, Tyminski allows apocalypse its right to become revelation. He shows us exactly how today's men are giving negative identities a chance to run their course and be replaced by a new existential resilience and fluid sense of the needs to define, to connect, and to survive that have always been important to men.

Tyminski offers us the image of masculinity as a containing power, co-equal to feminine empathy in its ability to accept both capacity and incapacity en route to being "good enough." One of his patients, a young man whom he was able to let know that he did not want him to keep cutting into himself, implying without saying so, that it was his masculine self that he was trying to puncture, referred with playful irony to his pleasure in this as "Dr. No," who had the temerity to try to prohibit him from such self-destruction. As he put it in what might be a coda to the impressive book you are about to read, his therapist was also "Dr. Know," and knowing that helped the patient find another way.

– John Beebe

Acknowledgements

When I wrote an acknowledgement for my previous book, I mentioned that writing it would not have happened without my crew. That is still very much how I feel about this book. Writing for me is like gardening or farming in that it takes considerable time, depends on things beyond my control, requires the help of others and is usually unpredictable. Many people besides myself play a role in what comes out of it: my patients, colleagues, friends, and family. I could not write convincingly without them in my life and in my mind.

First, I want to thank my patients for engaging with me in the challenging process of exploration that we call psychotherapy and analysis. The times when a patient discovers something unexpected are like gold, as Jung noted years ago. Even in moments when a treatment appears to go off track, there is much to be learned and opportunities to be found. I am grateful to my patients for letting me be a participant in what happens during this journey. I have significantly altered and disguised identifying information in the cases used in this book.

Several professional journals have been important places for lending me a voice on clinical matters. I thank the *Journal of Analytical Psychology* (for permission to use material in Chapter 2), the *International Journal of Jungian Studies* (for permission to use material in Chapter 3), and the *Journal of Child Psychotherapy* (for permission to use material in Chapter 4). In addition, *Jung Journal: Culture & Psyche* has accepted many of my articles and film and book reviews. These journals add substantially to any clinician's career because they offer through their contents a kind of friendly accompaniment in the relative solitude of practicing psychotherapy and analysis.

For the art work in this book, I thank the British Museum, the Tate Gallery, and Art Resource for permissions to use images in Chapters 6, 7, and 10. For two of the chapter epigraphs, I thank the publishers W. W. Norton for the translation of the poem "Archaic Torso of Apollo" by Rainer Maria Rilke (Chapter 3), and Farrar, Straus and Giroux and Chatto & Windus, the Random House Group, for the excerpt from Elizabeth Bishop's poem "Three Valentines" (Chapter 9).

I am pleased that both Princeton University Press and Routledge gave me permission to quote from C. G. Jung's *Collected Works*. In addition, Oxford

University Press allowed me to quote lines from a translation of Goethe's *Faust* (in Chapter 10).

The library of the University of California at San Francisco was a steadfast resource as I gathered research for this book. The librarians assisted me with locating journal articles and books, sometimes when these were quite a stretch to obtain. I admire and appreciate their tremendous commitment to research and higher learning.

Finding a place to contribute within organizations has been a mainstay of my professional development. I am proud to have a professional home in the C. G. Jung Institute of San Francisco. I have been fortunate there to find meaningful connections and friendships through a lively community, whose staff and members work hard to create something special and unique. I also want to express my gratitude to the many staff and families I came to know at Oakes Children's Center in San Francisco during my tenure as director. They taught me not always easy but often invaluable lessons about psychotherapy with troubled children and the therapeutic effects of community, about teamwork, the fluid nature of identity, and conflict.

I am thankful to John Beebe for his advice and guidance on my writing. He has never steered me wrong. Others who have encouraged my writing include: Joe Cambray, Linda Carter, Elaine Cooper, Diane Deutsch, Phil Moore, Sam Naifeh, Katherine Olivetti, David Sedgwick, Dyane Sherwood, Ellen Siegelman, Tom Singer, Charles Stewart, Til Stewart, Susan Thackrey, Dennis Turner, and Susanna Wright. They have been generous in reading drafts, some not ready for prime time, and giving me helpful ideas about how to revise and sometimes head in new directions. My copy editor for this book, LeeAnn Pickrell, has been nothing short of terrific in being a work partner who made me a better writer. I appreciate Susannah Frearson at Routledge for her openness to this project and her encouragement of it.

Many friends also read and listened to the ideas that have gone into this book. Lauren Cunningham, Gordon Murray, and Susan Williams have provided me through their kindness and friendship innumerable opportunities to blurt out ideas and see where they go. My friends Hope Selinger and Kim Hettena have read drafts of the material in this book and always offered helpful commentary. I have learned a great deal from the collaboration with my friend Mary Brady; the consultation groups we have co-facilitated have often helped to forge many of the intuitions that contributed to this book. Our group members – too many to count by now – have been a joy to listen to as we explore mysteries of the adolescent mind. The friendship of Mary's late husband, Carey Cole, whom we lost too soon, offered an ongoing conversation for exchanging ideas about men and fathers.

My friend Candia Smith has graciously given me helpful nudges with her insights into my writing. She never hesitates when I ask if she might take a look at something. That is an exceptional gift. Her husband Jon Winge has become a dear friend, although occasionally a bit wicked at pinochle.

My cousins Kathy Abruzzese and Janet Cormier frequently keep me centered with their humor, love, and reminders of why a shared past is so very important. Among many things, they have helped me to understand and appreciate the ups and downs of my own family better than I had. Barbara Wiechmann, my friend and Iyengar yoga teacher, who has instructed me for more than thirty years, has grounded me a lot, even when I've been standing on my head, literally and figuratively.

The two men whom I thank most for their love and for accepting me for who I am are my father, Frank, and my husband, Gady. Without both, this book would not have been written.

Robert Tyminski,
San Francisco

Note

1 C. G. Jung, "Mysterium coniunctionis," in H. Read, M. Fordham, and G. Adler (eds.), *The Collected Works of C. G. Jung*, Volume 14, Princeton, Princeton University Press, 1963, p. 179.

Chapter 1

The inner world and male alienation

Beware this house

> Fair youth, beneath the trees, thou canst not leave
> Thy song, nor ever can those trees be bare;
> Bold Lover, never, never canst thou kiss,
> Though winning near the goal – yet, do not grieve;
> She cannot fade, though thou hast not thy bliss,
> For ever wilt thou love, and she be fair!
>
> John Keats, "Ode on a Grecian Urn"[1]

Why begin a book about boys and men with a quote from John Keats, who died in 1821 at the age of twenty-five? This ode received, back then, mostly critical reviews for sentimentally extolling pagan times and for showing a complete lack of reason. Keats seems, in this quote, to be describing what happens when any of us becomes frozen with nostalgia, stumbling in our mourning, despite its admonition not to grieve, and finding it hard to move on with life. Through the years – over thirty now – I have listened as young men and older men alike struggle to make sense out of their inner lives. They often pine for something wondrous that appeared to get lost either during their adolescence or early adulthood. A spark seems to have vanished, and they can scarcely begin to account for its disappearance, although they often long to recapture it. Like the "fair youth" in Keats's ode, they find that they have aged and grown up – and yet are still held in place beneath some barely describable boyhood tree. If we interpret "she" in the ode as a representative of a boy's or man's inner life, then some of this dissonance, longing, and suffering becomes understandable. This inner life is there but not there, seen but not reached, promising yet disappointing, awakened though alienated.

At some point in life, every boy and man struggles in coming to terms with his inner world. Many break through to what it has to offer: emotional connection, being in touch with pain and suffering, a capacity for empathy, and a willingness to risk love and endure all its pitfalls. But many do not. They instead shut down and become hardened, alienated, and unable to describe what is going on inside them. These boys and men strike a deal, and this bargain, which they believe might protect them from feelings, drives them to live outside themselves. Some follow a heroic path, attempting to dominate their fields and perceived opponents.

Others withdraw into lonely isolation glued to various screens and devices seeking solace and relief. Yet others can only find these things through different psychoactive substances that they take to dull awareness of their situations. Much has been written about how boys and men tend to externalize their troubles onto their immediate environments in problematic ways, such as domestic violence, sexual assault, theft, addiction, terrorism, serious accidents, chronic unemployment (or underemployment), and falling behind educationally.

Keats lived 200 years ago when many of these issues also existed, but their scope was different. Certainly, there were wars, revolutions, abuse and demeaning of women and children, economic exploitation, and slavery. Yet, society had limited contemporary knowledge of what was happening, and for most, there was only sparse access to that news. Fast forward to now and the digital age. Today, we are swarmed with images and stories of boys and men who seem intent on destruction. It is nearly a cliché to dwell on how men disruptively live out their inner turmoil in the outer world and perhaps even a stereotype to claim that women are different in this regard. Still, how many mass shootings are done by women? How many girls play violent video games? How many terrorists are women? Although the answer is not exactly zero, it is close enough.

Explanations for male aggression and externalizing behaviors have proliferated. Some focus on how boys are raised and fathered.[2] Some consider so-called biological markers, everything from the shorter Y-chromosome to the effects of male hormones (androgens).[3] Cultural factors also play a role in how gender is perceived and in which expectations result from those perceptions.[4] This book cannot tackle the complexities of how boys and girls, as well as men and women, behave differently and similarly. Rather, it will take up the male side of the dilemma by looking at the extreme anxieties that introspection, self-awareness, and an internal window can evoke in boys and men. I will discuss many of the consequences that come about from an aversion to perceiving an internal life. These consequences often reveal a preference for "living outside" and are indicative of psychological problems when the inner world is felt to be full of fear, dread, and terror. Not at all hospitable as a place to exist.

Lying, cheating, and hiding

"I was 'NIFOC' when it started," John told me.[5] Not sure I heard right, I asked, "What's the problem with your knee?" He laughed and then explained, "No, it's *N, I, F, O, C*, and is just a term people use during online chats. It means 'naked in front of camera'." John had been having sex compulsively with various women online. He would meet them through Internet websites that connect people wanting to have a sexual encounter through sexting or video chatting.

John was a thirty-five-year-old straight man who had been married for five years. He had two young children. He had become addicted to Internet pornography, and his viewing habits interfered with both his job and his relationships. Initially, he would just watch pornography and masturbate. Then, he discovered websites that allowed him to connect remotely with women and have virtual sex using either chatting (just texting back and forth) or video (providing both visual and speech communication).

John thought his online activities were a problem, but when he first came to see me, he was defensive toward my questions about cheating and lying. He said, "Is it really that bad if she [his wife] doesn't know?" Later, he even took the position that "it's just another kind of 'don't ask, don't tell,' and I think it's better left unsaid." When I remarked that it sounded like hiding and that hiding over time usually has an emotional cost, he was somewhat more open to looking at what he was doing. John acknowledged that his feelings of depression and hopelessness might be associated with the "hangover" he noticed after an Internet hookup. He reported that he felt "in a haze" at these times, which I understood to be his description of a dissociated state. I commented that I wanted to hear more about this haze, and he replied that it was heavy and life-sapping. "There's absolutely no vitality left." When I asked him to visualize this, he responded, "I'm trapped in a corner with a black slick all around me."

This image of being trapped by a sticky darkness might have reflected John's depression. Additionally, I felt it represented something of the bind he was in from his addictive use of screens for fleeting pleasures – these screens eventually went dark. John was in many ways cornered by them, through his deception, his sense of emptiness afterward, and his lack of understanding about himself. Others have written about lying and its psychological purposes.[6]

Here, I introduce John as a man who was living outside himself and who feared what he might find inside. His first dream captures some of this terror at what he might encounter there.

> *I was in a jail cell awaiting arraignment. The guard won't tell me the charges. I just have to wait. I wondered in the cell, Is this even real? I went up to the bars and grabbed them. A bat fell down from the ceiling where it had been hiding. I was startled and told myself, 'Don't be scared; it's just a dream.'*

As this was John's first presenting dream, we spoke mostly about his anxiety in it.[7] He struggled to name even that feeling, which is not surprising, given that in the dream, his defenses tried to deny what was happening to him. John, like many boys and men, could not, at this beginning point in his therapeutic work, say very much about his feelings. He lacked words to describe them, preferring a dismissive attitude toward his inner world: "It's not real."

The picture of what might be inside is not at all inviting. Persecution lurks there, and it occurs within a claustrophobic space. These images in John's dream convey something of his psyche and its inner workings as being small, confining, and making him "batty." Indeed, many boys and men think that looking inside at how they feel could drive them crazy and that they would not be able to find their way out again; they'd be trapped. This belief supports an active avoidance of introspection and a fear at what will be discovered by spending too much time in the internal world. Considering such threats, we would understand John's reluctance to engage in a reflective psychotherapeutic process, because the internal space he imagines is terrifying.

Puberty

The physical changes boys experience at puberty can begin to outline some of the psychological barriers to self-reflection and curiosity about what happens inside them. This section in no way is intended to invoke a biological cause for why many boys and men learn to avoid their inner worlds. Rather, it will help clarify how they learn about change, how they make sense of it, and how they either accept it or do not. Change and growth are profoundly human processes that provide opportunities for meaning, symbolizing what is occurring, and opening the psyche for relating these experiences to others.

Puberty in English refers to the physical changes that occur when a boy or girl enters adolescence. The word comes from Latin *pubertas*, meaning age of maturity, and from Middle French *puberté*, meaning the period after childhood.[8] These changes are mediated by endocrine signals, which are transmitted by chemical compounds secreted by glandular cells that regulate distant tissues through the bloodstream. Examples of the functions of our endocrine system include temperature maintenance, glucose metabolism, and sexual development. The mean onset of puberty in boys is around age twelve.[9]

Pubertal changes are controlled by the interactions of the hypothalamus (H) and the pituitary (P) glands in the brain with the gonads (G) or sexual organs. This is often referred to the *HPG axis*. In boys, there are two phases to puberty: adrenarche and gonadarche. *Adrenarche* occurs when the adrenal gland begins to secrete more adrenal androgens, which lead to many of the secondary sexual characteristics, such as hair growth on the face, under the arms, and around the genitals. It usually precedes gonadarche by one to two years.[10] *Gonadarche* refers to the maturation of the sex organs for sexual reproduction (sperm in boys, ova in girls). Puberty in boys before age 9 is considered precocious and after age fourteen delayed.

There is about a thirtyfold increase in testosterone production in male puberty.[11] For example, blood testosterone levels can go from less than 10 nanograms per deciliter before puberty, to 300–400 nanograms per deciliter during puberty (*nanograms per deciliter*, or *ng per dL*, is a measure of how much of a substance is present in a given volume).[12] There is clearer epidemiological research that in the late 20th century puberty has been occurring earlier for girls, although this is less apparent for boys. Of note, there is little clinical evidence in the medical literature that testosterone level alone is associated with mood disturbances and behavioral problems in adolescent boys.[13]

The psychological aspects of puberty are complex. Under good-enough circumstances, we would hope for some combination of education, encouragement, and parental affection to guide boys and girls through this process of physical growth. Education is necessary to help a boy comprehend and explain what he is going through.[14] Mystification and strange imaginings occur when there is a lack of simple information. Encouragement is important for setting a time horizon that shows the process of adolescent growth as an emerging one that has some kind of endpoint. Encouragement also frames a message of making it through something challenging and moving forward with life. Adolescents depend on older adults in their families, schools, sports teams, and clubs to shape a positive attitude about growth to counter their anxieties about getting through this period of life.

Parental affection may seem so much a given aspect of what is needed that a reader may ask: Why do I even mention it? Too frequently, one or both parental figures move away emotionally when their son goes into puberty. Often, this withdrawal dates to a troubled adolescence in the parent, and it forms a generational repetition of something painful that has not been resolved. When asked about their own teenage years, many parents will tell stories of rejection, isolation, and embarrassing awkwardness. These stories retain emotional valence and unconsciously contribute to what can happen when a parent backs away from physical warmth toward a teenaged son. A somewhat newer version of rationalizing this stance emerges when parents "outsource" many of their parenting tasks to schools, nannies, and other extended family members. A boy can, nonetheless, be left questioning why this is so. He then creates a negative fantasy explanation that it is because of who he is and how he is growing up. This not only places an unfortunate burden on him but also reflects an abdication of necessary parental involvement in his life.

Even when education, encouragement, and parental affection are present, boys will still fantasize about the changes of puberty. These usually are particular fantasies that they do not themselves link to their growth, but rather are conscious attempts at expressing unconscious anxieties. For example, one sixteen-year-old boy I met had not yet gone into puberty. I asked him about this, and he replied that his family were "late bloomers." He had come to me because of insomnia and some evident obsessive-compulsive symptoms of checking things in the house (alarms, stove burners, doors and windows, and fuse boxes). His parents were concerned that he could not tell them why he did these behaviors and that he denied any awareness of anxiety related to them.

For this boy, his psychological state of mind was framed by a comparison with his peers, virtually all of whom had gone through puberty. When I noted to him that his checking behaviors were all located in his house, he confided to me that he was worried about one thing: that a burglar would break in and injure him and his family. He wanted to be sure that the alarm system was functional, that the doors and windows were locked when they left or went to sleep, that no one had gotten in and was hiding, having already disabled the electricity. In detail, he showed me through drawings all the different ways a burglar could gain entry to his house. What was I to make of the intensity of his emotional reaction around this specific fear?

His story is about a home invasion, someone nefarious getting inside and disrupting what has been a safe space for him. I felt that he was describing his fears, both about his delayed puberty and about what would finally happen when the intruders (hormones) finally gained the upper hand. He worried for his safety. He felt that he might no longer be secure when the change at last took place and that it − his eventual puberty − would also somehow endanger his family. This unconscious belief of puberty as a violent disruption is not uncommon in boys. It also reveals how a relatively secure space on the inside can suddenly turn into something that feels dangerous, even hostile. Might this be a potential motivation for some boys to turn away from their inner life to focus, instead, on what's outside?

Another 13-year-old boy who had just entered puberty told me that he was certain a ghost was haunting his house. I asked him how long the ghost had been there, and he answered six months. His parents had told me in our initial meeting when I took a developmental history that their son had started puberty six months prior. Interestingly, when I asked this boy to describe what he knew of this ghost, he said it was "definitely a woman" and "she had been murdered." Reflecting on his ideas about the ghost, I thought the timing of the physical changes in his body seemed associated to a feminine presence with a violent aspect about her that he did not like. If we view his "house" as a statement about his insides, he was telling me that this space had become dangerous and made him want to flee. He repeatedly asked his parents whether their family could move to a new place.

Other pubertal boys have described various phobias that seem to represent the evolution of a safe space into a threatening one. A twelve-year-old boy told his parents that he no longer wanted to participate in outdoor sports because he was suddenly afraid of dogs (cynophobia). When I inquired what he thought a dog might do to him, he replied that it would bite him. While I sympathized that this would surely hurt, he added that it was not just the bite, but rather that he might contract rabies. "I'd be crazy, foaming at the mouth, and raging." His conscious fear in this case again seemed connected to an unconscious fear of a violent change inside him that would cause him to lose control. Puberty can feel like a loss of control. The child's body no longer follows the comparatively innocent rhythms of boyhood, and it now forces upon him urges and changes that he might feel ill equipped to handle. His sexuality can feel too evident − too "out there" − and not as easily hidden as he would wish. This anxiety about a loss of control is reminiscent, too, of the various Wolf Man and werewolf tales, in which the appearance of a full moon − a feminine symbol − transforms the sweet teenager or young man into a violent monster.[15] In Chapter 4, readers will meet Anthony, whose puberty experience was so turbulent that he began cutting himself at that age.

The themes in these stories are of rapid changes, an increase in anxiety approaching panic, and a destabilizing of the boy's psyche. There is a definite shift from a known safety to a perceived threat of imminent danger. Often, this psychological threat is displaced outside and seen as coming in, and it seems to turn what is inside into, at a minimum, an unwelcome place and, more likely, a location of further persecution and loss of control possibly leading – in unconscious fantasy – to violence and explosive sexuality.

Psychological change

What makes psychological change, often accompanying distinct changes in boys' and men's bodies, so electric, amplified, and potentially disturbing? How do we square the more troubling reactions with the tendency for resilience? Psychoanalysts and psychologists have long thought about these essential human questions because they pertain to our existence as transient, limited, and temporal. We confront mortality, illness, death, ageing, and numerous losses as we each pass through our lives. At times, we might rebound strongly from one of these developmental inevitabilities, whereas at others, we might collapse into depression and lose sight of a way forward. Our attitudes about change are shaped by how our families dealt with adversity and by what we internalized from these incidents.

Jung's writing about death and rebirth cycles in human psychology, and his ideas about psychological transformation within analysis, give some understanding of the difficulties faced in trying to change and have some consciousness about it.[16] Jung describes how incest fantasies, as well as myths and folktales about incest, are often a figurative depiction of a return to the mother in order for a renewal to occur. In other words, a symbolic approach to this theme means understanding change as a reorientation of the personality and separation into an as-yet-unknown way of being. This is almost exactly what happens in puberty and also throughout adolescence and into early adulthood, when a boy or young man feels a regressive pull back to the safety of what he has known throughout boyhood, namely a stable house – identity, self-configuration – that had defined roles, norms, and expectations. During this supposedly halcyon time of life, the psyche appeared unclouded and undisturbed by sexuality, unpredictable growth, and the demands of being an independent adult. Rebirth or renewal occurs when a boy changes and accepts the "intruders" into his house, not as hostile, but as necessary guests and resources for physical and emotional development.

Jung's ideas about transformation are also useful in appreciating some of the reluctance that many boys and men express about going inside themselves. Such an internal process can feel uncomfortably close, indeed even incestuous, because it brings to awareness another world of feelings and relationships that are challenging, unsettling, and explosive. Precisely because of these difficulties, some containment is required, both internally and externally. This containment optimally comes from an interactive and reciprocal exchange between a boy's psyche and his environment so that enough experiences of being met psychologically build up over time, making the internal world seem safe and not so foreign and scary. To use the previous metaphor, this happens when a boy or young man can enter his own house, look around, and spend time there rather than quickly exiting to be outside again. Many cases in this book will show examples of when this happens; other cases illustrate what happens when a boy or man gets stuck outside and the risks that ensue from this alienation.

External containment often involves something Jungians refer to as an *initiation process*. I find this term quite helpful in thinking about change because it emphasizes the psychological dimensions of arriving at a distinct point in time when things in our life will become different moving ahead. We look back and see who we have been. There is a familiar sense, a kind of knowledge about the house as it has been constructed and run by its inhabitants who represent the different parts of ourselves as we have known them. When something initiatory occurs in life, like puberty or the launch into early adulthood, a point is reached when the house will be remodeled. We look forward, not knowing what will come next, how we will change, and whether we will be able to adapt. This is the essence of an initiation.

The Jungian analyst Joseph Henderson describes the psychological passage of initiation in his book *Thresholds of Initiation*.[17] He relates how many myths and folktales depict a seven-step process of initiation that encompasses a form of separation and submission to start off, when one crosses a threshold. This is the moment in time just described, when we know something is about to change and we will never be the same as before. Then, ordeals or trials of strength follow that test whether we can make it through to the end. During these steps, there must be some kind of containment. Imagine what happens nowadays to adolescents who are left unsupported in this phase of development. They often create their own unconsciously organized initiation process, which can be observed in gangs, fraternity hazing rituals, vandalism, and in many aspects of cutting, body piercing, and extensive tattooing.

When there is adequate containment for initiation, the process proceeds to an eventual liberation, which is not to be taken as an exalted position or inflated ending. Rather, this process concludes with a psychological appreciation for change and what is now different about the self. Further, it usually includes some aspect of being part of a community, although in a different way that expresses a changed identity. The end does not mean liberation as freedom to do as one likes. It means letting go of the weight of the ordeals and also letting go of the old, unrenovated version of the house from before the remodeling.

When successful containment becomes internalized, then we feel safer being introspective and trusting what we find. This is not nearly as easy as it sounds. We live in a manic culture that prefers external feats and accomplishments over the solitude of self-reflection. At the cultural level, looking inside is continually devalued. The psychological nuts and bolts of internal containment are something that Wilfred Bion writes about when he articulates the idea of container-contained.[18] He borrowed this concept from Jung's 1925 essay on "Marriage as a Psychological Relationship."[19] For Bion, the notion of container-contained arises out of developmental experiences in which an infant or child feels a receiving mind (container) to accept his projections (contained). Through good-enough parenting, we incorporate and internalize these repeated experiences. Staying with the metaphor, the house might become rowdy when unexpected elements rise from the basement, but we don't run out because there are resources upstairs to handle this situation. When boys and men cannot eventually rely on their inner container, they dash outside, preferring to enact a failure of psychological containment. Bion also describes episodes when the container bursts as representative of a catastrophic change.[20]

Apocalypse

What happens when the inner world of boys and men is thoroughly disregarded and devalued and, subsequently, they choose to live externally-oriented lives and seek out crime, mayhem, and destruction? Clearly, not all boys and men who struggle with their internal psychology do such things. Still, most murders, wars, acts of domestic violence, terrorism, and suicides are done by boys and men. *The Economist*, in an article titled "Men Adrift," notes that 93% of prisoners in the United States are male; 79% of murder victims worldwide are male; and 66% of suicides worldwide are male.[21] What circumstances might lead some boys and men to identify with these malevolent tendencies, resulting in violent behaviors gratifying their destructive and self-destructive impulses?

The word *apocalypse* is frequently used to describe some of the effects of male violence, for instance, in mass shootings, terrorist attacks, and gang violence. The word comes to us from ancient Greek. The word *calypsis* (καλυψις) means "to conceal." The nymph Calypso appears in the *Odyssey* to seduce Odysseus and detain him from his homeward journey, in this way concealing from him awareness of his goal.[22] *Apocalypsis* (αποκάλυψις) means something quite different in its original sense, namely, uncovering or unveiling. It referred to the revealing of knowledge. In the Book of Revelation in the New Testament, however, John describes the ultimate fight between good and evil, and it is this meaning of apocalypse that is now more commonly associated with an end-of-time scenario.[23] Although even here, apocalypse referred to the last judgment that was to be revealed, or unveiled.

The etymology of apocalypse with its dual meanings captures an inner-outer dichotomy that can apply to the male psyche when trying to understand how outside becomes preferred to inside and what follows when this occurs. Apocalypse is an extreme state of alienation, with everything falling apart into destructive chaos. This alienation can be linked to a breakdown in revealing what is inside the psyche and in accepting self-knowledge. Turning away from the complexities of what goes on inside their minds, a particular group of psychologically vulnerable boys and men may live out a form of violence as a solution to their alienation. Of course, not all alienated boys and men will do this, but those who lack the presence of older men and fathers to identify with, those who have themselves been victimized by men, those who are culturally dislocated, those who give in to various kinds of addiction, and those who fall behind economically, socially, and educationally – all may be at greater risk for behaving destructively and coming under the grip of apocalypse as an omnipotent expression of doom.

Although there will be more to say about this apocalyptic theme in later chapters, the idea that boys and young men are now especially at risk is not new. The Organisation for Economic Co-operation and Development (OECD) published results of an alarming study showing that fifteen-year-old boys are more likely than girls to fail a baseline level of proficiency in reading, math, and science.[24] This report looks at results from boys in developed countries such as the U.S., UK, Canada, Mexico, and many others (thirty-four OECD countries and thirty partner countries), using its Programme for International Student Assessment (PISA) data. Young men and boys are less likely to be engaged with school and more likely to endorse the idea that school is a waste of time. They spend more time video gaming and less time reading than girls and young women. This change has largely occurred within the last 10 years, and more women now obtain a college degree than men. Across the thirty-four OECD countries (like the U.S., UK, those in Europe, and so on), only 25% of boys have never played video games, whereas half of girls have not. This report documents that boys also spend more time surfing the Internet than girls do, and it cites research that video games tend to undermine cognitive abilities of focus and attention. In sum, this report presents a frightening picture of boys and young men in trouble educationally and falling behind in achievement because the Internet and video games on their computer devices consume too much of their time and cognitive capacity. *The Economist*, in discussing male unemployment in the twenty-one to thirty age group, notes research that over the past decade, unemployed young men have doubled the amount of time they spend video gaming to nearly seven hours per week, which may be a significant factor in male under-participation in the labor market.[25]

Another report, "ISIS in America," also provides information about young men specifically being drawn into sympathizing with terrorism.[26] The average age of these men is twenty-six (86% of the group studied are male). More than 250 individuals from the United States have either traveled or tried to travel to Syria to join ISIS.[27] This study attempts to answer why there has been a "surge in American Jihadi recruits," especially during 2015. One important factor is *hijrah* or leaving a non-Muslim society to be in a Muslim one. Another is the idealism of being part of a utopian group: "A search for belonging, meaning, and/or identity appears to be a crucial motivator for many Americans (and other Westerners) who embrace ISIS's ideology."[28] We can speculate that a state of alienation precedes this search and that psychological confusion, even disorientation, plays a role in this process.

Recruitment often begins on social media, which enables steps toward identification and commitment that eventually become tyrannical, overpowering vulnerable psyches much like the most effective propaganda. This report on ISIS notes that social media is primed for this effect because it is instantaneous, uses dramatic imagery (particularly black flags, lions, and green birds), offers no barrier to joining, and creates an echo chamber to reinforce ideological participation. The Internet is called "the turbocharger of the jihadi movement";[29] Twitter is described as the best social media platform for ISIS sympathizers. The FBI estimates there are approximately 900 active investigations into ISIS sympathizers in the U.S.[30]

Importantly, the "ISIS in America" report concludes that "most of the participants in this counter-culture will never make the leap from talk to action."[31] This acknowledges what Erik Erikson would term either *identity confusion* or *identity crisis*, when a young person seeks out a group to join in a fantasy that membership and a feeling of belonging will solve his internal problem.[32] Although we may be reassured that the majority will not act out the violence that membership in such a group requires, we still must be concerned about those who will. This latter group reveals a particularly serious alienation that likely shows preexisting psychological vulnerability, over-reliance on rigid and externalizing defenses such as denial and projection, an unrooted sense of identity, and a preference for concrete thinking – and a profound longing to fit in somewhere.

Substance abuse is another area in which boys and men externalize their problems and generally surpass girls and women with their observably disruptive behaviors. There are some exceptions – for example, opiate use among those older than the age of sixty-five – in which women are admitted for treatment more frequently than men.[33] Aside from this statistic, males are twice as likely to be admitted for substance abuse treatment as females, more likely to report marijuana and alcohol use, and men aged eighteen and older have twice the rate of substance dependence as women.[34] One gender variation in adolescence is that teenaged girls younger than eighteen use alcohol more often as their primary substance of abuse, whereas teenaged boys younger than eighteen report marijuana more frequently as their primary substance of abuse. This difference disappears by the mid-twenties. The National Institute on Drug Abuse (NIDA) reports, "Men are more likely than women to use almost all types of illicit drugs (SAMHSA, 2014), and illicit drug use is more likely to result in emergency department visits or overdose deaths for men than for women."[35]

Several of the cases discussed in this book involve substance abuse. Abusing drugs and alcohol is an effective way to dissociate and block awareness of one's inner world. Most psychoactive drugs (alcohol, marijuana, stimulants, sedatives, prescription pain medications, and other opiates like heroin) cause distinct cognitive impairments to perception, memory, language, and reasoning. Without these capacities, a mind is catapulted into an altered state, in essence, a state of alienation. Additionally, emotions are usually not experienced consciously or intelligibly when someone is intoxicated, high, or under the influence of drugs. These substances are frequently taken in attempts to dampen self-awareness, a so-called form of self-medication. For instance, one young man told me of his marijuana abuse: "It chills me out. I don't have any feelings except being chill." Another described his methamphetamine abuse this way: "I'm all sensation, no thoughts, and no feelings." They are describing ways to distance from and negate their own psychic experiences. In particular, opiate abuse has risen to the level of a social epidemic, as described by Sam Quinones in his book *Dreamland*.[36] There, he documents how a large pharmaceutical company exploited those who were vulnerable due to their own states of alienation secondary to social and economic upheavals.

The Internet as a dark blob

Another place where addictive tendencies show up is with the Internet and all things related to cyberspace. Nicholas Carr writes about how the Internet is changing how we read, understand, and perceive information.[37] He believes that our capacity for deep reading – sinking into a text and making meaning of it – is being eroded, and he shows research documenting what happens when we read webpages. We eventually resort to reading in a pattern like the letter F, more at the top, then a bit less, and finally skimming quickly to the bottom. This is indicative of superficial learning, and further studies illustrate that we are more confused, have less recall, and retain fewer images online.[38] Repetition of this pattern has neurobiological effects too, along the lines of Hebb's axiom, which states "neurons that fire together, wire together." Heavy and compulsive Internet use could, therefore, affect the biological foundations of how we use our cognition. Reflection, introspective thinking, and contemplation all decrease in this story of a tool (the Internet) becoming the master. This point reinforces the challenges that many boys and men, idling away hours online, might encounter in trying to rest inside their own minds with some degree of awareness.

Analysts and analytic psychotherapists have noticed this change in their practices and are trying to catch up because the acceleration of what happens in cyberspace, and the consequences for how it is used or misused, have outpaced their understanding of its emotional and relational effects. Alessandra Lemma and Luigi Caparrotta have edited a collection of essays and articles devoted to this subject.[39] The contributors look at attachment, affect regulation, desire, internal representations, and symbolization. They mostly express concern for what they describe seeing in their practices, and most of them have struggled to locate something positive in the march into cyberspace. Many repeat an admonition that for anyone who is already psychologically vulnerable, the Internet can become a hornet's nest of pain and trouble.

Paolo Migone, an Italian psychiatrist, explores the idea of adapting to the arrival of the Internet in our clinical practices.[40] He mentions that analysis on the telephone was happening much earlier than analysts were willing to acknowledge, and he reminds readers of Freud's letters with Fliess as another way of communicating analytically across distance. For him, the key question remains whether the transference is analyzed, or does cyberspace become a defensive barrier to that? He seems more accepting of the Internet's various effects on us as clinicians and concludes, "Virtual reality and real reality . . . are not superior one to the other, but simply two different kinds of experience."[41] I feel he is on to something we all might consider. I often find when a boy talks about video gaming that there can be a dream-like aspect to what he is describing. These tales are full of symbols (often of the hero-villain pair) and relationships (frequently about competition, domination, envy, and loss). The place of technology, the Internet, cyberspace, and video gaming will be topics that recur throughout this book in an effort to understand their impacts on analysis and on analysts working with boys and men. While remaining open to possible ways of appreciating these technological changes, I'll also address to what extent they define social and cultural alienation as a widespread phenomenon.

Addictive behaviors around the Internet can suppress the development of identity when cyberspace is used to satisfy emotional cravings. Luke was a thirty-five-year-old gay man when he came to me for help. He told me he had a history of panic attacks that interfered with his work in public relations. He often had to meet the press, and on occasion, he became so ill with sweating, nausea, and flushing, that he had to break off a meeting and leave. This symptom had gone on for many years, and he had tried other forms of therapy, but with little improvement. Luke and I would work together for seven years trying to sort through his panic and terror, which seemed linked to feeling a complete loss of identity.

Luke reported that throughout his childhood and adolescence his mother was always depressed. She seemed to be unreachable, lost in another world. He described his father as also distant in many ways. He showed little interest emotionally in his younger son (Luke had an older brother whom he felt his father favored). His father was busy professionally, traveled for his career, and was often away from the family home. Luke described an environment of emotional deprivation. He also abused cocaine and had done so over many years. When I asked him to describe how this abuse affected him, he told me he kept it secret from everyone. He would plan time off from work and rent a hotel room in another city. Using what is sometimes termed "the dark web," he would contact a dealer. He then spent his time in the hotel room getting high and watching pornography online. So he could return to work and appear not fully out of sorts, he allowed for a recovery day.

About five months into our work, he came rushing into a session. He sat down, breathing heavily. Waiting for him to speak, I remained quiet. He said he was feeling anxious because he had just come off "another episode" (of using cocaine). I listened as he jumped from topic to topic. During a pause, I commented that to me he felt desperate, like a lost boy. He nodded and then began to blush. He started to panic, stood up, and asked if he could go get some water. When he returned, I asked if he could tell me what he had been feeling before the panic set in. He said he was embarrassed to tell me, although he did. He had an image of me holding him as a boy and trying to comfort him. I asked how he felt telling me that, and he said "ashamed." I replied that maybe the boy is in pain and afraid no one will notice that he got lost in another city, losing himself with drugs and then online with pornography. Luke calmed down; tears welled up in his eyes.

A few sessions later, Luke told me his first dream. *I saw a dark blob come toward my house. I was afraid. It started to engulf the house. It was going to cover all of it.* He associated to *The Blob*, a film from the 1950s. He said the dream still made him anxious. I asked what he saw now when he looked at the blob. He was surprised and then replied that it felt like he "was losing my identity." As we discussed what that meant, Luke had many ideas, chief among which were his cocaine abuse and his pornography viewing. These were promising areas for him to look at in a more meaningful way, not simply as "bad habits." He was beginning to make some meaning out of his inner world, where he felt this terror of darkness overwhelming him. At the time, I wondered about his mother's depression as well as his father's emotional distance, which could have felt like a dark abyss to a young Luke. I considered the transference aspect of his dream, too. Was I potentially like a blob that would surround him? Or, conversely, were his needs going to be so thick and overwhelming that I'd not be able to contain them? As we were barely a half-year into his work, I was not yet sure of these ideas and kept them to myself. The dark blob also seemed a reference to the dark web, and how he sometimes used the Internet in self-destructive ways.

I did feel that Luke was telling me – even warning me – that going inside his house could be terrifying. That piece resonated from his dream, and I asked him to comment on his experience of me, especially as I had said I could see the lost boy in him. He seemed to appreciate this invitation and remarked that it helped him to know "there's a lot more inside me; I just wish I could do it faster and on my own." This response seemed both an acknowledgement of his need for me and his defense against that, a manic statement about speed (perhaps echoing his cocaine abuse) and isolation.

Anima

Jung had an idea about what a man might find in his house if he looked long enough – a woman. He viewed this woman as a feminine aspect of the male psyche. He described it as an unconscious archetype and believed it necessary to integrate a relationship with her in order to individuate and grow psychologically. He used a Latin term to describe this female aspect of the male psyche, as he so often did, calling her *anima*. In Latin, this word means "soul" – also "breath," "life," and "air." Aside from lending a seeming gender rigidity to this concept, Jung also left his followers with a terminology that others might not easily appreciate nor understand. For instance, Jung did not mean to imply "soul" in a theological or traditionally religious sense; he believed a man had to find his way into relating psychologically with that part of himself, and in some ways, this concept does provide an orientation as to why a boy or a man might prefer keeping it locked or hidden in an unused basement room of his house.

I will review some general notions about what Jung conceived the anima to represent. He notes that this concept appears in antiquity as a goddess and in later times, when the church was ascendant, as the queen of heaven; although in both these examples, he is referring to archetypal images coming from the unconscious. Here is where Jung writes about why the anima matters:

> After the middle of life, however, permanent loss of the anima means a diminution of vitality, of flexibility, and of human kindness. The result, as a rule, is premature rigidity, crustiness, stereotypy, fanatical one-sidedness, obstinacy, pedantry, or else resignation, weariness, sloppiness, irresponsibility, and finally a childish ramollissement with a tendency to alcohol.[42]

We have from this extended – and disparaging – description an image of older men who become cranky, irritable, dogmatic, and judgmental. This caricature also suggests how men may materialistically deal with their midlife crises, for example, by having an affair, taking up an extreme sport, or buying a flashy car. It is as if their internal world is sterile and barren, and they become desperate for an external compensation to defend against being aware of this state of mature alienation.

Jung sees the anima as a factor in how a man relates to others. Is he dry and only factual? Does he bring some liveliness to his interactions? Can he tolerate expression of his own feelings? He says that the anima "intensifies, exaggerates, falsifies, and mythologizes all emotional relations."[43] Her role in a man's house then is to enliven the atmosphere, to help bring others in, and to mediate a man's own needs and how these are voiced. It is in this sense a useful idea for understanding how boys and men may resist awareness of their internal states when and if these appear feminine, since they could then threaten a more traditionally role-bound definition of masculinity.

I wonder, however, whether applying this idea nowadays might be outdated. Is it still useful, since we now have a post-modern understanding of gender fluidity that is less binary? It is a difficult concept to explain to our psychoanalytic colleagues who may find this kind of personification of something internal as too static and conceptual. I would like to hold open this question about the contemporary applicability of Jung's anima concept and revisit it later in this book. There are specific qualities that Jung assigns to this feminine aspect of the male psyche that I find many boys and men struggle with.

Jung explains that anima is somewhat like a butterfly, "which reels drunkenly from flower to flower and lives on honey and love."[44] This image is striking for what many boys and men might find themselves openly disavowing: flowers, sweetness, and affection. Perhaps, there is something about these tender aspects of relating that call for a psychological openness implying vulnerability, which might feel too risky for some. Jung adds that the anima can potentially ensnare a man (think about infidelity, cheating, stealing), or alternatively, it can "entangle" a man, which could be a positive aspect of asserting a need for relationship.[45] In this regard, a feminine aspect of male psyche could be a useful consideration for understanding the importance for any boy or man of being in complex relationships, of taking risks for emotional entanglements, and of attaching to others. Moving forward, we might then consider how boys and men react when they become aware of internal states that seem feminine and long for these sorts of contacts – sweet, affectionate, and entangled. The psychological implications of this might parallel Keats's poetic imagination of a woman who "cannot fade," quoted at the opening of this chapter.

Overview

This book is organized into three parts. The first section (Chapters 2–5) will discuss circumstances that lead to and reinforce alienation from internal states.

I will keep returning to ways that technology and the Internet or cyberspace affect this discussion. Chapter 2 highlights the ways in which cyberspace is being used to negate relationships, and the risks surrounding magical thinking and omnipotent fantasies.[46] Chapter 3 focuses on issues of sexuality and gender identity, with attention to confusion about masculine ideals and stereotypes that seem rooted in a binary rigidity about gender.[47] In Chapter 4, I delve into what happens when there are serious issues arising from a lack of an emotional vocabulary, leading to a situation in which communication of feelings is suppressed, delayed, and garbled.[48] Chapter 5 looks at identity from the angle of race, ethnicity, language, and immigration. Many of the examples throughout this book will be reflective of my clinical practice over 30 years and, therefore, represent my experiences that have mostly been with individuals from ethnic minority backgrounds and/or with recent immigration histories. In this chapter, I also explore negative identities that present as outcasts, rebels, loners, and slackers.

The middle section of this book, Chapters 6 and 7, looks more deeply at external behaviors that can show up when some boys and men turn away from what is inside them and direct their considerable energies into their environments. Using the archetypal imagery of apocalypse, I explore destructive and self-destructive themes in the male psyche. Chapter 6 emphasizes the ways violence shows up online, for example, in violent video games, as well as in real acts of gun violence. It has become a platitude for many to assert that there is no causal link between these two; yet, it is apparently rare for a young mass shooter not to have played some kind of violent video game. The alienation behind such acts is frequently fueled by contempt, a problematic emotion to address therapeutically. What happens when a boy or man is alienated and has contempt for his inner world? Often violent fantasies of control, conquest, and destruction take hold and fester. Chapter 7 examines a different challenge in acting out: the pursuit of thrills and the accidents that often follow them. Seeking thrills is frequently an attempt at avoiding awareness of inner emptiness, and these thrills can be sought through drugs, sex, and self-harming behaviors, including recklessness with cars and physical activities.

The third section of the book, Chapters 8–10, will address the question, what happens when such boys and men who are avoidant of their internal world show up in our practices? Chapter 8 looks at the developmental side of this question, examining fathers and their roles in their sons' development. The history of every boy and man includes a father, whether present or not. I will discuss the fallout from fathers who are distant, as well as outright paternal abandonment, role rigidity, and punitive expectations. Chapter 9 explores both sides of the therapeutic encounter, examining effective strategies and difficult obstacles. How do we handle a countertransference challenge when our interest in our patient is actively repelled and devalued? And how do we as analysts and psychotherapists find a way in? Think again about the house metaphor: We want our patients to appreciate what the interior holds, and so we must search for ways in, while exploring our patients' attitudes about safety, openness, and expression of feelings. We can't barge in, although we may have to communicate that a sealed house is little different from a mausoleum.

Chapter 10 reviews the main themes of this book around alienation, looking at what can be found inside boys or men that can help them to heal, and discussing conclusions, however tentative, about this group of men and boys and our clinical engagement with them. My hope is to offer some answers to the many questions I pose in this book. I will circle back to some of the main tests we now face as analysts and psychotherapists, such as dealing with technology, cyberspace, and the psychological influences of cultural differences.

I will discuss psychological issues and clinical phenomena, and by extension, this book pertains to *a subset* of boys and men who are in distress. My methodology in this book is based primarily on the use of case examples. There is a long history of using case examples to illustrate clinical processes that often show common yet distinct factors. Use of this method implies that I attend to the limits of my conclusions, and I will try not to generalize widely from my observations. There is almost never a single independent variable that shows causality or determines what happens in a clinical encounter. Nonetheless, case examples can be rich explorations of commonly experienced situations that provide significant understanding of key elements. They are how clinicians learn.

I will also use examples from literature and contemporary media to amplify aspects of what certain case examples may suggest. These additions are to show further linkages with the psychological hypotheses emerging from the individual cases, not at a level of causation, but in a more explanatory and deepening sense. Finally, when available, I will include descriptive statistics from population studies, so readers can see problematic aspects of behaviors and trends that appear both clinically and socially. With these diverse sources of information, I will attempt to sketch out in greater detail the "house problem" that certain boys and men bring to us when they feel alienated and are looking for help.

Notes

1 J. Keats, "Ode on a Grecian urn," in *Complete Poems and Selected Letters of John Keats*, New York, The Modern Library, 2001, p. 239.
2 D. Kindlon and M. Thompson, *Raising Cain: Protecting the Emotional Life of Boys*, New York, Ballantine Books, 1999.
3 L. Brizendine, *The Male Brain: A Breakthrough Understanding of How Men and Boys Think*, New York, Three Rivers Press, 2010.
4 M. McGoldrick and K. V. Hardy, *Re-visioning Family Therapy: Race, Culture, and Gender in Clinical Practice*, New York, The Guilford Press, 2008; and C. Gilligan, *In a Different Voice: Psychological Theory and Women's Development*, Cambridge, MA, Harvard University Press, 1993/2016.
5 All case examples are substantially disguised. Identifying data have been either removed or altered.
6 A. Lemma, "The many faces of lying," *The International Journal of Psychoanalysis*, 2005, vol. 86, pp. 737–53, doi:10.1516/KN9J-2AU5-TB95-FRLH.

7   R. J. Maduro, "The initial dream and analysability in beginning analysis," *Journal of Analytical Psychology*, 1987, vol. 32, pp. 199–226, doi:10.1111/j.1465-5922.1987.00199.x.
8   As noted in the *Oxford English Dictionary*.
9   M. A. Sperling, *Pediatric Endocrinology, Fourth Edition*, Philadelphia, Elsevier Saunders, 2014, p. 701.
10 Ibid.
11 S. A. Duke, B. W. R. Balzer, and K. S. Steinbeck, "Testosterone and its effects on human male adolescent mood and behavior: A systematic review," *Journal of Adolescent Health*, 2014, vol. 55, pp. 315–22. Quote from p. 315.
12 Mayo Clinic Laboratories. Online, available: <www.mayomedicallaboratories.com> (accessed November 12, 2016).
13 Duke et al., "Testosterone and its effects on human male adolescent mood and behavior," p. 321.
14 Moving forward, I will refer to boys and men because they are the subject of this book; however, many of these comments about growth, adaptation to bodily changes, and need for understanding apply equally to boys and girls.
15 See, for example, Freud's 1918 case of the Wolf Man, about a young man who had many problems subsequent to a gonorrhea infection when he was 18 years old. Also of interest is the medical condition of *congenital porphyria*, the symptoms of which many believe associated with werewolf beliefs and the werewolf in folklore and popular fiction. See S. Freud, "Notes upon a case of obsessional neurosis," in P. Rieff (ed.), *Three Case Histories*, New York, Collier Books, 1909/1963. Also see "Porphyria," Medicalbag.com, April 3, 2013. Online, available: <www.medicalbag.com/profile-in-rare-diseases/porphyria/article/472320/>.
16 C. G. Jung, "Symbols of transformation," in H. Read, M. Fordham, and G. Adler (eds.), *The Collected Works of C. G. Jung*, Volume 5, Princeton, Princeton University Press, 1956; and "The Psychology of the transference," in *The Practice of Psychotherapy*, in H. Read, M. Fordham, and G. Adler (eds.), *CW* 16, Princeton, Princeton University Press, 1954/1966. Hereafter references to Jung's *Collected Works* will be cited as CW, Volume Number, date of publication (on first mention), paragraph number (¶), and page number (p.).
17 J. Henderson, *Thresholds of Initiation*, Wilmette, IL, Chiron, 1967/2005.
18 W. R. Bion, *Learning from Experience*, Lanham, Jason Aronson, 1962.
19 C. G. Jung, "Marriage as a psychological relationship," *CW* 17, 1925.
20 W. R. Bion, "Catastrophic change," *Bulletin of the British Psychoanalytic Society*, 1966, vol. 5. See also Chapter 12, in *Attention and Interpretation*, Northvale NJ, Jason Aronson, 1970/1995. pp. 106–24.
21 "Men adrift," *The Economist*, May 30, 2015, pp. 21–6.
22 T. Gantz, *Early Greek Myth: A Guide to Literary and Artistic Sources*, Volume 2, Baltimore, John Hopkins University Press, 1993.
23 The Bible, King James Version, hereafter referenced as KJV.
24 OECD, "The ABC of gender equality in education, aptitude, behaviour, confidence," OECD Publishing, 2015. Online, available: <http://dx.doi.org/10.1787/9789264229945-en>.
25 "Feel the force flow," *The Economist*, October 15, 2016, p. 70.
26 L. Vidino and S. Hughes, "ISIS in America: From retweets to Raqqa," in *Program on Extremism*, Washington DC, The George Washington University, 2015.
27 J. B. Comey, "Threats to the homeland," Statement before the Senate Committee on Homeland Security and Governmental Affairs, Washington DC, October 8, 2015. Online, available: <www.fbi.gov/news/testimony/threats-to-the-homeland> (accessed November 2, 2016).
28 Vidino and Hughes, "ISIS in America," p. 16.

29 Ibid., p. 18.
30 K. Johnson, "Feds have approximately 900 domestic probes about Islamic State operatives, other extremists," *USA Today*, October 23, 2015. Online, available: <www.usatoday.com/story/news/politics/2015/10/23/fbi-comey-isil-domestic-probes/74455460/> (accessed November 2, 2016).
31 Vidino and Hughes, "ISIS in America," p. 33.
32 E. H. Erikson, *Identity, Youth and Crisis*, New York, W. W. Norton & Company, 1964.
33 Substance Abuse and Mental Health Services Administration (SAMHSA), "Treatment episode data set," The TEDS Report, April 3, 2014. Online, available: <www.samhsa.gov/data/sites/default/files/sr077-gender-differences-2014.pdf>.
34 Ibid.
35 NIDA, "Substance use in women." Online, available: <www.drugabuse.gov/publications/research-reports/substance-use-in-women> (accessed November 2, 2016).
36 S. Quinones, *Dreamland: The True Tale of America's Opiate Epidemic*, New York, Bloomsbury Press, 2015.
37 N. Carr, *The Shallows: What the Internet Is Doing to Our Brains*, New York, W. W. Norton & Company, 2010.
38 Ibid., pp. 130–1.
39 A. Lemma and L. Caparrotta, *Psychoanalysis in the Technoculture Era*, East Sussex, Routledge, 2014.
40 P. Migone, 2013, "Psychoanalysis on the internet: A discussion of its theoretical implications for both online and offline therapeutic technique," *Psychoanalytic Psychology*, 2013, vol. 30, no. 2, pp. 281–99.
41 Ibid., p. 295.
42 C. G. Jung, "The archetypes of the collective unconscious," *CW* 9i, p. 71, 147, 1959. *Ramollissement* is French for softening.
43 Ibid., p. 70, ¶144.
44 Ibid., p. 26, ¶55.
45 Ibid., p. 26, ¶56.
46 This chapter is based on R. Tyminski, "Lost in (cyber)space: Finding two adolescent boys hiding from their own humanity," *Journal of Analytical Psychology*, 2015, vol. 60, no. 2, pp. 220–44, doi:10.1111/1468-5922.12145. Reprinted with permission of John Wiley and Sons.
47 This chapter will refer to material appearing in R. Tyminski, "Misreading Narcissus," *International Journal of Jungian Studies*, 2016, vol. 8, no. 3, pp. 159–67, doi:10.1080/19409052.2016.1201776. Reprinted with permission of Taylor & Francis Ltd.
48 This chapter will use material from R. Tyminski, "Lost for words: Difficulty articulating feelings in work with three adolescent boys," *Journal of Child Psychotherapy*, 2012, vol. 38, pp. 32–48, doi:10.1080/0075417X.2011.651842. Reprinted with permission of the © Association of Child Psychotherapists and Taylor & Francis Ltd.

Chapter 2

Online antics

Caught in the web

Online, nobody, nobody at all, really knows you.
—Twenty-year-old young man

It is a sophisticated game of hide-and-seek in which *it is a joy to be hidden but disaster not to be found.*
—D. W. Winnicott, "Communicating and Not Communicating Leading to a Study of Certain Opposites"[1]

Over thirty years have passed since William Gibson coined the term *cyberspace* in his 1984 science-fiction novel *Neuromancer*, yet his description of this domain as both a "consensual hallucination" and made for "disembodied consciousness" seems even more apt in our technology-focused world:[2]

Cyberspace. A consensual hallucination experienced daily by billions of legitimate operators, in every nation, by children being taught mathematical concepts. . . . A graphic representation of data abstracted from banks of every computer in the human system. Unthinkable complexity. Lines of light ranged in the nonspace of the mind, clusters and constellations of data.[3]

The Internet took off in the 1990s. We saw the Dot Com boom and bust of 1999–2001. Social media platforms exploded in 2007. Although video games have been around since the 1970s, the rise in Internet connections worldwide along with graphical user interface technologies has augmented their popularity, especially among boys and young men. These technological changes have, for the most part, preceded any evolution in social relationships. We are still just trying to catch up with what all these developments mean for the psyche.

Problems that arise in cyberspace range from hacking to violent video gaming, identity theft, and the temptations of the dark web, to cyberbullying, homophobia, misogyny, racism, and lying.[4] *Post-truth* was chosen as the 2016 word of the year by Oxford Dictionaries, in part, because of the widespread impact of social media and propaganda-driven Internet sites on national elections in the United States

(Donald Trump's surprise victory) and the United Kingdom (Brexit). The Oxford Dictionary defines post-truth as "relating to or denoting circumstances in which objective facts are less influential in shaping public opinion than appeals to emotion and personal belief."[5] Issues related to technology will be a focus throughout this book because they present psychotherapists, analysts, and psychology researchers with daunting challenges to previous assumptions regarding reality, human relationships, cognition, and emotional regulation.

My aim in this chapter is to explore an increasingly common clinical phenomenon in this technology-infused age. Two cases will show how young men can become lost in a computer world, so much so that they project massive psychic contents and thereby lose a sense of self. Erik Erikson thought of adolescence and early adulthood as a time for building identity and that failure to do so leads to the emergence of an identity crisis.[6] These boys and young men – for the most part, they are male – often have intellectual potential but underachieve because they are unmotivated by traditional academics. Instead, they divert their cognitive prowess into technology, especially computers, video gaming, programming, and hacking.

Their obsessions can appear schizoid, especially when accompanied by symptoms of withdrawal, escapism, dissociation, and omnipotent beliefs.[7] Getting to know these patients, one learns that their relationships with computer technology are experienced as holding many fragmented parts of their personalities, and they often label themselves as alienated, fake, and outsiders. These boys and young men (although nowadays, this observation can also be true for men in their thirties, forties, and beyond) seek out what appears to be hard, mechanical, and sharp-edged, and they struggle to shift toward another's receiving them softly or gently. Compulsive use of computers can stimulate an unconscious fantasy that the disturbing and disorganizing parts of the psyche are contained externally and not internally.[8] The psychological effect is psychic leakage through permeability of self and other, although here "other" is something perceived on a screen. There appears to be a loss of their psychological boundaries in how these boys and men use their computers – whether phones, tablets, laptops, or desktops – and frequently they struggle to articulate a coherent identity for themselves.[9] Sometimes such compulsiveness can even appear autistic, along lines that Frances Tustin and others have described as an attempt to encapsulate the self through autistic barriers.[10]

Contributing to the narcissistic disturbances that these boys and men struggle with is an affinity for magical thinking that is encouraged by what their devices offer. Computers reinforce magical thinking through speed, command-oriented actions, displacement, and the nullification of distance. When Freud and Piaget wrote about magical thinking a century ago, telegraph, radio, and telephone were major advances in human communication. Their insights into magical thinking still stand in providing us a perspective on how computer technology can become a catalyst for and an expression of fantasized power. *Technology* derives from the Greek word *techne*, meaning art or skill for accomplishing practical tasks. Nowadays, popular culture imbues this word with more numinous qualities that evoke power, control, success, and strength.

Often, these boys and men are alone and cut-off from others. They might pro-test when a psychotherapist brings up friendship, romance, or sex. One of the problems with magical thinking is that it predisposes us to interacting at a con-crete level. In cyberspace, the other can be regarded as a simple tool used for win-ning a video game, fulfilling exhibitionistic or voyeuristic needs, and generating "likes" for posts. Many adolescent boys and young men who spend hours daily online will lament that they find themselves isolated and friendless. Addressing their behaviors around computer technology now seems necessary to fully appre-ciate their disturbances in relating that show up in expressions of omnipotence and tendencies toward narcissistic self-absorption.[11]

Magical thinking

In his paper on two principles of mental functioning, Freud writes, "Neurotics turn away from reality because they find it unbearable – either the whole or part of it."[12] He introduces the term *pleasure principle* as a motive for what is sought in this turning away, although it is also characteristic of our dreams and moments in waking life when we recoil from "distressing impressions." The *reality princi-ple* acts as a check on the pleasure principle by prompting us to pause and take a moment to think, for example, to put off hasty gratifications and impulsive actions we may later regret. Freud notes, in addition, that fantasizing is spared the reality principle, as it is "subordinated to the pleasure principle alone," and it "abandons dependence on real objects."[13] Freud thus supplies an outline for magical think-ing. Elements include immaturity, discharge, immediacy, unconsciousness, grati-fication, and illusion or delusion. How many of these are nowadays characteristic of compulsive computer and Internet use, and when does this use become addic-tive? The British psychoanalyst Betty Joseph makes an important contribution to determining when something starts as a defense and then becomes addictive and self-destructive: "This type of self-destructiveness is . . . in the nature of an addiction of a particular sado-masochistic type, which these patients feel unable to resist."[14] She comments on the defensive aspect of addiction, which in such cases can seem to protect a person from tortuous emotional pain coming from his infancy or early childhood.

Piaget, too, considers magical thinking to be rooted in young developmental cognitive processes. He sees it as belonging to his pre-operational phase and specified the kinds of magic that it encompasses: rituals, telekinetic beliefs, spells, and use of enchanted objects. Piaget, like Freud, observed that magical thinking occurred more commonly with compulsive behaviors and narcissistic egocentricity:

> Reality is impregnated with self and thought is conceived as belonging to the category of physical matter. From the point of view of causality, all the universe is felt to be in communion with and obedient to the self. There is participation and magic.[15]

By "participation," Piaget means a psychological state in which there is limited self-object differentiation (poor interpersonal boundaries) and a primitive fantasy of control or influence over the external environment. He adds that usually there is "no spatial contact nor intelligible causal connection between the person or objects believed to be in this mysterious relationship of 'participation.'"[16]

Piaget asserts that magical thinking underpins a wish for absolute power, unbridled egocentrism, and defiance of causality. These aspects call to mind the vulnerabilities that may arise for many on the Internet. At their best, the Internet and computers are tools for creativity, knowledge, and expression. Yet the Internet can also be like a blank canvas on which we ask a four-year-old to finger-paint. On occasion, such a possibility goes awry and leads to anxiety-producing messes that are more complicated than ever intended. Which psychological and behavioral tendencies are observed when magical thinking predominates in how someone uses his computer and the Internet? This question is being asked in psychotherapy practices much more frequently.

Dark zones

Trying to understand computer technology's impact on analytic practice goes back over twenty years. Sherry Turkle was one of the earliest psychoanalytic writers on this topic, and she later explored how computer culture affects perceptions of identity and self-image.[17] She believes that Internet use encourages a multiplicity of selves, a phenomenon that alters psychoanalytic understanding of terms like *identity* and *relationship*. She remarks, "If one is afraid of intimacy yet afraid of being alone, a computer offers an apparent solution: the illusion of companionship without the demands of friendship."[18] This illusion frequently includes an unconscious fantasy of power and control.

Others have focused on therapeutic presentations of Internet use that appear linked to dissociation and negative effects. For example, Vittorio Lingiardi discusses how a computer becomes "a tool for emotional regulation" when a patient uses it to cope with shame and abandonment by seeking protection coming from a non-human object.[19] Richard Frankel writes about "digital melancholy" occurring when Internet users become obsessed with non-alive objects, just as mourners can feel haunted by those they've lost.[20] Robert Galatzer-Levy explores the dissociated frame of mind that happens sometimes in adolescent boys who view a lot of Internet pornography.[21] These boys dehumanize what they see in order to disown their experiences of arousal, desire, and masturbation. Aaron Balick cites a case in which Internet use seemed intrusive and persecutory to the therapeutic frame. At a time when the use of search engines such as Google or Bing has become a handy way to preempt first impressions, the Internet provides instant information that would once have been relatively difficult to obtain. Balick regards this kind of search by a patient of the therapist online as "pathological."[22]

Zack was nineteen years old when we met; his college required him to seek psychotherapy for depression. He had been spending hours alone in his dormitory room and stopped attending classes. He went out only for meals and, already skinny, had lost ten pounds. He spent his time on the Internet, surfing various social media websites and imageboards. Perhaps feeling that he had no other choice, he contacted me for psychotherapy.

He was the second child of immigrants from a Southeast Asian country. His parents divorced when he was 4 years old, and his father moved to another part of the United States. Zack rarely saw him. Zack's sister was nine years older, and they were not close. His mother later remarried, and both his mother and stepfather had busy careers that required much foreign travel. Zack also had an older stepsister who lived in a different city.

During high school, Zack studied hard and learned a great deal about computers. He taught himself a computer programming language and built his own PC. He reported that he wanted "the fastest processor" so he could quickly download video content and navigate the Internet. He was not that interested in online video gaming, although he had occasionally played some massively multiplayer online role-playing games (MMPORGs) like *World of Warcraft*. Zack's priority was to explore the Internet in a way that would be stealthy, fast, and undetectable. Speed mattered to him as a strategy for eluding someone's notice, trace, or discovery – in short, to hide. The hidden child. Who was looking?

When I met Zack, he appeared unhealthy and like a boy years younger than his actual age. I wondered if he had an eating disorder. When I asked about his weight, he informed me that he enjoyed running and had always been thin. He had even belonged to a running club before his depression worsened and then he quit. Still, he reported that he had lost "a few pounds, nothing serious." He intentionally downplayed my interest and concern, and I felt he was hoping I would not pursue him. This initial feeling further coincided with an observation that he seemed to want to disappear right in front of me. He sunk into a large chair in my office and wiggled nervously, as if searching for a gap in the cushion to slip through. He averted his gaze, staring at the floor when he spoke. His voice was so soft it was barely audible. His eyeglasses steamed up because he was sweating. Acting as a veil the steam made it difficult for me to assess his expression. I asked whether he was nervous, and he said no. When I commented that it was hard for me to see him, and perhaps even hard for him to see me, he shrugged silently. I offered him a tissue in the hope that he might wipe off his glasses, but he seemed confused that I was handing it to him. I had an intuition that if I did not look for him, Zack might not return, concluding that I had not found anything of interest in him. I felt it important to make an effort to seek for this slippery hider. This feeling of trying to find Zack right before my eyes persisted for months into his psychotherapy.

Over the first six sessions, it became more evident that he was severely depressed, although Zack did not endorse my view of his mental state. Blandly, he told me, "It's how I've always been. I'm just not very emotional. I have a very narrow bandwidth for emotions." He saw himself as a bit deadened – like a flat line on a heart monitor. When I asked about his future, he replied that he "wasn't excited about anything because there's really nothing to look forward to." He told me he would likely end up working a menial job, living alone in an apartment in an unsafe neighborhood. When I suggested that his outlook sounded deflating and gloomy, he agreed but said he had no feeling about it. I began to sense that much of Zack's emotional life occurred completely unconsciously. I was aware of thinking that he saw himself in his mind as like a failure-to-thrive infant, neglected and underdeveloped. What held him in this deprived inner world?

At the start of our seventh session, when I provided him with more feedback about what I was seeing, I expressed an interest in finding out more about what he might feel about his life, as he seemed unaware that he could have feelings about what he was telling me. He replied that he liked facts, news items, and technology because these things felt more real to him than feelings or emotions. Considering his defensiveness, I asked if he might complete a short questionnaire about depression (QIDS-16; see www.ids-qids.org), so we could see what the facts might be about his emotional state. He was intrigued and said yes. I chose to meet Zack here at his more concrete level of operating by using a technology instead of pursuing, at this point, an interpretative approach to his psychological problems.

The QIDS-16 is a sixteen-item rating scale with good psychometric properties for the diagnosis of depressive symptoms.[23] It can be helpful with adolescent boys who are in a state of alienation, either unaware of or resistant to looking at their internal depressed mood. It functions as a tool to show what their conscious minds might not perceive internally, and the format invites a shift in perspective on what is being warded off. Zack's responses put him in the high range of depression, and when we looked at his score together, for the first time, I felt I could see more of him. He looked frightened. At the time, I did not realize that I had stumbled on one of his "dark zones." I suggested he consider antidepressant medication in addition to his therapy with me, and he agreed. Shortly after this, he consulted his physician and began taking an SSRI.[24]

As I got to know him better, I commented to Zack that sometimes I felt he was hiding in plain sight, as if he was looking for a way to withdraw from interacting. He seemed surprised, asking if I thought he might have Asperger's syndrome. I asked why this question came to mind, and he said he found relationships difficult and always had. He explained that, while he had friends, much of his socializing took place online, either through instant messaging or Skype. I reflected that he was questioning how he related to other people by wondering whether he might keep too much distance, as someone with Asperger's might do. He went on to say, "Maybe I'm just a cynic about relationships," and I asked why he thought that. He replied, "People get into relationships just to compensate for their shortcomings and insecurities." This struck me as a transactional attitude about relationship, not one with a lot of meaning and depth. I wondered how he might be commenting on our relationship, and I offered that maybe he felt worried about our getting closer and what I would see, maybe parts that he himself had doubts about. He smiled slyly at this comment and nodded. I had the sense that he felt relieved, although his question about Asperger's made me think that he wondered what it felt like for me to experience his withdrawal. Perhaps this dynamic of approach-avoidance reflected something of how Zack felt in relation to his parents. If so, then I might have represented the child part of him feeling that his parents kept too much distance. His question about Asperger's may also have been his unconscious expression for how he was feeling about the emerging analytic narrative between us – that he was unsocial and unlikely to change much and that I would pull back, not looking for him beyond a diagnosis.

About six months into his therapy, Zack began talking with me about his earlier years. He spent much of his childhood alone, studying and reading books. He indicated that family meals with his mother and stepfather seldom occurred because of his parents' work and travel schedules. In this climate of emotional unavailability and absence of contact, he became an avid reader of fiction. This interest, as it can be for many boys and young men, seemed an opening to explore what went on inside him. He mentioned a contemporary novel that particularly got his attention. Its tragic story revolves around a sixteen-year-old boy with paranoid schizophrenia who descends into a spiral of madness from which he cannot save himself. Zack identified with the character's fragile hold on reality and his alienation. I felt that he also recognized something from his experience in the lack of emotional support and missing nurturance from the boy's parents. Zack's parents seemed flat and vague in his mind, and I was reminded of Anne Alvarez's idea about "the stupid object," a kind of internal parental figure that offers a child nothing of positive value.[25] This kind of internalization leaves a child feeling adrift, empty, and without resources inside himself to draw on. I asked Zack to describe one time when he felt affection from either of his parents, a time when they might have shared a closeness that he could recall fondly. As he stared ahead blankly, tears welled up in his eyes. He eventually said, "I'm sure it must have happened; I just don't remember."

A lack of nurturing and emotional holding early in life appeared to have contributed to Zack's missing something inside during adolescence, when he began to distrust others and to disregard his own emotional needs. He effectively turned away from his inner world. These flimsy, weak parental internalizations seemed another "dark zone" in his personality. I felt that the remnants of this unfortunate attachment experience made Zack's relationships operate from a paranoid-schizoid position, although at times I also felt he resembled some autistic boys who become encapsulated in peculiar ways as adolescents and feel unreachable. Nonetheless, I didn't believe that Zack had Asperger's syndrome. Instead, the more I got to know Zack, the more surprised I was by what went on inside him, where I found the parts that he had carefully hidden from others and from himself in what he called "dark zones." Zack had a hidden sense of aliveness.

Getting to know him was not easy. For many months, the process felt emotionally fraught and tiring, much like the child's game hide-and-seek, but I never got a turn to be found and always had to seek. Perhaps Zack was just demanding, as a child has a developmental need to do, "Find me!" Sometimes, I was exhausted after a session with Zack because I felt that I got so little back from him. I found it challenging to keep us together at the same metaphorical dinner table. I continued, however, to develop my early observation about Zack hiding from me – and from himself – as a prominent feature for how he withdrew, even when the person he was with might have something emotionally nourishing to offer him. I noted to Zack the times when I felt his hiding in different ways – his coming late, his not looking at me, his silences, his cutting off a lively interaction between us – and he gradually began to affirm that he could see these behaviors happening too. He told me how he liked to hide in Internet communications, for example, keeping his webcam turned off during a Skype call, although he preferred seeing the person to whom he was talking. I suggested that this detail about himself reminded me of hide-and-seek, but with him always having the advantage. He smirked, "I got that," and it seemed here that he was slowly revealing more. Like a young boy, he appeared to awaken to a hope that he now had a human partner to play a game with.

About one year into Zack's treatment, he asserted that he wanted to make sure "everything in here is private, right?" I noted that he seemed worried about something he wanted to tell me, and that what we discussed stayed between us, unless I felt that he might hurt himself in some way. "It's not that," he said. After some restless silence, he continued, "I wonder if you know about imageboards on the Internet." I replied that I did not and asked if he might explain. He answered, "They are a dark zone of the Internet. Some of them are harmless, like the ones about *anime* and *manga*. But there are some of them that aren't very reputable."[26] Zack explained that imageboards are sites on the Internet where content, written and visual, can be posted, but because the post expires, it can often disappear within minutes.[27] According to Zack's understanding, once the content disappears, it is simply gone and irretrievable. I wondered if Zack was telling me about his projection of how slipping away and disappearing occurred in relationships, a situation leaving no one sure or steady. I thought he could be describing attachments that are never meant to last because sticking around was too risky. Essentially, he was describing aspects of an avoidant attachment pattern.

I asked why these sites are "dark zones." Zack said, "They are the shadow of the Internet."

In some of these conversations, he became overtly paranoid. I noted his suspicions about trusting me and his anxiety about what he was telling me. At times, he became irritated with my curiosity, and I suggested his upset might come from feeling that I was discovering something about him that he wasn't sure he wanted me to know. He agreed with this idea and later told me he believed that, in twenty years, everyone's lives would be an open book. I said that this prediction sounded disturbing because we would not be able to trust one another. I added that he might now worry about what I was getting to know about him and his dark zones, his secrets. He shrugged; perhaps I had said too much, or put it too clumsily, because he appeared to brush me off. I felt that his description of the dark zones suggested he might have used these online imageboards as lifeless containers for his projections, although he never got any human feedback and was only left with web-based crumbs devoid of meaning. It seemed that Zack was describing, in a dream-like manner, how he felt about opening his dark zones to me. In this Internet-infused dream, I was never quite sure when our connection might break, although he clearly liked getting live attention and empathic responsiveness from me.

Well into his second year of psychotherapy, Zack became less anxious in discussing his preoccupation with these imageboard sites, which he followed daily. On occasion, he was drawn to violent content, for example, right after the terrorist bombing of the Boston Marathon. He was intrigued by conspiracy theories about this event. His thinking could seem quite shaky, and I wondered what psychotic process might lie underneath his fascination with these sites. I inquired whether he ever believed any of these ideas, and he replied, "No. Sometimes, they're outrageous and funny. I have to laugh when an absurd claim riles a lot of people. It's like someone's mental masturbation turns into a circle jerk." Zack had never made such an explicit sexual comment to me, so I asked him about his own sexuality – possibly this was another dark zone.

During high school, he had a girlfriend, and they occasionally shared some physical intimacy. He portrayed their relationship as one of convenience – transactional – happening because, "Everyone else we knew was going out, so we figured why not?" He didn't convey any sentiments of adolescent infatuation or early romance in how he spoke about her. He was embarrassed in talking to me about his sexuality. I remarked on his frequent blushing, and he said that he worried whether young women would find him attractive. "I look like a boy, so I've told myself I may have to wait for that [i.e., sex] to happen more." Zack thought of himself as rather impotent and undesirable. When I asked if he could imagine getting "more of that" sooner rather than later in his life, he replied by referring to another contemporary novel. His response was probably a displacement of his heat-of-the-moment feelings that talking with me about sex brought up because he was uncomfortable. But again, fiction provided an entry.

The story of this book sardonically portrays modern relating during late adolescence (it is about a prolonged adolescence, and the male protagonist is in his early twenties). It tells of an emotionally deadened romance that occurs largely through online chatting, emails, and texting. As I heard more about his high-school relationship and his interest in this novel, I wondered to Zack why there would have to be so much distance between him and a girlfriend – was he worried about what she might see in him? It sounded not only transactional but also alienating. He answered, "This is just how I imagine it could be safe, and how I would not feel pressured to be something I'm not." In our relationship, I felt that Zack was anxious to see whether I found him to be inadequate, too, perhaps in a way that he imagined his biological father had seen him when Zack was 4 years old and he left. I began to consider that Zack's involvement with the online world of imageboards, where messages disappeared quickly, worked psychologically to give him a defensive hideaway for projections of himself in which he felt two-dimensional and weaker in relation to others. Although this idea framed some of my experience thinking about Zack, I also felt more hopeful about him as I could sense that his feelings for me were growing.

During this phase of his therapy, Zack told me the imageboards that he followed were frequently filled with vulgar, obscene, and racist content. He stated that he liked to read, "These outrageous ideas people put up. Maybe they're crazy or criminal. Some of these posts are beyond sketchy – they're plain creepy." Thinking about the imageboards as projective spaces for Zack's dark zones, I continued to encourage him to tell me his feelings about them. This discussion led to a moment when I could comment on his anxiety about where my interest in him might be leading us. I noted he had taken a risk by showing me more of himself. As I thought about his wafer-thin internal parental objects, I felt he had now become anxious that I would lose interest, or that I would give up on him. When I mentioned this idea, he laughed nervously, although he nodded in agreement. He paused for a while, then said, "I am wondering, what assumptions do you make about me?" He blushed after saying this, watching me carefully, making eye contact, which was unusual for him. I felt a boyish longing for contact in his look, for contact with a father figure who would not disappear on him. He was not hiding in this moment.

Many sessions later, I commented that he might be worried that my curiosity about him could disappear, that whatever I felt toward him would vanish, and that he would be left alone to sort it out. I also thought of his earlier remark about "circle jerks" as possibly being related to an unconscious fear that he had about my view of him – that when he felt he was exposing himself, I would find him small and laughable. I didn't interpret this latter idea, however, because it felt more important to comment on the fear that I could vanish rather than why I might. Also, with many disturbed late adolescent boys and men in general, special care should be taken with what could be regarded as "saturated interpretations" that increase defensiveness.[28] Zack remarked, "I'm surprised that you see what you do, because I still think I'm playing my cards close in. But I think you have a point about the disappearing. I wonder if anyone cares. Sometimes I ask myself: why would anyone pay attention to you?" I said that I felt the hopelessness and alienation in that question and that I understood some of where it might come from. I continued that I felt he now could tell that I liked what I saw of him when he stopped hiding from me. He nodded, "I do see that." This was a healing exchange for Zack, a time that I also felt close to the frightened and skittish boy whom I had found.

Following this interaction, Zack was more open to discussing ways in which he neglected himself. This dialogue during the final months of our work seemed to work through some of the residues of the inadequate parental internalizations that had left him often feeling depleted and inadequate. After two-and-a-half years of therapy, Zack returned to his college, where he decided to pursue a degree in a technology-related field of study. This decision seemed to be not only a sublimation of his preoccupations with social media and imageboards, but also a statement about asserting an identity that included his dark zones. He appeared more actively engaged with what he might create or produce and more open to how his plans could show a complexity about who he was. In one of our last sessions, Zack mentioned that he no longer understood why anyone would spend so much time on the Internet using sites like Tumblr (for what is called *microblogging*) or Pinterest (for *visual bookmarking*). He remarked,

> I used to spend hours on these sites, but now I see them as not being about creativity at all. They're more about curating, using other people's content for your own purposes. That doesn't seem like what I'm interested in anymore.

Here, Zack expressed what can happen in psychotherapy when a young man still caught in adolescence is able to integrate split-off aspects of the self and when he can open to feeling cared for. Although I felt Zack was in a better place psychologically, I wished for more time with him. I could see that he was really beginning to look into himself, to spend time inside his house, and that he had further to go. I would like to have accompanied him for a while longer. This situation represents a recurring dilemma in work with adolescents and young adults: they decide it is time to move on, and we are left wanting more.

"Better to be alone than have to put up with idiots!"

Brad was fifteen when his school referred him to me because of attendance problems related to his feeling ostracized by classmates. He believed that other students were making fun of him behind his back by gossiping about him. The third son of immigrants from a Mediterranean country, Brad had recently self-identified as gay. It is important to note that this is another immigrant story that will, like Zack's, weave in threads of identity, alienation, and acculturation. Brad felt his mother had accepted his coming out better than his father. Brad spent many hours, both day and night, on his computer. In our first meeting, I experienced a result of this compulsion firsthand when he told me, "I have social anxiety. I did a checklist on a website, and I scored high on it. And I also am depressed, and another website says I have body dysmorphic disorder." Brad seemed to be telling me that he felt there was a lot wrong in him and that he required a lot of attention. He also signaled that he had figured it all out by himself. Brad was overweight, lethargic, and moved as though dragging himself through the world. I initially felt that Brad viewed me as someone to be controlled, and I found many of his verbal behaviors geared toward boxing me in, for example, by repeatedly cutting me off mid-sentence. He came across as tyrannical, putting me on notice that he expected I would fix his various problems.

Because his sleep schedule was erratic, I asked Brad how much time he spent daily on his computer. He said that it was "easily ten hours . . . probably more than that most days." I asked if he had ever tried to limit this time, and he replied, "Why? It's my main social outlet." When I followed up on how long this had been the case, Brad proudly told me that he, again like Zack, had built his own PC. "I ordered all the parts and assembled it myself because I wanted the biggest hard drive I could afford . . . for a lot of memory." He added, "I also got an expensive video card, like one gaming programmers use, because I want the best graphics." Brad's statement about memory and the graphics card made me think about what he might have needed in terms of maternal and paternal containment for his projections. It appeared that he was telling me something was missing in his development, and now he coped through a manic fantasy that he could make it himself. Brad's expressions were often grandiose, especially early in his psychotherapy, and I often felt he expected my role in our relationship to be confined to admiring him, mirroring him, and not disrupting his wish to control me.

Brad's need to express omnipotent feelings also characterized his interactions on the Internet. He chose gaming websites where he could feel powerful and domineering by creating avatars or pseudo-identities that were the polar opposite of a boy who professed to be shy and socially phobic in the real world. He was an avid player of *League of Legends*, which is a multiplayer online battle arena (MOBA) strategy game. Briefly, *League*, as it is known, is a role-playing game in which two teams battle each other, seeking to advance and destroy the other team's "nexus," a structure at the heart of a team's home base. Players adopt hero identities ("champions") and try to acquire experience points to level up by adding more powers and skills for their heroes. They battle to win gold when they defeat opponents. The game's play requires a team effort so that no one player can claim ultimate success for winning (or responsibility for losing). Tournaments are organized in many locations with ranked teams competing against one another; an official website showed 11.5 million players worldwide in a previous month.[29]

Going online did not solve any of Brad's social problems, as I learned after four months of intensive psychotherapy. He found it difficult to be a member of a team, as the game requires. He called other players "stupid" and sometimes faulted their English-language skills. He would become angry and swear at them (players often communicate through some type of Voice over Internet Protocol – VoIP – such as Skype or Ventrilo). He felt frustrated at not being able to control the choices and moves that other players made in the game. In short, he could not modulate his omnipotent thinking, which continued to interfere with how he related to teammates. At times, he was banned from the game for various intervals, one of which was on the order of several months, for his inappropriate comments. When we discussed what had happened that time, Brad became angry with me for questioning how he had behaved. He said, "I thought therapists always sided with their patients." I responded that he felt troubled by my lack of understanding for his position, and he agreed. He then became impatient at having to explain aspects of the play that I did not understand. I noted that I wanted to hear from him how this game was played. Dismissively, he replied, "You can go online and read about it." When I suggested that this kind of conversation was how he might build a relationship with someone like me, he rolled his eyes. Then he said, "Better to be alone than have to put up with idiots!" Although I realized this remark referred to his opinion of me, as well as the *League* players whom he had insulted, I responded only by noting how frustrated he had become at my not already knowing what he knew. He could not appreciate that I had a separate mind.

Brad's anger at me would be a focal point in our work during this phase of his therapy. I first addressed his hostility by naming the ways in which I could see and feel his anger: how curt he was, how he talked down to me, how he scowled at me, and how his comments indicated I did not measure up. At the time, I felt that in doing this, I was giving him short observations and then verbalizing the impact of projective identifications about what it felt like to be belittled by someone who saw himself as bigger, more powerful, and controlling. I was unsure whether how Brad treated me represented a reversal of a maternal or paternal transference, or some combination, because both his parents had, at times, been overpowering to him during his early childhood and latency years.

His father had frequently ridiculed Brad for various ways that he expressed himself, so in one sense, I felt what Brad was showing me was a version of a negative paternal transference. However, Brad mostly complained in his psychotherapy about his mother, whom he described as constantly "sticking her nose into my business." It seemed that his conscious hostility stemmed from experiences of feeling her intrusiveness toward him. He repeatedly described her as "judgy." I wondered whether we were then navigating a negative maternal transference of times when he had felt intruded upon and persecuted by her. His hostility to me, in either of these transference situations, seemed based on his identifying with one or both of his parents as aggressor and with me in the role of his child self – a hapless boy having to take it.

After seven months of psychotherapy, Brad resumed attending school. His contempt and hostility found new targets. In session, he lambasted other adolescents in school for being "loud," "annoying," and "uninformed." Thinking he had previously felt outcast at his school, I brought up with Brad how difficult it can sometimes feel after coming out as gay to others, because there can be a hope that taking this step will automatically resolve many of life's problems by ending a period of hiding. This belief is not infrequent among gay adolescents, who often experience a coming-out process as liberating and freeing but then also expect that it should make real a utopian fantasy of acceptance and inclusion, which, of course, it never does. Brad, however, remained profoundly disappointed that he could not connect even at a level of friendship with other boys, and he took this lesson quite hard. As he told me how upset this made him, I found an opportunity to suggest that perhaps their distance, which he felt as hurting him, might go two ways since he often seemed to indicate disapproval for their behaviors, a disapproval that they might experience as his distance from them. Although he argued some about this interpretation, he gradually became gentler and less grandiose in talking to me about these boys. After this, he made this self-reflection, "I think at my previous school I thought I was better than everyone. This is how I cope with feeling rejected." He appeared here, uncharacteristically, to recognize that his taking a superior attitude to others was both defensive and alienating.

I saw an opening to suggest that this pattern of imagining my disapproval, rejecting me, and distancing himself also happened between us. Brad associated to my comment by bringing up the topic of whether I was gay or not. He said when he thought that I was not gay, he wanted to argue more with me – "to yank your chain." Although I thought his wording had sexual undercurrents, I replied that I felt he liked the idea of being able to rattle me that way. I then wondered instead what his reactions were when he thought I was gay? He answered, "Like it matters that you like me. I don't want to come across as mean. It doesn't feel right to argue with you so much." Brad could tolerate feeling closer to me when he saw me as a gay man accepting him, but the image of me as a heterosexual man judging him brought up fears that I would fight and try to attack him. He relaxed considerably as we talked about this over the course of several sessions.

After this and nearing a year of therapy, Brad discovered a way to use the Internet that provided a solution for his social isolation. He found other gay teens online, and he began to chat with them. Some of these contacts were one-offs; some lasted a week or two; some lasted far longer. For example, he developed a sort of "pen pal" friendship with a boy his age who lived in a South American country. They used Skype to talk, and this way of communicating seemed promising for Brad. First, it gave him a feeling of belonging, because he saw that there were many gay teens who struggled in similar ways. Brad felt less stigmatized about being gay because he quickly identified with this virtual community. Second, this mode of communicating helped him not to impulsively and defensively say the first thing that crossed his mind. He learned he could take time to reflect a bit before speaking too bluntly or hotly in a way that put others off. Third, it was conceivable that his knowledge of the physical distance between them lowered Brad's persecutory anxiety about how he was being perceived. In this virtual environment, he described feeling less threatened by his own paranoid thoughts. Conceptually, we might think of Brad as learning to use the computer less concretely (like a symbolic equation) and instead more as a transitional space along the lines of Winnicott.[30] In making this shift, Brad, therefore, showed that the Internet offered a continuum of potential psychological uses, stretching from the pathological to something positive in a developmental sense.

His friendship with the South American boy developed over many months of conversations. When I asked Brad what he felt was different about this friendship, he replied that he was "becoming a good listener." He seemed to be acquiring some basic understanding of empathy as crucial for relationships, and I suspected that his awareness for this came in part from his experience of containment from me in his psychotherapy, especially around his anger and rage. Brad's earlier omnipotent thinking about using the Internet as a space for domination and control over others appeared to have been somewhat modulated, so that he could begin to experiment with it as a way to connect with others, rather than merely planning how to defeat them. Brad found that instead of just playing violent online video games on his computer, he could also use it as a tool for communication.

Online 24/7

95% of U.S. teens now use the Internet, and 81% of them use social networking sites.[31] The median teen Facebook user has 300 friends.[32] We live in a much different social-cultural environment than we did fifteen years ago, and psychoanalysts have struggled to keep pace with what these changes mean for our practice. Glen Gabbard comments on two potentially problematic features of Internet usage, its immediacy and its disinhibiting effects, both of which often result in more personal disclosure than intended.[33] Florence Guignard sees the virtual realm as exciting expectations for instantaneous wish fulfillment, similar to magical thinking.[34] She notes that in "vulnerable children digital reality could reinforce the idealization of action over reflection."[35] This situation accentuates a kind of cognitive flattening in which magical thinking overtakes reality testing.

Alessandra Lemma discusses alienation from the body when adolescents use the Internet to retreat into "an order of pure decision."[36] She mentions how Internet use, although not causative of these symptoms, is nonetheless frequently associated with problems such as loneliness, low self-esteem, and shyness. At a minimum, compulsive use of video games with avatars for role-playing, questing, and violent combat raises a question about the consequences for a still maturing ego, which Freud noted long ago "is first and foremost a bodily ego."[37] What happens to awareness of the developing body for boys who spend hours daily on virtual gaming or surfing websites? Do they lose touch with their vitality and become dissociated from a basic flow and rhythm of life? This was true for Zack and Brad, whose compulsive Internet behaviors seemed related to their own difficulties with body image and awareness of their physical needs. We might consider all the time spent on computers as adding up to time that is not available for sports, being in nature, and playing outdoor games. These boys risk becoming alienated from their own bodies and their basic biological functions.

Didier Anzieu notes that the skin and brain derive from the same embryonic structure.[38] His ideas are useful for conceptualizing changes that occur in adolescence when the body develops to sexual maturity and when interpersonal boundaries are renegotiated and given newer, more intimate meanings. Anzieu attributes many functions to the "skin ego," which operates as a hypothetical psychic structure to contain our sensations, images, and affects. A failure in this structure leads to intense anxieties, a propensity for discharging aggression (frequently a problem for adolescent boys), and a leakage of mental contents that are projected outside. When this happens, it results in a Swiss cheese effect, in which there are inexplicable holes and gaps in psychic experience. This circumstance applies to many adolescent boys and young men in treatment, for example, when they seemingly cannot find words to articulate their emotional pain and instead act it out, frequently in bizarre ways, as will be shown in Chapter 4. Returning to the house metaphor, it is as if their houses are not sealed properly, with leaky roofs, missing windows, and holes in the walls. This is an image of a psyche at risk because of perforations, fissures, and cracks that do not separate inside and outside effectively. I once had a patient, a young man, report a dream in which *he was walking on a pink surface with holes like Swiss cheese. He was in a state of increasing panic that he would fall through one of them.* The pink color might represent skin or mucosal membranes, and this dream might represent the terror of experiencing such a house/psyche where one is never comfortable at home.

What happens psychologically when someone substitutes his computer for relating to the real world? We might think of compulsively surfing the Internet and video gaming as unconscious attempts to find substitute surfaces, behind which there would be a fantasized container that would be an alternative to a decrepit house. Without a secure boundary between inside and outside, ego capacities can suffer, such as understanding the limits to one's desires, flexible thinking about choices, delay of impulses, verbal expression, and affect regulation. Reinforcement of magical thinking in cyberspace also inflates an omnipotent attitude about the self. This omnipotence undercuts one's ability to relate in cooperation, mutuality, and acceptance of reality-bound limitations. Instead, one becomes fixated on a transactional attitude about relating, an attitude that is focused on tangible exchanges and benefits and is starved of deeper meaning.

For Zack, the "dark zones" of the Internet seemed to become a place where disturbing parts of his personality found a temporary home, because whatever he believed to be put there would soon be erased and untraceable. He was just a fly-by renter. Imageboards represented a kind of containing – and disembodied – surface that Zack felt he could use for various projections about identity, sexuality, hostility, and rejection. This would be an example of developmental projective identification gone awry, which Bion believes to result when there is no real containing object as a nurturing person to metabolize these projections for the infant or child.[39] Zack's problem was that there was almost no way to integrate his actual identity into whatever appeared on these sites because the content always disappeared. He was in a state of chronic depletion that manifested in his many depressive symptoms. Only when he began to talk about what truly interested him – on these sites, in books, in his relationship with me – could he begin to use me therapeutically to find a way into claiming his own house and begin its repair. Although at times he was troubled in this process, especially by paranoid ideas of what I might make of him, Zack gradually responded to me offering him a living container, not a technology-laden substitute. For patients like him, the idea that an analyst or psychotherapist has a containing mind with a memory and with empathic attunement often comes as a surprise. More than once, Zack remarked that he was astonished I could remember what he had talked about in prior sessions. Two persons using their memories in face-to-face interaction and meaningful conversation provide solace for alienation.

Zack's magical thinking showed in how he used the imageboard sites and, to some extent, social media. He unconsciously believed that using these sites allowed him to eject disturbing aspects of his psyche – to post them, in the vernacular of social media. Zack was in a state of what Piaget calls "participation," in which his boundaries were loose and which invited massive projective identification; Jung termed this condition "participation mystique." Zack had a childlike belief that imageboards were magical – now you see it, now you don't – because the contents disappeared. This disappearing act fostered an attitude in Zack that he could hide from the more disturbed states of his mind that he saw reflected in the "crazy stuff" posted on imageboards. The imageboards, unfortunately, fit his alienation all too well.

Brad, because of narcissistic defenses, was thin-skinned, especially when it came to social interactions in which he perceived slights and rejections that other adolescents might handle with resilience. Brad dealt with his insecurities around his identity through a defensive inflation of self. His contempt could be formidable, dismissive, and hostile, and it led him to adopt a transactional attitude toward relating, in which what mattered was his score, his status, and his power. At first, he barely could acknowledge how alienated and lonely he felt. Magical thinking appeared to be part of his motivation to build his own computer – he could make an enchanted device that would be powerful, and it reinforced a fantasy of control. He discovered, however, that his wish to dominate others was not so easily achieved in the multiplayer online video games that he liked. Similar to Zack, he suffered from a magician's delusion that the trick was real. Brad believed that because he was master of this fantastic machine with expensive and sophisticated components, his wishes should come true. Early in his relationship with me, he often became angry when he saw me representing something of the real world, rather than merely mimicking an imaginary virtual world that he pretended to have at his beck and call. While he vented anger at me, especially as we explored his misfortunes online, he used me as a therapeutic container for powerful negative emotions around his disillusionment. A deflation of powerful infantile impulses loosened the hold of magical thinking on his actions, although it still shaped his expectations. Later in our work, after questioning who I might really be to him and feeling realistic hope in seeing me as a gay man, he began to use his computer as a communication device to connect with other boys online.

Writing about these experiences gave me fresh perspectives on some of the challenging countertransference feelings that Zack and Brad evoked in me. Zack often exhausted me and left me feeling resentful whenever he gave so little – frequently nothing – back in the relationship. On one occasion when he canceled because of illness, I felt relieved at not seeing him. In retrospect, I believe that he had to constantly test whether I would give up my search for the hiding boy. I imagine that he sometimes sensed my tiredness. Brad more overtly angered me, especially when I experienced him wanting to tightly control me. He at first rejected most of my suggestions that we think together about his relationships, and I felt disempowered, which of course was what he wanted in order to feel safe with me. His intense need for domination made me question whether I could ever get through to anything vulnerable in him. He feared that being gay meant hiding, and he used me to explore some of his unhappiness around that idea. Both these young men had spent too much of their development directing their considerable mental energies into alienated cyberworlds filled with hard-edged caricatures of people. I felt that they disowned their humanity in doing this. They were frightened by what I would call the soft touch of human contact: an emotional attitude for connecting. My countertransference did inform me about severe father-son alienation and perhaps how cyberspace could be sought out as refuge from that pain.

An ongoing issue for psychotherapists and medical practitioners is the explosion of information now available online. In many ways, this access empowers patients to learn and advocate for themselves and, therefore, is largely positive. Yet, when narcissistic disturbances are present in someone, the Internet can become a feeder for magical thinking that a "do-it-yourself" approach can solve most, if not quite all, of life's troubles. I have had adolescent boys protest to me that poor grades in mathematics do not matter because "that's what computers are for." Many psychotherapists now have stories of young patients who copy text from the Internet and present it as their own without ever considering this to be plagiarism. And I have found, in recent years, that several parents who did not like my evaluation of their child went online to make their own diagnosis and prescribed a course of treatment based on what suited their opinion. For instance, a mother told me that, despite what I thought, her seven-year-old boy was not depressed, but rather "a touch moody and just needs CBT" (Cognitive Behavioral Therapy). Little did it matter that CBT has not consistently been demonstrated to work with such younger children, whose intellectual capacities may benefit less from such a targeted, narrow approach. These could all be viewed as instances when the Internet contributes to magical thinking. This egocentric strategy reinforces an illusion of magical solutions to difficult problems. It is probably no coincidence that Oxford Dictionaries selected *post-truth* as word of the year for 2016. According to its definition, facts do not matter because "appeals to emotion and personal belief" are what count in shaping an opinion.[40]

For the purposes of this discussion, I emphasize that magical thinking can be exaggerated by use of the Internet through its speed, nullification of distance, immediacy of responses, flattening of cognitive complexity, and exposure to self-affirming ideas and gratifying imagery. Many of these characteristics are consistent with what Freud and Piaget wrote about magical thinking long ago. The nullification of distance is akin to telekinesis in that it underpins a belief that objects can be influenced or controlled without regard for their spatial relationships. This idea explains, in part, the significant popularity of online shopping and cyberporn.

What else might these two cases reveal? In both, there was an attempt to use the Internet to modulate disturbing affective states, in Zack through the image-boards and in Brad with his video gaming. It is noteworthy that their compulsiveness around the computer occurred in isolation, meaning they were essentially left alone in states of affective arousal that can put vulnerable adolescents and young adults at risk for acting-out behaviors, such as self-harm, substance abuse, and violence. Additionally, both young men struggled with identity issues, perhaps because they used their screen time for so much projection. Zack felt himself to be empty and without a future, whereas Brad had such an inflated sense of himself that he lost perspective on his actual capacities and limitations. Significantly, neither of them gained what relief they sought from their time online. In fact, Zack's depression steadily worsened with the time he spent surfing the Internet and Brad's social problems followed him right into the virtual world.

Many young men and boys with insecure attachments may now compulsively use cyberspace in a desperate attempt to blot out the pain of what they have missed emotionally growing up. With the predominance of the Internet and social media, will this phenomenon become increasingly prevalent in our practices? Young men and boys like Brad and Zack are not as uncommon as we would hope. They have not had satisfying and enriching developmental experiences of another aspect of the soft touch, namely the basic need for human skin-to-skin contact. Their deprivation in this regard makes them not only lonely, but also socially clumsy at making real contact with peers for any kind of intimate expression or exploration. We know from attachment research, contemporary neuroscience, and a wealth of analytic case material that intervention to repair deeply damaged relationship patterns usually succeeds best when begun at younger ages. Even then, developing and practicing the emotional skills required for more intimate relationships takes considerable time. None of us wants to believe that the Internet will rewire our human attachment needs, but we must be open to how it may be altering what our patients are capable of when they first appear in our offices.

Often, what we see in clinical settings is a transactional attitude about relationships, defined by score keeping, cost-benefit terms, terms of service, stereotypes, and narrow perceptions of desirability. This attitude is difficult to engage with in psychotherapy because a young man can counter with what he finds to the contrary online and then argue about what is "really" important. Faced with this defensiveness, we might, instead, note the serious psychological problems of alienation (depression, anxiety, neglect of the physical body, loneliness, isolation, online compulsions, and so on) and continuously reflect our observations about these back to our patients as reasons for why they came to us. Their avoidance of meaning and what is inside their houses ought to be taken up as primarily contributing to their suffering, but we must time these statements so that they can be taken in gradually. Neither Zack nor Brad improved over a course of weeks. Depth psychotherapy offers an antithesis to a transactional approach, and it, therefore, requires explanation, comparisons with what happens online, and contrasts to offset established beliefs about interacting. With young men like Zack and Brad, I may repeatedly ask versions of, "How is it different in here than online?" Then they can begin to see and verbalize alternatives in relating and come to value these.

Finally, in both cases, there was a creative urge behind some of the manifest problems. Building and creating are parts of growing up, and children and adolescents have long toyed with making model planes and cars, radios, kites, and rockets. Building a computer, creating online avatars, and posting on social media are perhaps contemporary versions of this desire. Computers and the Internet can be used in many constructive ways such as when Brad began to explore social media to find other gay boys. boyd (sic) believes that new technologies offer different ways to learn and to socialize and argues that they are largely positive.[41] She views adolescent fabrication on social media as a form of creativity, play, and rebellion. In myth, Prometheus is regarded as both rebellious and creative, a figure who overturned a petrified establishment so something new could emerge.[42] A creative urge is usually disruptive because it aims at expressing human experiences that sometimes are hidden, painful, and dark – often waiting to be found. It is important for us, as clinicians, to consider the psychological interactions and effects that computers and the Internet have on adolescent and young adult development. We can now see a rather uneven continuum for pathological and creative expressions, and we must be willing to move along this complicated spectrum that switches between the human and nonhuman. The Internet can function like a deep dark forest where children can be lost and abandoned but must be found.

Notes

1 W. D. Winnicott, "Communicating and not communicating leading to a study of certain opposites," in *The Maturational Processes and the Facilitating Environment, Studies in the Theory of Emotional Development*, pp. 179–92, New York, International Universities Press, 1965. Quote from p. 186, italics in original.

2 William Gibson, *Neuromancer*, New York, Ace Books, 1984, pp. 4 and 51.

3 Gibson, *Neuromancer*, p. 51.

4 R. Tyminski, "Techno-theft," in *The Psychology of Theft and Loss: Stolen and Fleeced*, pp. 120–31, New York and East Sussex, Routledge, 2014.

5 A. W. Wang, " 'Post-truth' named 2016 word of the year by Oxford dictionaries," *The Washington Post*, November 16, 2016. Online, available: <www.washingtonpost.com/news/the-fix/wp/2016/11/16/post-truth-named-2016-word-of-the-year-by-oxford-dictionaries/?utm_term=.70c7871fbe54> (accessed online November 18, 2016).

6 E. Erikson, *Childhood and Society*, New York, W. W. Norton & Company, 1963; *Identity: Youth and Crisis*, New York, W. W. Norton & Company, 1968.

7 J. H. Rey, "Schizoid phenomena in the borderline" (1979), in E. Bott Spillius (ed.), *Melanie Klein Today: Developments in Theory and Practice, Vol. 1: Mainly Theory*, pp. 203–9. London and New York, Routledge, 1996.

8 D. Meltzer, *Sexual States of Mind*, Perthshire, Scotland, Clunie Press, 1973.

9 When I refer to computers, I include any electronic device that can function in this way such as laptops, tablets, and smartphones. Even gaming consoles are computers.

10 F. Tustin, *Autistic Barriers in Neurotic Patients*, New Haven and London, Yale University Press, 1987.

11 H. Rosenfeld, "A clinical approach to the psychoanalytic theory of the life and death instincts: An investigation into the destructive aspects of narcissism" (1971), in E. Bott Spillius (ed.), *Melanie Klein Today*, Volume 1, pp. 239–55, London and New York, Routledge, 1988.

12 S. Freud, "Formulations on the two principles of mental functioning," in J. Strachey (ed.), *The Standard Edition of the Complete Psychological Works of Sigmund Freud*, Volume 12, London, The Hogarth Press and the Institute of Psychoanalysis, 1911/1955. Hereafter reference to Freud's work in the Standard Edition will be cited as *SE*, with volume number and page. This quote is from p. 218 of this volume.

13 Ibid., p. 222.

14 B. Joseph, "Addiction to near-death" (1982), in E. Bott Spillius, *Melanie Klein Today*, Volume 1, London and New York, Routlege, pp. 311–23, p. 323.

15 J. Piaget, *The Child's Conception of the World*, trans. J. Tomlinson and A. Tomlinson, London, Routledge & Kegan Paul, 1960, p. 167.
16 Ibid., p. 132.
17 S. Turkle, *The Second Self: Computers and the Human Spirit*, New York, Simon and Schuster, 1984; "Whither psychoanalysis in computer culture?" *Psychoanalytic Psychology*, 2004, vol. 21, no. 1, pp. 16–30.
18 Turkle, "Whither psychoanalysis in computer culture?" p. 21.
19 V. Lingiardi, "Playing with unreality: Transference and computer," *International Journal of Psychoanalysis*, 2008, vol. 89, no. 1, pp. 111–26. Quote from p. 111.
20 R. Frankel, "Digital melancholy," *Jung Journal: Culture & Psyche*, 2013, vol. 7, no. 4, pp. 9–20.
21 R. M. Galatzer-Levy, "Obscuring desire: A special pattern of male adolescent masturbation, internet pornography, and the flight from meaning," *Psychoanalytic Inquiry*, 2012, vol. 32, no. 5, pp. 480–95.
22 A. Balick, "TMI in the transference LOL: Psychoanalytic reflections on Google, social networking, and 'virtual impingement'," *Psychoanalysis, Culture & Society*, 2012, vol. 17, no. 2, pp. 120–36. Quote from p. 133.
23 A. H. Rush, M. H. Trivedi, H. M. Ibrahim, T. J. Carmody, B. Arnow, D. N. Klein, J. C. Markowitz, P. T. Ninan, S. Kornstein, R. Manber, M. E. Thase, J. H. Kocsis, and M. B. Keller, "The 16-item quick inventory of depressive symptomatology (QIDS), clinician rating (QIDS-C), and self-report (QIDS-SR): A psychometric evaluation in patients with chronic major depression," *Biological Psychiatry*, 2003, vol. 54, no. 5, pp. 573–83.
24 Selective serotonin reuptake inhibitors, such as Prozac, Zoloft and Celexa.
25 A. Alvarez, "Types of narcissism and apparent narcissism: Some questions concerning the stupid object," paper presented during "A Day with Anne Alvarez," San Francisco Center for Psychoanalysis, San Francisco, California, 2005.
26 *Manga* are Japanese comics and graphic novels; many deal with adult themes involving sexuality, violence, and moral transgression. *Anime* are the animated versions; they are popular with boys and young adult men.
27 For further information, see Imageboard, available <http://en.wikipedia.org/wiki/Imageboard>.
28 A. Ferro, *The Bi-Personal Field: Experiences in Child Analysis*, London and New York, Routledge, 1999.
29 See Riot Games, available: <www.riotgames.com/tags/number-players> (accessed August 9, 2016).
30 D. W. Winnicott, "Transitional objects and transitional phenomena," *The International Journal of Psychoanalysis*, 1953, vol. 34, no. 2, pp. 89–97.
31 A. Lenhart, "9 things you need to know about teens, technology & online privacy," Pew Internet Project, Washington, DC, Pew Research Center, 2013. Online, available: <www.pewinternet.org/2013/11/07/9-things-you-needto-know-about-teens-technology-online-privacy/> (accessed May 7, 2014).
32 Ibid.
33 G. Gabbard, "Cyberpassion: E-rotic transference and the internet," in A. Lemma and L. Caparrotta (eds.), *Psychoanalysis in the Technoculture Era*, pp. 33–46, East Sussex, Routledge, 2014, p. 34.
34 F. Guignard, "Psychic development in a virtual world," in A. Lemma and L. Caparrotta, *Psychoanalysis in the Technoculture Era*, pp. 62–74.
35 Ibid., p. 72.
36 A. Lemma, "An order of pure decision: Growing up in a virtual world and the adolescent's experience of the body," in A. Lemma and L. Caparrotta, *Psychoanalysis in the Technoculture Era*, pp. 75–96, quote from p. 75.

37 Freud, "The ego and the id," *SE* 19, 1923, p. 26.
38 D. Anzieu, *The Skin Ego*, trans. C. Turner, New Haven and London, Yale University Press, 1989, p. 96.
39 W. R. Bion, *Learning from Experience*, Oxford, Jason Aronson, 1962.
40 Wang, " 'Post-truth' named 2016 word of the year by Oxford dictionaries."
41 d. boyd, *It's Complicated: The Social Lives of Networked Teens*, New Haven and London, Yale University Press, 2014.
42 R. Tyminski, *The Psychology of Theft and Loss: Stolen and Fleeced*, New York and East Sussex, Routledge, 2014.

Chapter 3

Narcissus in the locker room

Sexuality and gender

> We did not know his legendary head,
> in which the eyeballs ripened. But
> his torso still glows like a candelabrum
> in which his gaze, only turned low,
> holds and gleams. Else could not the curve
> of the breast blind you, nor in the slight turn
> of the loins could a smile be running
> to that middle, which carried procreation.
>
> Rainer Maria Rilke, "Archaic Torso of Apollo"[1]

The locker room. Many a boy's and young man's place for banter and playful teasing. But for many others, it's a place of dread, where a wet towel is twirled into a whip that is flicked at a target, and if it hits, there is usually a momentary sting; it's called towel snapping or being whipped with the rat's tail.

"Man, that move you made was so gay. I can't believe you dropped the ball like that." The towel snaps from the hand of the first boy.

"Screw you, you're gay! You didn't even score. That's real gay." The second boy snaps back with his towel while a third boy named Bill watches the two of them, unsure what to say or do.

"Hey, Bill," the first boy says with a touch of menace, "you weren't so good today either." He twists the towel tighter in his hands. "You held back too much. You know what that is?"

Bill looks at his backpack wondering if he dares change into his street clothes. He has his towel wrapped around his waist to give an extra layer of privacy while changing his shorts. Before he decides, the towel, with a loud snap, strikes him on his butt. His towel falls, and he stands there in his underwear. His attacker says, "Gay, it's totally gay to not go for it. And those underwear are so, so gay." The two boys laugh loudly, and Bill fumes but eventually mumbles, "Right. You're the gay one hitting everyone with your towel so you can see their junk."

I've heard variations of this story countless times from many of my male patients. John, whom I discussed in Chapter 1 and whose story you'll learn more of in this chapter, told me that he walked into the locker room to find his oldest son engaged in such a scene of towel snapping and taunts of "you're gay." Charlie, a fifteen-year-old whom you'll meet later in this chapter, avoided locker rooms because of similar experiences when he was the target. The locker room presents a plausible theater for male dominance, posturing, and bullying. A boy's or man's nakedness can seem wrong when it means exposure, when there's a threat and the naked male body becomes a target. Frequently, a locker room gives an actor the stage to express some of the worst homophobic tendencies of domineering and aggressive masculinity. Ken Corbett discusses how, for boys and young men, "faggot" can come to mean "loser." This word then provides a spiteful definition for what is ultimately demeaning in the male psyche, namely, seeming small.[2] Nowadays, the word *gay* can work just as well in a certain male vernacular that perhaps reflects some education around not using the word *faggot*, because of its more overtly derisive and ridiculing connotations. Political correctness may have lessened the prevalence of the latter word, although the former one can clearly substitute for the same meanings of small, feminine, soft, and loser when used an insult among boys and men. Towel snapping, with a hard sting against soft skin, seems an apt game for mimicking this masculine dilemma of toughness defined by rejection of anything delicate or sensitive. To what degree do these games represent internal concepts of masculinity?

Masculinities and sexualities

Ronald Levant notes that there are four contemporary debates about masculinity: 1) essentialism versus social constructionism; 2) mutability; 3) biological, social, and psychological differentiation between masculinity and femininity; and 4) affirmative and negative perspectives shaping intervention and research.[3] The complexities of this field illustrate how segmented it is and how difficult a big-picture approach might be. My house metaphor about the trouble many boys and men have with what is inside them seems, by contrast, a bit flimsy, although I hope to bring an analytic clinician's perspective into this area.

In another article, Levant lays out the important contemporary research questions he sees in the field of masculinity and its implicit gender roles.[4] Here, he uses "the gender role strain paradigm" to evaluate how men relate to their sexuality and gender ideology, clarifying that sex refers to biological characteristics and gender to psychosocial ones. He mentions how men have long been researched, because of their high numbers relative to women, for problems such as being estranged from their families, addicted, homeless, violent, imprisoned, suicidal, murderous, and self-destructive. He notes that "a masculinity crisis began in the mid-1990s and continues today."[5] Gender ideologies reflect beliefs about what is male and what is female, although, notably, much research shows that the genders are more alike than different. Gender ideologies are fundamentally derived from social construction and social learning.

Traditional "masculine ideology" incorporates four elements: 1) not being feminine, 2) being successful, 3) not appearing weak or small, and 4) being adventurous and taking risks.[6] Both men and women carry gender ideologies about their own and other gender expressions. Gender role strain among men has been linked to problems with self-image, restriction and inhibitions in relating to others, and crushing expectations fueled by social comparisons. Not surprisingly, aspects of these difficulties appear throughout the clinical material in this book, and this model offers a descriptive conceptualization for what many boys and men describe as highly challenging when they feel they do not fit in. Levant also proposes what he calls "normative alexithymia" as a byproduct of traditional "masculine ideology" to explain some of the common complaints about boys and men not communicating, not sharing, and withholding. I will explore clinical aspects of this concept in the following chapter. Levant cites evidence that infant boys are quite expressive, but that "they become less verbally expressive than girls at about the age of 2 years and less facially expressive by 6 years."[7] This observation seems to support the social-construction hypothesis for shaping gender roles. It also underscores why many boys and men might take refuge in the alternative environment of cyberspace, which can appear controlled, limited, and flat.

Psychoanalytic understanding of boys and men has lagged in this area. Bruce Reis and Robert Grossmark, in their 2009 edited book on masculinity, remark, "Heterosexual masculinity has yet to be approached from a view that understands gender as fluid, multiple, and emergent."[8] Corbett echoes this view, writing that "masculinity remains largely undertheorized" and that analysts and psychotherapists have either focused on problems boys have in "separating from and dis-identifying" with their mothers or, more recently, on the attachments they form with their fathers.[9] He formulates an intriguing idea about phallic narcissism that transcends a pathological viewpoint and instead looks at its developmental importance as well as its positive erotic dimensions. He asserts that too much in depth psychology's ideas about gender is overly embedded in the mother-child dyad, turning "us away from the fantastic construction and materialization of the body and mind beyond infancy and early childhood."[10] Mentioning that newer parenting-help books rarely mention the word *penis*, he says this is representative of a "phallophobia" in our thinking about boys.

Corbett writes the following:

> I think many boys present a particular dilemma for parents . . . through their persistent activity and aggression, through the pitch, push, punch, and pull of their muscular eroticism and expansive narcissism, an eroticism that is often overshadowed by aggressive and sadomasochistic dimensions, an eroticism that is often fueled by the endurance of pain, an eroticism that is often laced with violence or the near violent.[11]

The sexual excitement and desire for bigness that he discusses here are, to his mind, attempts at relating in a "fantastic" way – in other words, that this aspect of masculinity strives to expand into the world with challenging, dramatic, and potentially problematic gestures. Instead of seeing merely narcissistic traits in these kinds of behaviors, Corbett postulates them to be more like operatic displays of masculinity.

Irwin Hirsch discusses how moral judgments and fears of appearing feminine constrain not only men in therapy but also many of the analysts and psychotherapists treating them.[12] He openly describes one of his own mistakes in interpreting a male patient's cross-dressing as immature and reflective of a girly attachment to his mother, comments that resulted in a premature termination. The bounds of what we as analysts and psychotherapists find normal can, if turned into explicit suggestions, formulaic interventions, and moralistic interpretations, preclude many boys and men from getting the help they are seeking to explore their feelings that seem feminine, girlish, or maternal. Hirsch believes that ideals we hold about acceptable masculine behavior and fidelity might limit our openness to non-normative and seemingly imperfect patterns of relating that many men struggle to understand. "The more we think in diagnostic or in other universal splits and binaries, the more we are inclined to be disapproving with our patients and to impose our own personal moral judgments [and] standards on them."[13] A historical problem with psychoanalytic theory has been to favor a moralistic internal father – theoretically as superego – to the exclusion of digging into nonnormative behaviors and the feelings under them. Hirsch also offers his own idea that infidelity can be a way for men to regulate emotional distance, to feel control over their dependency needs, and to show a bit of "revenge for childhood humiliations at the hands of powerful mothers."[14] I am less sure how often infidelity fits the latter category, however, because many men I have treated who struggle with their sexual behaviors often describe a different dynamic based primarily in emotional problems with their fathers.

Puberty is usually a time when a boy begins to recognize his emergent sexuality as also shaped – socially constructed – by external things such as transmitted masculine gender ideologies, family dynamics including sibling relations, and the demands of one's peer group. The overview of puberty in Chapter 1 emphasized many of the changes that occur rapidly in a boy's endocrine system contributing to physical and sexual development. Recall that there is a thirtyfold increase in testosterone production, a figure that suggests a dramatic reorganization of both body and psyche. This period of significant change typically creates sexual urges that feel confusing, unstable, and are directed at the opposite sex as well as the same sex.

Freud believed that bisexuality is somewhat inherent to our development. He called "anatomical hermaphroditism" as belonging to the "normal," and fetal development certainly could be viewed as endorsing that view since there is a bi-potentiality in the early embryo before fetal endocrine hormones begin influencing the sex of the fetus.[15] Freud has also been accused of anatomical determinism in his theories of sexuality and gender. Certainly, many of his ideas about sex have not been validated, and especially in regard to gender, they can appear too essentialist in the face of what we have learned about environmental and cultural variables and their roles in constructing gender. His original idea about bisexuality, however, may still tell us something about the conflicts boys and men face when rejecting what seems feminine in them in order to adopt behaviors consistent with culturally sanctioned gender ideologies.

Sneaking around

You met my patient John in Chapter 1. Recall that John used Internet sites to find partners he could have cybersex with. He rationalized his behavior as an escape from his marriage where he felt trapped, like being in the jail cell of his first dream. He read a lot and would sometimes lecture me about various problems with monogamy, citing articles from anthropology, philosophy, and psychology to explain, in his view, why it made for a dull life.

John and I worked together for several years. Part of John's job involved checking his employees' written documents for errors. He once described how he relished this, especially when he discovered something they had plagiarized. I asked him to describe the feeling he had, and he said, "It's a funny mix of anger, excitement, and . . . this is hard to say . . . victory, like I've uncovered their sneakiness." I asked if that sounded at all familiar to him, someone sneaking or hiding to cover up an indiscretion, and he blushed. "I don't like what you're implying, but now it seems obvious." As we talked more, he said, "Someone has to be the policeman." I wondered if there was anything in his past he might link to that idea, and he recalled how his father would burst into his bedroom when he was a teenager saying, "Just checking you're okay," but John resented the uninvited intrusions and suspected his father was trying to catch him masturbating.

John described his father as self-centered; the whole family revolved around his needs. John had two sisters and one brother and was the third child, but that position did not prevent his father from demanding his obedience and compliance, a form of parenting that can feel crushing to a child. Indeed, John described how his father came home one day when he was about ten years old to tell him he'd bought a new lawnmower. His father threw away the old one and presented John with a push-along model, telling him, "This will build character, don't whine." They had a big yard, and John told me it took hours to mow with the push-along. He also cut his sneakers repeatedly on the blades when he wasn't paying attention. His father would smile and tell him not to expect a new pair because he should learn to mow better. I felt that John needed my help in remembering his feelings of impotence and humiliation when he was at the mercy of his authoritarian father.

I asked John how he recalled feeling then about the mowing, and he said, "So, so small. He decimated me." During this time, we spoke often about John's inner policeman and his close association with his father. This persecutory father showed up in John's dreams as various "agents" from the *Matrix* movies who would chase and nearly kill him. In discussing one of these nightmares, John cried for the first time when he remembered his father tearing up his report card. John was about 12 years old and had received all *A*s except for a *B* in physical education (PE). "He looked at it and said, 'What's the matter with PE? You a sissy?'"

John told me his father made his mother take him to see a doctor when he was thirteen because he'd not yet gone into puberty. John had heard his father tell his mother that he was concerned John "might have some girl hormones in him." John went into puberty a few months after this incident.

During these years, he was steadily taking on board a battered image of himself as weak and effeminate, even though he tried hard to please his father, for example, by playing baseball throughout his childhood and into high school. As a teenager, John began to worry about his appearance not being masculine enough, so he insisted on crew cuts for his hair and only wore black, white, gray, and navy-blue clothes. John described his mother as "dutiful" but "protecting us as much as she could" from his father. With four children, there were limits to what she could do to shield them from her husband's emotional cruelty. John developed a stereotyped image of women as appeasing, weaker, and overwrought. Interestingly, when John spoke about his own wife, she seemed to resemble his father more than anyone else from his past life: competent, bossy, and with very high expectations.

His feeling judged and berated by his wife contributed to John's belief that cybersex was his only outlet for emotional satisfaction. He rarely had sexual contact anymore with his wife, who traveled frequently for athletic events she participated in. As we talked about his relationships with his father and his wife, John noticed how closed off his mind felt to him. He commented, "I can fill it up with ideas and stories, but where am I?" He voiced how his identity seemed wrapped up in his father and his wife and what they expected from him. Many of his dreams during this time involved his wife literally turning into his father as part of the storyline. In one of these, *she angrily told him he was late paying the rent, and as he started to write a check, she became his father shouting, "Get out of here!"* John broke into deep sobs. Later, he was able to explain: "I don't have a right to my own mind? How fucked up is that?"

John seemed caught within a self-defeating internal structure of following his father's edicts. He believed that exploring his feelings or delving into what was inside him was "sissy" and effeminate; I am somewhat simplifying John's psychological predicament to illustrate the extreme defensiveness he experienced around a rigid self-image and fears of what could be feminine in his psyche. At times, he became critical of psychotherapy for "seeming too much like mama-ing." He did not consciously endorse me as a maternal figure, but my interest and liveliness, which felt nurturing to him, also confused him and caused him to worry I was feminizing him. In these moments, I invited him to tell me what he saw in me and how it made him feel.

After one such exchange, John came to the next session in a buoyant mood. His overt depression had lifted, and he was beginning to reclaim aspects of what he called "my lost self." He lay on the couch and smiled, telling me, "This is hard to say. Driving here . . . well. I had this fantasy about you." He paused for a bit. "A sexual fantasy." Another pause. In a loud voice, he said, "I wanted to bang you!" He blushed and apologized, but I encouraged him to keep talking about it.

John continued, "It's real intimate here. It's not like with my wife, or those women I have sex with online. I feel . . . like I'm waking up." He told me this felt exciting but assured me he was not gay. I wondered with him how he might make sense of the fantasy about us. He replied that he felt more open, sensed something "moving inside," and "all these crazy things pop into my head, and they're okay. I don't have to push them away." John indicated here that, through his work with me, we were freeing him from some old beliefs about himself. He didn't have to be in jail – which is a constricting model of a psyche. His desire to bang me may, at the time, have given him the freedom to express that I was a feminine object for him, but it was not simply that.

Jung had the idea that a conjunction (he used the Latin *coniunctio*), a marriage of sorts, occurs in deep psychotherapy or analysis when both parties are affected.[16] He saw this process as our combining, in a symbolically erotic way within the unconscious, so that something new develops. "The real meaning of the *coniunctio* is that it brings to birth something that is one and united."[17] Masculine and feminine aspects unite; the potential for creation emerges, perhaps integrating split-off parts of our psyches. I felt John was saying something similar – that our work created possibilities for him to reach inside himself and that this process involved his imagining something feminine between us. I discuss more about John's sexuality in Chapter 9. Speaking about his fantasy of "banging" me provided him an opportunity to explore his feelings of submission and sneakiness, which had troubled him for so long.

Finding Narcissus

How have certain myths become enshrined in our understanding of psychology? Freud certainly made the myth of Oedipus into a cornerstone of his theories about sexual development, and his idea about this unaware young man climbing into bed with his mother has been so convincing that it has migrated into popular culture, humor, and media.[18] Jung concentrated his focus in myth largely on rebirth, and in a way, that expanded how analysts and psychotherapists appreciate what happens in adult development when we might feel lost, aimless, adrift, and empty.[19] We might think of these explorations as selected myths that reveal something about the authors, along the lines of Jung's personal equation, and about the times when they wrote, for example, how contemporary cultural attitudes determined perceptions of development and individuality.

What happened then with Narcissus, whose legacy has contributed to a pathological diagnostic term (*narcissistic personality disorder*), as well as to a more general form of insult when we refer to another person's selfish behavior as narcissistic? It is as if all that psychology took away from the myth of Narcissus was the single moment when he pined away at his own reflection in the pond to the point of himself dying. This moment is important in the myth, but there is much preceding it, and something following it, too. What does the backstory of Narcissus reveal that has been perhaps forgotten or swept aside? Jung neither took one image of engulfment by the Terrible Mother to illustrate the power we may feel behind our own wish to be reborn, nor did Freud simply reflect on Oedipus's blinding himself to moralize about the dangers of family desires. They both flushed out these myths in considerable detail and did not rest with a static interpretation. Narcissus, on the other hand, appears to have undergone a quite different fate in how his story gets used psychologically.

Jung makes no reference to Narcissus in *The Collected Works*.[20] There are only five references to narcissism, mostly in connection with criticism of Freud's reductive approach to analysis that would compare introversion with a troubled form of narcissism.[21] In *Mysterium Coniunctionis*, Jung argues against meditation being viewed as a kind of narcissism, emphasizing that what superficially appears as self-absorption can instead have healthier meanings.[22] According to the OED, the word *narcissism*, meaning "selfish, grandiose, self-centered, and vain," came to English in the early 19th century, although notably this occurred about a century after the word *egotism* showed up in English.[23] Extreme egotism or ego-inflation might have been a more accurate term for what Freud was describing when he wrote about narcissism in 1914. Paul Näcke used "narcissism" in 1899 to refer to a sexual perversion, and Havelock Ellis, around the same time, defined it as excessive masturbation.

A linkage between homosexuality and narcissism dates to Freud, whose writing gave us the psychological terminology of narcissism thanks to his amplification of one scene from the myth of Narcissus.[24] In a paper that begins with a definitive repudiation of Jung, Freud describes a model of sexual libido like a closed hydraulic system in which there is a fixed quantity of liquid flowing through it. A problem arises when too much flows toward the ego. Writing about homosexuals, he says,

> They are plainly seeking *themselves* as a love-object, and are exhibiting a type of object choice which must be termed 'narcissistic.' In this observation we have the strongest of reasons which have led us to adopt the hypothesis of narcissism.[25]

His circular logic – that his assumption is true because he believes he sees the hidden truth in it – led to decades of psychoanalytic theorizing that harshly stigmatized gay men and women.

The psychoanalyst Richard Isay, in his 1989 groundbreaking book *Being Homosexual*, writes, "On the whole, analytically oriented psychotherapists have little understanding of the importance of these attachments [between gay men in their community] for the enhancement of self-esteem."[26] Isay argues that anyone can respond negatively to narcissistic injury, especially when it takes the form of stigma. Freud, the man who gave us a careful description of Oedipus, was cursory in his portrayal of Narcissus because he neither mentions the myth nor the character of Narcissus in his 1914 paper. Although the term *narcissism* is likely to remain with us for some time, it represents, at best, something of a shallow version of the myth.

Before turning to Ovid's widely appreciated telling of the myth of Narcissus, it makes sense to reiterate that Jung did not see a particularly salient connection between narcissism and anything of significance in his own theories. After breaking with Freud in 1913, he did not take much interest in giving developmental aspects of sexuality a dominant place in his ideas about the psyche. In Jung's *Collected Works*, there are only six references to adolescence and an additional twenty-two on "puberty," of which six refer to puberty-initiation rites and another six originate before Jung's final break with Freud.[27] Where Jung is most candid about the adolescent stage is in Chapter II, "School Years," of *Memories, Dreams, Reflections*, when he describes a series of events – the outbreak of neurotic fainting spells at age eleven and a teacher's insistence, when he was fourteen or fifteen, that he had plagiarized a paper that was the best in his class, indicating how painful adolescence must have been for him, with little sustained adult guidance to assist him in sorting through his private obsessive conflicts.[28] Jung portrays a bleak picture of his family, his school, and his social environment.

In a letter to Freud, moreover, he revealed that when he was "a boy," Jung was "the victim of a sexual assault by a man I once worshipped."[29] Then, as in childhood, his creative fantasy life provided him with refuge, though one might wonder whether that significant compensation or the fact of his profound alienation and depression during those years was more decisive in shaping a theory that presented internal objects as so much more reliable than outer ones. Brian Feldman discusses some of what we know biographically about Jung's adolescence, and he proposes that Jung's troubled dynamics with his father during that period set in motion unconscious forces that later played out with Freud.[30] There has been much more written by post-Jungians about adolescent boys and their struggles with sexuality and identity.[31] Semantically speaking, it is fair to say that we have subsumed psychoanalytic terminology about narcissism without entirely questioning its origination, although Marie-Luise von Franz did offer analytical psychology a reframing of the topic in her writing about the *puer*, which she described as an archetype characteristic of a man who "remains too long in adolescent psychology."[32]

Ovid's Narcissus

Ovid lived from about 43 BCE to 17 CE. His great poem *Metamorphoses* includes a tale of Narcissus, in which we learn that Narcissus's parents were water creatures; his father Cephisus was a river god, and his mother Liriope was a nymph.[33] This watery heritage is important to recall when considering Narcissus's death beside a pond, as if something in his relationship with his parents became part of what trapped him there, not just a fascination with his own reflected image.

The prophet Tiresias – also famed for his prophecy to Oedipus – told Liriope that, ironically, Narcissus could only live long if he never knew himself. Psychologically, here we have a conceptualization of dissociation within the myth, something that can occur often in adolescence and early adulthood when boys and young men often struggle with how their identity is forming, for example, adjusting to how their bodies might be developing, how they feel perceived by male peers, and difficulties with their own sense of autonomy. Narcissus, a young man of sixteen, becomes an object of infatuation for Echo, who herself has been cursed by Juno for previously assisting in a cover-up of Jupiter's sexual indiscretions. As a result, Echo cannot speak for herself except to repeat the last word spoken. She thus represents a silenced feminine aspect of the psyche that pokes at awareness, like perseveration, to eventually capture some of our attention.

Ovid's Latin text allows for an ironic misunderstanding between the words "meet" and "mate," with Narcissus agreeing to the former and Echo believing the latter. Here, we might consider the myriad miscommunications that nowadays occur online and in text chatting, or even when meeting can also be equated online with mating through hookup dating apps. Narcissus rejects Echo's advances, and she withers to nothing more than a voice. This rejection is not unlike how many male adolescents and young men react to awareness of their sexuality, especially when some aspect of it feels potentially feminizing to them. In the myth, Narcissus is eventually cursed when the gods respond to a prayer from another scorned boy who desires him. We might thus view Narcissus's stubbornness and insistence on exerting his own will as largely what undoes him.

The effect of the curse is what popularly remains of the myth, a boy languishing, unable to move away from his own reflection in a pond. This image corresponds with what Freud, too, chose to take from the story. But for a sixteen-year-old to be self-absorbed with his looks is hardly new, surprising, or radical. We have only to think about today's ever-changing hairstyles, trendy clothing, colorful sneakers, piercings, and tattoos to realize that appearances weigh mightily in an adolescent boy's (or girl's) mind. This preoccupation with self-image characterizes an emergent psychological process revolving around central developmental questions: who am I to others, and what do they see of me? It is about trying on identities to see what feels right and wrong.

When Narcissus realizes that he is staring at himself, then Tiresias's prophecy comes full circle. Self-knowledge is frequently painful at this age of being on the cusp of adulthood. Narcissus exhausts himself, and his death pond-side recalls his parental habitat, as though he was not able to fully separate from them. In that sense, Narcissus typifies a failure to launch, to become more meaningfully independent, which is a common problem that many analysts and psychotherapists encounter when treating their patients in late adolescence and early adulthood. This seems to be part of the mythic "lesson," namely that Narcissus could not successfully separate from his parents. The water's reflecting capacity may give us a clue about what was missing. Perhaps he could not get beyond what he saw of himself through his parents' eyes. That discovery frequently leads to an identity problem for many in late adolescence, when a wish to psychologically kill off the parents can be great. Hugh Gee writes about this as a manic attempt to assert self-sufficiency in adolescence, although often well before one is ready.[34] However, versions of one's internal parents do usually undergo a transformation, if not a killing, when a young person no longer sees them from a position of dependence, and they have much less power.

The Narcissus myth conveys one more detail. A flower emerges where Narcissus's body laid, one with white petals encircling a gold cup. This hopeful image of springtime might represent what Narcissus could not ultimately have – fertility as a natural part of a lifecycle that includes elements of sexuality with both masculine and feminine parts. The sensuality of this particular flower comes not only from its striking visual appearance but also from its penetrating fragrance. The myth ends with Narcissus's death and with this symbol of what he might have become as a young man if only he had been able to separate from the hold of the pond's reflection and to build a relationship with someone like Echo or the last boy he rejected. A key part of this myth, and a neglected one in the way it is used for psychological theory, is Narcissus's turning away from the feminine, which in a mythic sense – the flower named for him – belongs to him in any case.

Case example – coming out, maybe

Charlie was fifteen when he came to me because his parents were concerned by his social isolation and awkwardness. They mentioned in passing that they suspected he was gay and added that they were "fine with that." Charlie was a shy, soft-spoken boy, fully in mid-adolescence, who enjoyed technology and spent a lot of time online, often late into the night. When I first met Charlie, who was wearing a torn black t-shirt, scruffy jeans, and sneakers with holes in them, he struck me as depressed and lonely.

He admitted to feeling sad much of the time, and he was quite aware of not having many friends. Exploring his social connections, I asked if he ever thought about dating. He said sometimes, but when I followed up by inquiring whom he might like to date, he became stone-like. My question seemed to have petrified him. His fear was palpable, and I felt a need to tread carefully in our conversation.

I commented on the apparent tension my question caused, and I asked if he could say why. He replied, "I don't want to think about it." Seeing his downcast eyes, I could sense his shame. He then blurted out, "I can't be gay. I just can't." He relaxed some into the pillows and cried a little.

The depth of his sadness moved me, and I also wondered why he felt so rejecting of himself if he were indeed gay. I remarked how forcefully he told me that and asked why that was. Charlie answered, "There are so many ways I am not normal. I can't take there being another one." At this time, Charlie's sexuality was charged with painful emotions. He used a litany of negative beliefs to subject himself to punitive self-criticism that drained any good feeling he might have had. It was no wonder he was depressed. His biting self-commentary mostly centered on his self-image that he wasn't enough of a boy, by which he meant strong enough to stand up for himself, to fight, and to make others respect – or fear – him. Much of our initial work involved my questioning these ruminative beliefs, asking him what else he saw in himself that might be different and positive, and helping him to better articulate his feelings within his family and at school. His perspective on who he was shifted ever so slowly. During this time, we only occasionally took up the issue of his sexuality, which still felt like a wound too tender to yet consider.

After a year of therapy, Charlie began to link his harshness toward himself to his parents' subtle ways of conveying their disapproval. Speaking about his father, he said, "He's old. Not just in years. He's old in ideas, in what he believes is right." I sensed an opening here, and I wondered how problematic it would feel for a gay son to relate to the father he was describing. I posed a hypothetical scenario, asking how his father would take it if someone in the family came out as gay. He replied, "Not well. He'd be all PC [politically correct] in what he said, but I think he'd disapprove underneath." I wondered why his father would be homophobic, and Charlie explained that he came from a traditional and conservative family. When I pointed out that his father had a different background from Charlie's, he agreed. He then blurted out this question: "So why am I so hard on myself?" He was trying to put some psychological distance between himself and his parents, which seemed growth-oriented and assertive.

For some time following this exchange, Charlie spoke about the homophobia that he saw at his school, in popular culture, and on social media. It seemed we were now working through a core aspect of his identity by addressing his anxieties about being gay and social perceptions about homosexuality. This process of circling the topic of homophobia and social attitudes and gradually edging closer to a central aspect is something many gay male youth and young adults go through to locate themselves in a world where they can see themselves as gay. Charlie came in one day and told me he'd been chatting online with another boy. He told me this boy was openly gay at his high school. Charlie admired this. Then he told me, "I guess you probably have known this. I'm gay, too. I told K [the other boy], and he said, 'Dude, that's way cool!'"

I told him I felt pleased to hear him tell me this because he was naming something about himself, seeing it was important, and showing courage in voicing who he was. This statement might sound too positive to some analysts and psychotherapists because it implied I was taking a side in Charlie's struggle. And they would be right about that. For many children and adolescents, feeling that someone is on their side can seem foreign and unfamiliar, and perhaps in reaching across such alienation, we have to show a willingness to bear allegiance. I asked Charlie how he felt hearing me say this. He looked at me for a while and then replied, "Relieved. Like a weight's gone."

His disclosure subsequently allowed Charlie to admit why he felt so ashamed about being gay. His internal homophobia reflected ideas he had about stereotypical constructs of a hard masculinity and a soft effeminacy, the latter of which implied weakness and powerlessness to him. Charlie repeatedly mentioned fears about his physical safety. He was not sure he could defend himself. Several years earlier, he had been bullied at school, and he recalled that the teachers and administrators had intervened only half-heartedly. He had felt "left out to hang," a particularly gruesome image evoking the murder of Matthew Shepard in 1998. Charlie was troubled by another gay bashing reported in the news. Describing it, he became tearful and told me, "I wouldn't be able to fight back either. I'd be like that boy and end up in the hospital on life support." In processing this sadness and terror about his survival, Charlie was able to verbalize a need to protect himself. He began to understand that if he were open about being gay, then it might be safer than hiding. He reasoned that if others saw him for who he was, they might recognize when he needed help and come to his aid. He'd be visible to others. I continued to support him in claiming his gay identity, although we talked at length about the anxiety this created for him. He made an invaluable connection that by accepting my help he was learning how to find it elsewhere too.

Charlie gradually decided to come out to his friends. After this, another boy at his school invited him to a school dance. A few days before the dance, Charlie showed up at our session wearing a floral-patterned shirt. I had never seen him wear anything like it. He was excited, telling me that he planned to wear it to the dance. When I mentioned he looked good in it, he blushed. I said that perhaps I had embarrassed him. He responded that he felt "two things at once and that's weird" – both a bit embarrassed and "psyched." I wondered privately if his use of the word *psyched* was an unconscious response about what we had worked through together in exploring this part of his psyche, where gay and male were "two things at once" about his identity. I hoped he felt freer because of this.

Reality about sexual orientation

Charlie's story about coming out ended in a meaningful and positive way for him. This is not true for many other boys and men who feel variations in their sexuality, especially for what appears feminine. The Centers for Disease Control and Prevention (CDC) published a 2016 report based on over 15,000 responses from high-school youth in the United States about sexuality and high-risk behaviors.[35] The sample covered twenty-five states. This report found that sexual minority youth have a higher prevalence for many health-risk behaviors when compared to nonsexual-minority students. These behaviors include exposure to violence, HIV infection, sexually transmitted infections, and substance abuse. Table 3.1 summarizes several selected statistics from this report.

In the total sample, 88.8% of high-school youth identified as heterosexual, 2% as gay or lesbian, 6% as bisexual, and 3.2% as not sure. Extrapolated to a nationwide tally of just over 16-million high-school students, more than 1.28 million would be gay, lesbian, or bisexual, and more than another half million would be in the "not sure" category.[37] The "not sure" group may include many who, because of shame, religious reasons, family pressures, and cultural factors, do not want to perceive yet that they are gay, lesbian, or bisexual. In addition, high-school dropouts and homeless youth are not be counted in this sample, thus underestimating the numbers of gay, lesbian, and bisexual youth. This CDC report did not include numbers for transgendered youth, who may not have known how best to respond to this survey.

Coming out is difficult under even apparently supportive family circumstances such as Charlie's. Brian Willoughby, Neena Malik, and Kristin Lindahl have

Table 3.1

	Prevalence Among All Students Nationwide	Prevalence Among Male Gay and Bisexual Students	Prevalence Among Male "Not Sure" Students
School avoidance due to safety concerns	5.6%	15.5%	NA
Cyberbullied	15.5%	22.4%	22.3%
Being a victim of sexual dating violence within last twelve months	10.6%	20.9%	21.7%
Suicidal ideation within last twelve months	17.7%	32.7%	30.9%
Suicide attempt within last twelve months	8.6%	19.4%	16%
MDMA ("ecstasy") use, ever tried one or more times	5%	16.3%	22.2%
Methamphetamine ("crystal") use, one or more times	3%	14.8%	16.5%
Tested for HIV infection	10.2%	16.7%	N.A.
Computer use, longer than three hours daily for other than school work	41.7%	48.8%	59.1%

Nationwide figures include both male and female respondents. Table 3.1 is adapted from statistics in the Center for Disease Control and Prevention's *Morbidity and Mortality Weekly Report*, August 12, 2016.[36]

found that a main difference in sons' coming out experiences pertains to family functioning.[38] Families that are warm, cohesive, and communicative offer their sons a better opportunity to adjust and integrate their coming-out story into the family without feeling negative judgments about their sexuality. Families that are cold, rigid, and authoritarian are especially unhelpful to sons who are coming out. Although not surprising, this finding does underscore that negative beliefs about being gay or bisexual are reinforced within many families. These same beliefs weighing on a young man's self-image can likely be associated with many of the high-risk behaviors shown in Table 3.1. The statistics for being a victim of another's aggression, for self-destructive tendencies, and for substance abuse show a twofold increase or greater in prevalence among gay and bisexual male youth.

Narcissus at the pond of adolescence

I believe that we could consider the myth of Narcissus somewhat differently from what the psychoanalytic literature has handed down to us. Narcissus was a self-absorbed young man like most men who are that age. Part of this developmental preoccupation stems from the integration of many aspects of the personality into something with coherence, which includes sexuality. Shame can be activated when a boy perceives a socially defined difference to his sexual feelings. Mario Jacoby notes the intense loneliness and alienation that shame brings on, particularly when someone feels it as a judgment that he is an unapproachable freak.[39] For many boys and young men, dawning awareness of their sexuality can be clouded and obscured by shame, subject to peer pressures about normative masculine behaviors and compounded by terror of the feminine, including what is within themselves. Adolescent peer culture is frequently unforgiving around perceived differences, and the scapegoating process is something all adolescents are sensitive to.[40] Boys and young men can feel emotional turmoil, with their self-image suffering when their sexuality does not conform to normative standards of traditional masculinity.

Shame can cause boys and men to hide, not only from others but also from themselves. This hiding process was apparent in how John, at a mature stage of his life, and Charlie, much younger, both dealt with their sexual feelings. For a boy or a man, sexuality that strays from masculine ideals about penetration, dominance, and phallic conquest can seem "sissy" and feminine, although too often this perception is defined by a corresponding stereotype of femininity as submissive and passive. This misattribution can evoke shame of difference, of weakness, and of not being "man enough." In the myth, we might consider Narcissus's rejection of Echo as representing these male anxieties about relating to his feminine side. Although she acts in the story with insistent pursuit, she could also be viewed as a projected part of the male psyche from which it flees. Why bother listening to Echo as she fades away?

Interestingly, the curse that dooms Narcissus is brought on when another "youth" feels rejected by him. In this detail, Narcissus refuses a homoerotic advance, although he clearly spurns heterosexual ones as well. One reason to reassess this point is that it reminds us of the variation in sexuality that the original myth referred to – something forgotten in subsequent psychoanalytic interpretations. David Engels, discussing psychoanalytic psychology's misuse of the Narcissus myth, comments,

> Thus, Freud's handling of the myth is characterized by his uncertainty of how to integrate narcissism, not Narcissus, into his growing complex of theories, so that he, quite understandably, prefers to ignore the precise details of the myth itself and retains only the abstract idea of "narcissism" as a somewhat shadowy form of self-love.[41]

According to Engels, the psychological term *narcissism* tarnishes the mythic character Narcissus. I would add two points: 1) that it conflates severe egotism or ego-inflation with adolescent self-absorption, which may be tediously typical and explainable without psychopathology, and 2) that it completely misses the masculine-feminine dilemma posed in the original story. A short detour about the genesis of Freud's "On Narcissism" essay illustrates that Freud misinterpreted Narcissus, although he did see an archetypal underpinning to radical selfishness and extreme egocentrism.

Sonu Shamdasani asserts that Freud's "On Narcissism" was a reworking of his drive theory, and Freud's speculations demonstrate "extended attempts at damage control."[42] A reader can infer Freud's irritation at Jung from his polemical attitude throughout part one of his essay. Freud refers to "barren theoretical controversy," his feeling "obliged" – because of Jung's *Symbols of Transformation* – to discuss what "I would gladly have been spared," and his correcting Jung's "erroneous interpretation" of defining "libido with psychic interest in general."[43] Freud tries to refute authoritatively Jung's conception of libido, in part because Freud could not explain psychotic disorders with his own energic theories. He required a new concept to account for breaks from reality that were untreatable with psychoanalysis: "The libido that has been withdrawn from the external world has been directed to the ego and thus gives rise to an attitude which may be called narcissism."[44]

Jung saw that Freud's drive theory was circumscribed in accounting for the richness of human motivations if everything psychological is reduced to mere sexual origins. Instead, he writes, "Libido is appetite in its natural state" and equivalent to "psychic energy."[45] Shamdasani notes that this formulation "broke free of the pansexualism with which Freud's libido concept had been charged."[46] Accordingly, Freud's ideas in "On Narcissism" amount to an attempt to use a thin slice from the Narcissus myth with no further reference to it, nor to the story behind it, to corral recalcitrant clinical observations about the psyche back into the stable of his drive theory. The myth of Narcissus is, however, worthy of a more discriminate reading, which tells us much about the developing male psyche coming to terms with the feminine within, separation from parents, and the development of a meaningful relationship with one's self. I find it curious to consider if the bad feelings leading to and following the split between Freud and Jung may also have contributed to Freud's narrow reading of the Narcissus myth, perhaps as a way to distance himself from memories of the tender feelings these two once shared for one another.

Gender out of the shadows

Rex Harrison voices it loud and clear in the film version of *My Fair Lady:* "Why can't a woman be more like a man?"[47] He sings of men's fairness, rationality, kindness, and so on. His song is as much a lament about the unconscious as about feelings; it is also a grievance about gender. He denigrates women because they express their feelings and frighten a man's sense of control. Of course, he could be equally speaking about what goes on inside a man as well as about the character Eliza Doolittle. The song refers to what many men, perhaps adhering to traditional masculine beliefs, but not entirely so, can't stand in themselves – feelings, irrationality, changes of mood, whims, needs.

The converse would be just as ill advised, that is, to claim that boys and men "be more like" girls and women. This wouldn't help anyone with his identity issues. I think it is simplistic to assert that in every man there is a woman, and she just awaits discovery. Yet, the figure of Echo does communicate something that can be a trouble spot in the developing male psyche. Echo – showing explicit needs for intimate relationship, connection, friendship, and conversation – represents a feminine aspect within the Narcissus myth. These qualities of relationship might acknowledge male receptivity without threatening Narcissus's masculinity, or that of any other man. This reciprocity is what many boys and men sometimes find challenging because the openness it requires can seem potentially, though misguidedly, feminizing and too vulnerable.

Traditional, norm-based masculinity usually operates in a binary fashion when it comes to gender and gender roles; one is either male or female. The recent and public fluidity of contemporary gender definitions can seem disruptive to many men's sense of identity. They may protest that they cannot keep pace with these changes, that they wish for the old days when their roles felt more clearly defined by social institutions, and that they long for unquestioned support for them within their families and society. They appear to hold a gender grievance. If we consider that in the U.S., same-sex marriage has been legal nationally only since 2015, and in the UK since 2014, then we can see we are in the midst of a period of rapid social changes around gender roles, legal definitions of marriage, and social attitudes about sexuality. This shift is welcome for many boys and men. But for others, it can seem uncertain, turbulent, and even apocalyptic. Charlie's grievance about not wanting to add to a list in his mind how he wasn't normal illustrates the endurance of binary belief systems about gender. John too expressed a gender grievance when he spoke about therapy as "mama-ing" and making him a sissy.

Returning briefly to the end of the Narcissus myth, what should we make of the flower, which blossoms where Narcissus's body laid? I think this flower could symbolize a reemergence of a transformed feminine aspect that one hopes will be accepted in the male psyche. The sensuality of flowers, often used in romantic courtship, conveys softness, seductive fragrance, and color, all of which stand in contradistinction to traditionally masculine ideals of hardness, pungency, and muted emotion except when aroused to climax or fight. This flower in the myth, itself called a narcissus, might represent a more integrated sexuality, one that is not conventionally restricted and can locate feminine qualities within a masculine psyche. I realize that, in this discussion, I too am relying on an understanding of masculine and feminine that uses certain binary notions; these may be unavoidable for now.

John and Charlie each worked through their fears – even terrors – about what could seem feminine within them, because this was strongly associated with a difference that they felt, not atypically for boys and men, was shamefully weakening. These clinical examples indicate a new way to think about the myth of Narcissus and to apply it to what might happen when male sexuality reveals itself in surprising ways. Narcissus could be understood in this story as failing to listen to the feminine within him. Depth psychotherapy and analysis involve access to intimate, internal processes. In order to avail themselves of such an approach, many boys and men struggle to learn that looking inside does not mean they are forsaking their gender identity to become like girls and women. By working through this alienation, however, they might then be able to listen to what's there.

Notes

1 "Archaic Torso of Apollo," from TRANSLATIONS FROM THE POETRY OF RAINER MARIA RILKE by Rainer Maria Rilke, trans. M. D. Herter Norton. Copyright 1938 by W. W. Norton & Company, Inc., renewed (c) 1966 by M. D. Herter Norton. Used by permission of W. W. Norton & Company, Inc.

2 K. Corbett, "Faggot = loser," *Studies in Gender and Sexuality*, 2001, vol. 2, no. 1, pp. 3–28, dx.doi.org/10.1080/15240650209349168.

3 R. F. Levant, "How do we understand masculinity? An editorial," *Psychology of Men & Masculinity*, 2008, vol. 9, no. 1, pp. 1–4.

4 R. F. Levant, "Research in the psychology of men and masculinity using the gender strain paradigm as a framework," *American Psychologist*, 2011, vol. 66, no. 8, pp. 765–76, doi:10.1037/a0025034.

5 Ibid., p. 766.

6 Ibid., p. 769.

7 Ibid., p. 772.

8 B. Reis and R. Grossmark, *Heterosexual Masculinities: Contemporary Perspectives from Psychoanalytic Gender Theory*, New York and London, Routledge, 2009, p. xvi.

9 K. Corbett, *Boyhoods: Rethinking Masculinities*, New Haven, Yale University Press, 2009, pp. 5–7.

10 Ibid., p. 217.

11 Ibid., pp. 228–9.

12 I. Hirsch, "Imperfect love, imperfect lives: Making love, making sex, making moral judgments," in B. Reis and R. Grossmark (eds.), *Heterosexual Masculinities: Contemporary Perspectives from Psychoanalytic Gender Theory*, pp. 89–104, New York and London, Routledge, 2009.

13 Ibid., p. 103.

14 Ibid., p. 102.

15 S. Freud, *Three Contributions to the Theory of Sex* (1905), The Project Gutenberg eBook, 2005. Online, available: <www.gutenberg.org/files/14969/14969-h/14969-h.htm#p7> (accessed January 24, 2017). Originally published by The Nervous and Mental Disease Publishing Company, 1920.

16 C. G. Jung, *The Psychology of the Transference*, Princeton, Princeton University Press, 1954.

17 Ibid., ¶458, p. 86.

18 Freud, *Three Essays on the Theory of Sexuality, SE* 7, 1905, pp. 125–243; and S. Freud, *The Interpretation of Dreams, SE* 4, 1900.

19 Jung, "Symbols of transformation," in H. Read, M. Fordham, and G. Adler (eds.), *CW* 5, Princeton, Princeton University Press, 1956.

20 Jung, "General index to the *Collected Works*," *CW* 20, 1979.

21 See Jung, "The state of psychotherapy today," *Civilization in Transition, CW* 10, 1934, ¶340; "Psychological commentaries on the 'Tibetan Book of the Great Liberation,'" *Psychology and Religion: West and East, CW* 11, 1939, ¶770; and "On the relation of analytical psychology to poetry," *The Spirit in Man, Art, and Literature, CW* 15, 1922, ¶102.

22 Jung, "Mysterium Coniunctionis," 1963, ¶709.
23 See *Oxford English Dictionary* (OED). Online, available: <www.oed.com>.
24 Freud, "On narcissism: An introduction," *SE* XIV, pp. 67–102, 1914.
25 Ibid., p. 88, italics in original.
26 R. Isay, *Being Homosexual: Gay Men and Their Development*, New York, Farrar Straus Giroux, 1989, p. 62.
27 Jung, "General index," *CW* 20, pp. 9–10, ¶559.
28 C. G. Jung, *Memories, Dreams, Reflections*, ed. A. Jaffé, New York, Vintage Books, 1965, pp. 24–83.
29 W. McGuire (ed.), *The Freud/Jung Letters. The Correspondence between Sigmund Freud and C.G. Jung*, trans. R. Mannheim and R. F. C. Hull, Princeton, Princeton University Press, 1974, p. 95.
30 B. Feldman, "Identity, sexuality and the self in late adolescence," *Journal of Analytical Psychology*, 1996, vol. 41, no. 4, pp. 491–507, doi:10.1111/j.1465-5922.1996.00491.x.
31 F. Bisagni, N. Fina, and C. Vezzoli (eds.), *Jung Today: Volume 2 – Childhood and Adolescence*, New York, Nova Science Publishers, 2009; M. Sidoli and G. Bovensiepen (eds.), *Incest Fantasies and Self-Destructive Acts: Jungian and Post-Jungian Psychotherapy in Adolescence*, New Brunswick and London, Transaction Publishers, 1995.
32 M-L. von Franz, *The Problem of the Puer Aeternus*, Toronto, Inner City Books, 1970/2000, p. 7.
33 A. D. Melville, trans., *Ovid Metamorphoses*, Oxford, Oxford University Press, 1986.
34 H. Gee, "The Oedipal complex in adolescence," *Journal of Analytical Psychology*, 1991, vol. 36, no. 2, pp. 193–210, doi:10.1111/j.1465-5922.1991.00193.x.
35 L. Kahn, "Sexual identity, sex of sexual contacts, and health-related behaviors among students in grades 9–12 – United States and selected sites, 2015," *Weekly Morbidity and Mortality Report*, Centers for Disease Control and Prevention, August 12, 2016, vol. 65, no. 9, pp. 1–202. Online, available: <www.cdc.gov/mmwr/volumes/65/ss/ss6509a1.htm> (accessed June 6, 2017).
36 Ibid., pp. 14, 15, 17–18, 19, 20, 40, 52, 69.
37 Ibid., p. 77.
38 B. L. B. Willoughby, N. M. Malik, and K. M. Lindahl, "Parental reactions to their sons' sexual orientation disclosures: The roles of family cohesion, adaptability, and parenting style," *Psychology of Men & Masculinity*, 2006, vol. 7, no. 1, pp. 14–26, doi:10.1037/1524-9220.7.1.14.
39 M. Jacoby, *Shame and the Origins of Self-Esteem: A Jungian Approach*, London, Routledge, 1994.
40 M. Waddell, (1998). "The scapegoat," in R. Anderson and A. Dartington (eds.), *Facing It Out: Clinical Perspectives on Adolescent Disturbance*, pp. 127–41, New York and London, Routledge.
41 D. Engels, "Narcissism against Narcissus? A classical myth and its influence on the elaboration of early psychoanalysis from Binet to Jung," in V. Zajko and E. O'Gorman (eds.), *Classical Myth and Psychoanalysis: Ancient and Modern Stories of the Self*, pp. 75–95, New York, Oxford University Press, 2013, p. 95.
42 S. Shamdasani, *Jung and the Making of Modern Psychology: The Dream of a Science*, Cambridge, Cambridge University Press, 2003, p. 227.
43 Freud, "On narcissism: An introduction," *SE* XIV, pp. 77, 79, 80.
44 Ibid., p. 75.
45 Jung, "Symbols of transformation," *CW* 5, p. 135, ¶194.
46 Shamdasani, *Jung and the Making of Modern Psychology*, p. 225.
47 "A Hymn to Him," in *My Fair Lady*, directed by G. Cukor, screenplay by A. J. Lerner, produced by Warner Brothers, 1964. Based on the play by G. Bernard Shaw, *Pygmalion*, 1913.

Chapter 4

Breaking it

At a loss for words

> I know what you're asking . . . I can't put it into words . . . I can't even find the
> words for it.
>
> —eighteen-year-old young man

When language fails us, we say we are at a loss for words, as my patient above
indicated. But what happens when, like thirteen-year-old Jason Taylor in David
Mitchell's novel *Black Swan Green*, this occurs routinely around communicating
feelings?

> It must've been around then (maybe that same afternoon) that my stammer
> took on the appearance of a hangman. Pike lips, broken nose, rhino cheeks,
> red eyes 'cause he never sleeps. . . . But it's his hands, not his face, that
> I really feel him by. His snaky fingers that sink inside my tongue and squeeze
> my windpipe so nothing'll work.[1]

In this chapter, I summarize clinical findings from the cases of three young men,
each of whom suffered from an inability to communicate deep states of alienation
and depression. Furthermore, they each had an urgent need to puncture an aspect
of inner and outer reality, breaking an important and vital boundary. Within the
analysis, questions arose about their capacity to verbalize and about their difficulties in relating to their internal experiences.

Damage to or loss of alpha function, as conceived by Bion, helps us as analysts and psychotherapists account for an inability to access, metabolize, and
ultimately express painful states of being.[2] *Alpha function*, as Bion theorized, is
a psychological capacity for turning raw life experiences into more meaningful
pieces of psychic ideation, imagery, and dreams. It is like physiological diges-
tion that separates food and liquids into nutrients our bodies need, dividing them
into smaller parts that are recombined for our use. Bion believed this function
emerged in early development out of an attuned relationship with a caregiver who
could accept, hold, and eventually express the continuous projections of an infant
and young child without overwhelming him or her. In a chronologically older

mind without this capacity for alpha function, meaningful thinking and communicating can both become impossible, and such a deficit creates profound mental disorganization.

The three young men I discuss in this chapter had disturbing experiences of *puncturing* an exterior surface of some kind. Although the psychological background for each instance of puncturing differed, this behavior can be considered in relationship to a loss of language. Puncturing can be associated with acting out, with nonverbally communicating pain that is not yet ready to be spoken about, and with giving expression to a broken self-image. The act of breaking is a common feature of puncturing, and this perhaps describes how whatever minimal sense of containment there is gets shattered. A simultaneous casualty appears to be expressive language. As noted in the *Oxford English Dictionary*, the word *puncture* derives from the same Latin root as the English word *punctuate: pungere*, meaning "to prick." Although this is just an etymological connection, I suggest these young men needed to internalize a psychological editor that would help them to express – and punctuate – painful experiences. This internal editor helps to organize raw pieces of reality like unpleasant sensory stimuli and transform them into meaningful images, dreams, and ideas. Interestingly, a medical colleague told me that when she was working in the emergency room, she had become rather skilled at splinting and bandaging the broken hands of young men because so many of them had punched through walls in states of emotional upset.

In adolescence, breakdowns of varying degrees typically occur in communication with adults, who are regarded by adolescents as out-of-touch, authoritarian, intrusive, oppressive, and so on – this list could grow rather long. In analytical treatment, this breakdown appears as a mixture of defensive retreat during times of silence or one-word answers to questions and of a seeming inability to say more, which may reflect turmoil over struggling to separate while still depending on others. Language in adolescence can become more conflictual than in latency or puberty because it reveals the workings of a mind that is not entirely sure how revealed it wants to be. This is especially so given the inner pressures of developing sexuality, which strongly reactivates oedipal themes. In some sense, why would any adolescent want to share details about this process, except perhaps with a few trusted peers?

A competing adolescent and young adult need that brackets this question is a desire to be seen. Looking inside oneself is a stepping-stone to forming an identity and to creating a capacity to relate to others whom one loves, hates, or aspires to know better. During this confusing period of life, language operates increasingly as an expression of self, although what is proclaimed one moment might be hidden or recanted in the next. Evolving problems of adolescent communication are now underscored by endless stories about how the Internet is used for cyberbullying, sexual exploitation, pornography, and violent videogaming in virtual reality. These represent new venues for communicating, with words and images, but without face-to-face contact. Adolescents have fully appropriated the Internet in ways both innocent and sinister, demonstrating its unappealing aspects.

Words can be used cruelly and viciously, but their disappearance is even more troublesome. An adolescent or young adult can hide or be unseen while significant danger unfolds and actual risk to his wellbeing increases. When acting out, an adolescent often verbalizes little or nothing. During latency, this capacity to verbalize, along with the defense of repression, helps internally to stabilize a developing child to support growth in social relations and academic learning. But with the onset of adolescence, a storm begins that often derails communicating, and the urge to act can seem like a better alternative to telling anyone about what is happening inside. How many times have I heard a parent of an adolescent say in my office, "I just don't understand him any more"? Or, more aptly, "He never talks to me." It is as if the adolescent becomes cryptic, a riddle unto himself and others. For many now, this period persists beyond early adulthood into the late 20s; a person in it sometimes called an "adultescent."[3]

Donald Winnicott describes one phase of adolescent development as the *doldrums*, one that he believes is survived by the passing of time perhaps more than anything else.[4] This is when adolescents sit around outdoors, "hang out" in cellars and bedrooms, have sleepovers that can last days, and appear content letting time elapse. These experiences may help contain restlessness, impulses for acting out, and seeking thrills. They create a model for containing growth in time, especially when shared with friends, since these peers then reinforce mutual value in waiting for the next phase of life to begin.

Bion's ideas about containment, and their elaboration by Meltzer, Alvarez, Ferro, Grotstein, Mitrani, Ogden, and others, have helped me to understand what additionally – besides time – allows for adolescent growth and maturation.[5] The right balance of internal and external containment underpins the development of a self with a future, with satisfying relationships, and with dreams and aspirations. It is also important to keep in mind here the Jungian contribution around initiation, since nowadays this archetype can seem woefully lacking in the outer social supports provided young men and women. We might ask, "Which psychological forces disrupt the internal containment needed for development to move forward?" A big question indeed, and certainly external trauma, deprivation, and family instability all play pivotal and decisive roles. Is there, however, an internal component that can undermine Bion's concept of alpha function, something destroying language and expression and coming from a darker layer of the psyche?

Adolescent and young adult development can be undone by what appears to be an ominous, uncontainable force from deep within the personality. From a Kleinian perspective, a young person in this state might be seen as using manic defenses, losing his standing in the healthier part of his personality, and becoming immersed in omnipotent, negative fantasy. This psychological decline refers to what psychoanalysts Donald Meltzer and Robin Anderson have described as being in the grip of the destructive part of the personality, which can frighteningly overtake the developing mind and body of the adolescent, leading to self-destructive behaviors.[6] A Jungian viewpoint emphasizes a failure of initiation structures leading to an upsurge in a malevolent trickster archetype, the hero turning into the anti-hero or villain. This energy potentially inflates a susceptible ego, especially when there are not adequate environmental correctives such as limits, real-time feedback from peers and adults, and other outlets for trying on an identity within a group. An example from literature is the creature in Mary Shelley's novel *Frankenstein*, which I discuss in Chapter 6. An outcome of this developmental course might be the adoption of what Erik Erikson terms negative identity.[7]

The following case examples of three young men illustrate the internal disarray when destructive and self-destructive aspects of personality become powerful and consuming. Thinking of Bion, I view this as a hijacking of alpha function in a developing mind, when internal resources are inadequate, and states of alienation predominate. In this process, a young man is left expressionless and *unable to communicate*. To cope, he searches for something to break because breaking provides a form of temporary relief – the symptom itself conveying a misguided attempt to cure the young man's psychological distress. As Jung says, this is an aim – *telos* – within the symptom. Typically, such breaking can be a kind of puncture. The relief gained, however, is ultimately unsatisfactory. The danger is that a vicious cycle might be unleashed, wherein further relief is sought through even more destructive breaking. The mind becomes psychotically disorganized by this unraveling, and a young man runs a risk of self-destruction.

A broken condom and alienation turning into psychosis

Edward asked to come to me at age fifteen. His mother had phoned me in an urgent state and said, "He needs to see you today if possible. He won't tell me why, but I know something is seriously wrong." I agreed to see Edward later that day. His mother told me a few facts about their family, and I offered to meet her and Edward's father the following day. Edward lived with them and two younger sisters, who were ten and seven years old at that time. Both parents were employed.

Edward presented in a troubled and disturbed way. He mumbled to himself incoherently, and his eyes darted to and fro. I feared he was overtly psychotic and asked if he were hearing voices. He said, "Yes," and I asked if he might tell me what they were telling him. He answered, "They say, 'You're bad, you're evil, you're disgusting.'" He appeared agitated and was bouncing on the couch in my office. I said that sounded painful, that I imagined he'd be feeling awful hearing voices speaking so badly about him like that. He relaxed somewhat then and replied, "You got that right." In response to other questions, however, Edward just mumbled, "I can't say. I just can't say." He was at a loss for words, and those that he could utter were often garbled.

In the first several sessions, I noticed that Edward kept touching the crotch area of his pants. I thought to ask about it, but as he was still considerably distressed, I opted to wait a little. He explained some paranoid ideas about his school and society. Hearing him ramble, I began to feel slightly off balance, as though I were disoriented and looking for a way to steady myself. I found that when I focused on Edward's hands, my feeling of disorientation eased. I wondered what story his hands might be telling in their frenetic and compulsive touching of his groin.

As we got acquainted, Edward ranted about consumerism and materialism, both of which he said were controlled by our government. I tried to follow his train of thought but felt this was pulling me away from something more central. He wished "that life could be harmonious like on *Star Trek*." He believed his school principal was "racist" and "homophobic." I asked why, curious because this remark about homophobia brought sexuality into our discussion. Edward responded that the principal "singles out Hispanics" for punishment. I enquired about the homophobia, and he added that the principal had refused to allow the publication of a school picture for "The Best Couple That Never Was," which included Edward and a male friend. He told me he was not gay, but he was "sick and tired of how bad gays are treated." As I considered this, I observed that the dance of his hands persisted and wondered privately if there might have been a sexual experience that Edward felt guilty about and was now inflicting on himself hallucinated recriminations. These sessions were difficult, as I weighed whether to refer him for medication. I noticed that he seemed to pull together psychologically by the end of a session. He made good use of me, and this observation led me to wait and see what his story was.

We soon spoke about his history of drug use, which alarmed me, because it included hallucinogens. I questioned whether he was presenting in the aftermath of a drug-induced hallucinosis or psychosis. However, he didn't show other cognitive or behavioral signs of either being intoxicated or immediately post-intoxicated. For example, the movement of his hands wasn't sloppy and uncontrolled; on the contrary, it conveyed a sense of intention. I gently pressed him about recent drug consumption, and he assured me that, lately, his use had been limited to marijuana. He denied ever having a negative experience from his use of recreational drugs. During this initial period of meeting twice weekly, his hands continued their nervous display around and near the crotch of his pants. He pulled and tugged at the cloth, sometimes reaching his whole hand under his genital area as if rearranging a source of discomfort. As we spent more time together, he felt less psychotic to me, and his parents confirmed that they saw him doing better at home and school, completing chores and assignments and even cleaning his room. He told me he still occasionally heard voices, but they were "less than before and quieter like a song fade."

I realized how helpful it was to focus on Edward's hands, and I wanted to ask about them at the right moment. If I asked too quickly, he might feel I was being intrusive and could react by becoming defensive and inhibit himself. I had a concrete notion that perhaps Edward's underwear was too tight. But I also believed there was more to it. After a month, when I felt our rapport was relatively good and he seemed much less tense in sessions, I said that I kept noticing his hands – that I thought they were trying to draw my attention to his body. Was there something he wanted to tell me about that? He blushed a bit and nodded yes. I said that he hadn't talked with me yet about sex, and I wondered if this was on his mind and making him worry.

At this point, Edward dropped his head into his hands, which were propped on his knees. He sobbed, running his hands through his hair as if he might pull it out. He muttered softly about not knowing what to say. I sat with him for several minutes while he cried. His hands were now devoted entirely to massaging his head, rubbing his eyes, pressing his forehead, and twirling his longish hair. They seemed to confirm a move away from compulsively touching his genitals and his trying to get into his head and mind. I said that I thought there might be a story about sex he was waiting to tell someone. He looked at me with swollen eyes and said, "I don't know how you know that, but that's true." I am reminded in writing this now of Freud's observations about fortuitous actions performed "unthinkingly . . . for something to do with one's hands."[8] Freud explains how actions and movements with our bodies often tell an unconscious story if we pay attention to them.

In the following sessions, Edward then told me a complicated story about his first sexual encounter, which had occurred several months before with an eighteen-year-old young woman. He explained because it was "my first time, I was kind of clumsy. I didn't know how to use a condom." He tore two condoms while putting them on, and eventually his partner helped him with the third one. Before he ejaculated, however, this condom also broke, and it was too late to do anything about it. The young woman became pregnant from their sex with this punctured condom.

Throughout this recounting, there were many interruptions, when Edward would sit silently or sometimes mumble, "I can't say more." He was lost for words. His hands no longer moved frenetically, and his thinking seemed to stall into a cold emptiness at these moments. I was aware of how alone and alienated he felt even sitting with me, and I commented that perhaps he felt unsure how much to trust me. But that comment was off the mark because Edward really did want to tell me everything that had happened, just at his own meandering and slow pace. As the British psychoanalyst Patrick Casement notes, patients will often give us unconscious consultation when we are open to it.[9]

Edward gradually told me the whole story. Weeks before coming to see me, Edward learned about the pregnancy, which he and the young woman kept secret. She decided to have an abortion, and together, they went to a clinic, where they found out how much the procedure would cost. They raided their meager savings, and not having enough, they proceeded to sell valuable personal items to other teenagers to collect the necessary sum. Edward went with her on the day of the procedure. Shortly after this, he reported, "My mind went crazy. The voices came to me, and I got fucking scared I'd never be the same."

As I summarize Edward's story, I realize that it makes more sense in this summary than in his original telling. Within those sessions, there were conversational gaps when he stopped and started talking, interruptions with various paranoid ideas, and unarticulated feelings of profound sadness. I worried about his sanity and the depth of his psychosis. I suggested he consider a medication to help stabilize him during this rough time, but he declined my referral. Repeatedly, I was struck by the level of his guilt and a heavy gloom that he brought into the room with him. His alienation was intense and deep. I thought at these times that he was punishing himself for the broken condom, and I said that he seemed to believe this accident was completely his fault.

He agreed, revealing that he believed his penis was "too pointy." He added, "Maybe that's what happens when you're circumcised," which then led him to share paranoid thoughts about why circumcision is widespread in the United States. He said that his penis had "tiny, invisible prickers on it."[10] "That's what broke the condom." He feared he had also injured the girl, somehow mutilating her insides with his sharp spiked penis. He said he was haunted by an image of the aborted fetus. He described it as "a mutant, damaged beyond recognition, missing brain cells, and with an extra limb. It'd be a fucking mess." This image might have represented Edward's mind when he first came to see me. A destructive force had taken over, and he couldn't contain a storm of primitive sexual forces following all that happened after his first sexual experience. Edward's imaginary "penis with prickers" was a source of destruction; it not only caused the condom to break but also impregnated his partner with "a mutant." This penile monstrosity left Edward with "a fucking mess," in which his mind deteriorated into senseless recriminations and psychotic ideas.

After six months of intensive psychotherapy, Edward recovered from the acute phase of his psychosis. Although pharmacotherapy probably would have helped him not feel so miserable, his psychotic symptoms diminished without it. He continued in treatment with me for another six months during which he worked more on issues about his identity and self-image. He was worried he would be "a loser" and felt especially upset with his father for "not being a better role model." Edward remained a troubled young man, but he did learn to articulate many aspects of what had terrified him and made his mind feel like a trap for punishment. Language and the expression of emotion were no longer such formidable barriers.

Cutting and taking alienation in a perverse direction

When we met, Anthony was twenty-one years old, though still very much in adolescence. He had finished college and was working fulltime. He was a wiry, jumpy fellow who didn't seem comfortable in his skin. He had long struggled with psychological difficulties that included serious depression with psychotic features, and he had been cutting himself since age twelve, as I mentioned in Chapter 1. He grew up in a small town with his mother and younger brother, who had severe physical disabilities. His father, an immigrant, abandoned the family when Anthony was five, soon after his brother's birth. His father subsequently led a transient lifestyle, living out of a van that he drove around the country. Anthony later told me, "I think my father might have Asperger's."

He rarely saw his father and, at the start of treatment, had not seen him in four years. Anthony spoke about the onset of his cutting at age twelve as stemming from being bullied and teased by other children. "I was a total wuss, a wimp, too timid to stand up for myself. I'd never let my son behave the way I did. No spine."[11]

He thought, however, that his cutting proved that he was secretly "strong – that I could stand the pain." Yet, disturbingly, he also said, "It was also to let the evil out of me." Anthony believed he was "possessed" by "evil energy" and that bleeding was one method to release this. In other words, his puncturing of his skin was a mistaken attempt at self-healing. Jung wrote about this meaning hidden in a symptom: "It is correct that neurotic symptoms and complexes are also elaborate 'arrangements' which inexorably pursue their aims, with incredible obstinacy and cunning."[12]

Anthony described his belief about this: "When I'm bleeding, sometimes I think it lets evil out of me. The first few drops look black; because when you first bleed, the blood is darker. When it absorbs more oxygen, it gets redder. I imagine those first drops are the beginning of an evil stream." When he talked this way, I felt jarred and incredulous; it was strikingly at odds with his appearance: angelic, timid, and boyish. Listening to him, I felt my skin crawling. He could sound creepy and sinister. In terms of projective identification, I thought the sensation of my skin crawling gave me a hint of why he cut himself. I felt as if I were being scared by a clever monster in disguise, leaving me helpless and desperate. This monster, I came to think, was in Anthony and was part of what he felt helpless against.

During an early session, I talked at length with Anthony about his cutting. He relished telling me about it, and when I commented on his excitement, he blushed. I mentioned that possibly something about it felt like a turn on, and he agreed. "It makes me feel powerful. It's kind of exciting."

As I heard this, I wondered if Anthony's cutting was a source of perverse sexual satisfaction. I inquired, "Has a therapist ever just asked you to stop doing it?"

He looked amused and surprised. "No. Actually, no," he said.

I replied, "I'd like for you to stop it."

He asked if I intended to medicate him if he didn't.

I thought his question conveyed that he saw me as someone potentially punishing him. I said no, but that I'd like a chance to take care of him in a different way. This involved our trying to understand together how his mind worked; I believed there was another pain that I needed to hear about, instead of only what came from his cutting. I add here that I didn't believe him when he said no other therapists had tried to place a limit on him. I think he lied to test me about whether I took it seriously and to see what I'd do if he didn't stop.

Anthony cautioned me, "I'll think it over." In the next session, he brought in several drawings that he'd made of himself, self-portraits, that depicted him as a gargoyle. These were drawn with artistic form, expressed through detailed shading and good three-dimensional perspective. There was a series of five drawings, beginning with one of Anthony as a baby gargoyle in an egg. This baby creature's most prominent feature was its large claws. The "adult" gargoyles were likewise characterized by long, powerful claws. Their bodies were sinewy and naked except for loincloths. The heads were bald; the noses protruded; and the mouths were filled with pointed teeth.

As we looked at his drawings, I asked Anthony how he felt showing them to me. He said he had shown them to a previous therapist who seemed frightened by them and told him he was psychotic. His opinion of her was that "she overreacted." I wondered if he might have a similar worry about me. He asked, "Well, what do you think?" I answered that I thought these drawings contained many possible meanings about how he saw himself. He rolled his eyes, warning me, "They're just drawings." I said that was true, but these drawings seemed to be about someone who might have felt lonely and outcast. He argued, "You're reading too much into them." His repeated negation of my observations felt as though he were cutting off our interaction, to keep it from going anywhere, using his imaginary claws to tear away at our communicating more meaningfully.

I replied that perhaps he thought I was now overreacting like the other therapist, when I hoped instead to understand his feelings. I continued by saying that maybe these feelings seemed like they were too much for him. He paused, then nodded. "That's a possibility. I can't even describe my feelings." When it came to questions about his feelings, Anthony would usually stare blankly ahead, speechless. More than once he said his feelings were "like tiny insects I can hardly see."

At the end of this session, Anthony wanted me to keep his drawings. I made what seems, looking back, a relational error because I suggested he take them and bring them next time. This decision bothered me when I considered how frequently younger children might ask me to keep their drawings in the office, and I usually would agree as a way to hold and contain something of importance. Why didn't I do this for Anthony?

At the time, I felt that I wanted to see how he handled this limit, similar to my request that he not cut anymore. Now, I think that I enacted a countertransference anxiety around how close I wanted to let him get to me. As I later learned, Anthony's perverse behaviors extended quite far, and possibly intuiting some of this, I chose to create some distance by giving him back the drawings. He didn't bring them again.

After this session, we occasionally discussed the gargoyles, although thematically we stuck with the direct ways in which Anthony felt alienated from others, from me, and from himself. He continued in treatment with me for another three years, and during this time, he eventually stopped cutting himself. He often referred to the encounter of my asking him not to cut as "meeting Dr. No." Although this moniker might represent a projection of his negating self, he more than once joked, "Dr. No could be N-O, or it could be K-N-O-W." I thought by this he meant that he saw I might know when putting a limit on himself was good for his mental health.

The pictures of the gargoyles offered Anthony an opportunity to communicate profound loneliness, alienation, and his belief he was an outcast, cut off from others. They showed me aggressive and monstrous aspects of his self that drove him psychotic. They also brought him into our relationship as a clawing creature that, he likely fantasized, could rip me to shreds. I felt that I had to find ways for us to feel close to each other. This was a challenge.

Anthony's perverse world included a women's underwear fetish that involved stealing underwear and wearing it while he masturbated. He saw himself in this fantasy as a triumphant thief who fooled his victim into a degrading situation over which she had no control. He imagined the woman would feel humiliated when she discovered what he had done. His other sexual fantasies were often about adolescent girls, perhaps indicative of the time in his life when his development went off course around his own puberty, when he was bullied, felt weak, and began cutting himself.

Anthony's gargoyle identity, like Edward's mutant baby, represented an alienated state of mind when he began treatment. Although quite bright, Anthony had been an under-achiever because his psychosis disrupted his capacity to think over long stretches. The gargoyle, capable of tearing apart his mind with its claws, made him seem more stupid than he really was. It shredded not only Bion's alpha function, but also representations of other good internal objects that could contain him. It made his interior world unsafe. Although Anthony obtained short-term relief from his suffering and isolation through self-harm, he was consumed by this identification with the destructive side of his personality.

Gillian Straker, in an article about adolescents who cut, hypothesizes that cutting is an attempt to build self-structure through being one's own mirror, trying to exist outside of interpersonal experience (she refers to this as "auto-mirroring").[13] She believes this fails because the person is never truly seen by anyone else. Anthony retreated into a perverse world that had many of the omnipotent, autoerotic qualities that Straker describes. This dynamic changed during his treatment with me because I saw other explanations for Anthony's "evil," and I indicated I wasn't put off by learning about that. I wanted to see as much of him as I could. He sometimes resisted my appeal at greater involvement, but he also seemed to like it. After working through the tension between us about limits, Anthony began to shift psychologically in how he viewed his sexual behaviors. Much of this work occurred through my labeling his feelings (such as loneliness, rejection, intimidation, inferiority) and encouraging him to express them in his own words. Gargoyles are inarticulate beings (except in comics). Anthony's path in therapy went straight through learning an emotional vocabulary to communicate what happened inside him, especially when he felt hurt, cast aside, and furious.

Alienation leading to mania

Manic states are, by psychological definition, geared toward action, racing thoughts, and excessive talking that is difficult to follow.[14] Melanie Klein described a relational triad often seen in manic states characterized by control, triumph, and contempt.[15] It doesn't help that our culture supports manic inflation in so many contradictory ways. Many boys and men idealize elements of mania because of the supposed strength, authority, and power implied in it. In a way, mania is an invitation to take whatever is inside a person's house and put it outside, come what may.

Tom was twenty-one years old when we first met. He had been sent home from college because he was severely depressed and abusing marijuana. Tom was the younger of two sons. Although intelligent, he frequently underachieved and had an erratic academic history. He appeared to have recently woken up and had dark circles under his eyes. Overweight, he was dressed in loose athletic clothing. Both of Tom's parents had been employed during his childhood, and they relied on nannies to care for the children. Tom seemed to have felt some emotional abandonment around this situation. He only began experimenting with drugs and alcohol when he was at college.

He spoke loudly and defensively. "I don't need to be here. The university is making a big deal about nothing." He tried to impress me with how intelligent he was and told me his scores on college admission exams. When I asked what he enjoyed learning at school, he replied, "Not much. The professors are idiots, most of them. They just want you to regurgitate their pet ideas back to them, and I'm not into that." I felt he was judging me to be another "idiot."

After Tom had finished his first term at university, he began to sleep all the time. I asked what had happened. He replied, "I don't know. Er, I can't put it into words." I wondered whether he had been depressed to be asleep so much. "I don't know," he said. "What's depressed?" He looked perplexed and was at an uncharacteristic loss of words for someone who often proclaimed how much he knew.

Tom continued to abuse marijuana and alcohol despite my warnings that this hurt him physically and psychologically. He questioned my knowledge, asserting, "I looked it up on the Internet. It's not as bad as you say. If it was, the whole country would be a mess." He often used this excuse – "the Internet says" – to contradict me and proclaim his own disturbing beliefs. This selective use of false information from the Internet has become a factor in working with many patients who want to confirm personal biases and to dispute my professional perspective when it relates to science, clinical experience, and evidence. Tom came in after this exchange with a bandaged hand. He told me he had slipped and fallen into a window at home when he was high.

He came to a subsequent session visibly high, with dilated pupils, slurred speech, and hypomanic affect. I said that although he might have wanted me to see him like this, I had little way to help him when he was high. The next time we met I suggested he consider a twelve-step program like Alcoholics Anonymous (AA). He became angry and then missed several sessions. When he returned, he told me he'd lost his job at a grocery store for insubordination. He derided the boss as "a bonehead." I imagined Tom probably felt similarly toward me for suggesting AA and another intensive drug treatment program.

Tom soon got into trouble for smashing car windows with a friend when they were high. It was late at night; someone phoned the police; and they were arrested and charged for property damage, disturbing the peace, and resisting arrest. Tom tried to brush off this incident with a hypomanic attitude that led him to believe he'd get off without any serious consequences.

I challenged him, wondering if we could think together about my helping him so he wouldn't put himself at such risk again.

He answered, "It's just a fucking joke."

I thought he was waiting to see if I'd give up. I said that what happened to him was no joke to me.

He paused, growing somber, "Oh." After a long silence, Tom sighed. "So what are we going to do?"

I noted that he'd just said "we."

He became suddenly anxious, fidgeting on the couch and stuttering, "Er, I . . . I . . . I guess that's, that's, that's what I said. Yeah, yeah. You and . . . and . . . and me." This moment is when Tom's therapy started to move in a more meaningful direction. In describing what had happened the night he was arrested, Tom told me that he'd been so high he began to hallucinate. He saw "alien zombies" inside parked cars, and he began to strike these car windows, trying to make these terrifying visions disappear.

In the weeks after this, Tom became more openly depressed, sleeping a lot, crying for reasons he couldn't understand, and saying, "I think this must be what sad is." He described how lonely he often felt. He told me he was certain that he'd never find a life partner. He began to speak differently about his harshness, his bragging, and his arguing with others as problems that isolated him. He told me that he didn't know how to be affectionate toward anyone. He did know about shattering things. His frequent breaking and hitting expressed something inside him that was constantly breaking too – a mind barely held together. His internal house was kept in a shattered state, with cracked windows, walls with holes, and broken doors.

Like Anthony, Tom used his body to express how extreme his emotional pain was and how damaged he felt himself to be. Despite these considerable challenges, he remained in treatment for another two years and was able to stop his use of drugs and alcohol. In addition to his therapy with me, he completed an intensive outpatient substance-abuse program, and he began attending AA meetings regularly. Tom's clinical presentation was complicated initially by the legal fact that as a twenty-one-year-old, he had a privacy right to keep any of his doctors from communicating with one another or with his parents. Only later in his treatment would he permit me to speak with his parents, though he doubted any

good would come of it. I continually reminded him of the value of open communication, and I often used what happened between us as an example that he could
understand for why it mattered.

A lost ability to name feelings

At a special school where I previously worked, the children, mostly boys, had
significant social and medical problems.[16] Many were survivors of violent trauma.
When I began to work there, I often observed them in their classrooms and on the
playground and found myself thinking that these boys reminded me of nursing
home patients. They had trouble speaking; many walked in funny ways, dragging
their feet or bumping into walls; and most were socially awkward, clumsy, disoriented, and forgetful. It was as if these children were stroke victims, especially in
how they moved so oddly. I mentioned this observation after a lecture that Anne
Alvarez gave in San Francisco.[17] She found this comparison interesting since her
lecture had been about how, in children with autism or psychosis, problems in
walking often mirrored problems in thinking. Because of experiences of deprivation, poverty, violence, and other trauma that impinged on their brain's hardware,
the boys at this school were understandably at a loss for words. Consistently,
two-thirds of them required intensive speech therapy to address their speech and
language disorders, which interfered with articulation, communication, expression, and fluency.[18]

Loss of speech can be a feature of many psychological conditions, for example,
an obsessive avoidance of certain words, truncated word usage found in many
psychotic and autistic states, and elective mutism. Certainly, in adolescence, communication can become sparse. An intense need for privacy, keeping secrets, and
a move to separate from family: these all influence how much is said and to whom
it is related. The adult world is particularly suspect and regarded as a likely source
of intrusion and misunderstanding. The phenomenon of brooding in adolescence
is characterized by withdrawal, moodiness, and few words. Language is perceived
as a source of unwanted exposure because it can become a possible avenue for
uninvited infiltration into an adolescent's psyche – a key to a locked door.

The psychological problems described in the cases of Edward, Anthony, and
Tom arose in different circumstances, yet they each shared a feature of being at
a loss for words to describe emotions and feelings. This is sometimes referred
to as *alexithymia*, a clinical and descriptive term also characterized by concrete
thinking and lack of much imagination or fantasy life.[19] In Chapter 3, I referred to
alexithymia as being associated with certain traditional masculine behaviors, and
I will consider it further in Chapter 9's discussion about effective psychotherapy
and analysis with boys and men. Here, I believe these cases describe a somewhat
different phenomenon because each young man had an active, visually oriented
imagination along with good intelligence. They struggled to convey to others
what happened inside emotionally. Edward's initial incoherence ("I can't say")
indicated an extreme end of this spectrum. Anthony's seemingly articulate and

intelligent nature showed another variation of difficulty in communicating, when, for example, he referred to his feelings as "insects" that were "alien" to him. Similarly, Tom was capable of intellectual conversation that he used to attack others and defend himself, although he experienced a peculiar loss of words ("What's depressed?") when it came to describing how he felt. In these three cases, the range of not communicating emotionally stretched from incoherence (Edward) to dissociation (Anthony) to confusion (Tom), and it affected how they related to language.

Some of these clinical observations could be classified as defensive; the boy or young man does not want to let someone inside, and he does not want to look inside himself: withdrawal and avoidance. Communicative aspects of language are shunned to protect an inner fragility and to guard entry to their house. But I think their loss of a vocabulary for feelings extended beyond defensive purposes. In their states of alienation, each young man showed how a destructive part of the personality undermined a capacity to communicate. Their evocative yet disturbing imagery (mutant baby, gargoyle, alien zombies) afforded glimpses of how this destructive part produced internal chaos, cutting them off from relating to the wider world.

A loss of internal containment goes hand in hand with enabling a destructive part of the personality to become dominant. Although I have not discussed each boy's family history in detail, there was a prevalent failure to internalize resourceful, good-enough parental objects. The absence of these, in a process that has been described by Bion, Ogden, Ferro, and others, creates a lack of internal containment that leads to severely disturbed states of mind.[20] For example, Edward's parents grew marijuana at home, and Edward described their house as being in "a haze" so thick that he feared for his own lungs. His father was almost always high. Anthony's father was for him "a sad case," and his mother diverted her attention from him to his disabled brother whose care exhausted her. Tom's parents both traveled extensively and left their children in the care of relatives and nannies. Each case shows a profound disturbance emerging when secure parental objects are missing and unavailable or, instead, are seen as attacking. What becomes internalized is itself dangerous and perhaps defies accurate representation and description because it feels too scary to know.

Breaking it

Puncture is not necessarily related in a causal way with loss of words in these young men. In each of these clinical examples, puncture involved a broken surface in contact with the young man's body – a condom on penis, a knife cutting skin, and hands through a window. A boy's body in adolescence, and a young man's right after, is charged with sexual energy and many conflicts around what to do with it. Masturbation as an outlet does not involve a conscious act of penetration, and in at least two of the cases (Edward and Anthony), there were reports of compulsive masturbation. Masturbating was experienced as comparatively safe, whereas penetration seemed to signify an elusive, dangerous form of masculinity. Edward was guilt-ridden with an idea that his "prickered penis" broke the condom and created a mutant baby; the act of penetration became traumatizing for him. Anthony cut as a form of self-penetration and imagined that he was no "wimp," but instead tough enough to take it. This act may have made him feel stronger than his own father, a kind of oedipal victory over a father who seemed mentally ill and disabled.

Perhaps, in these three cases, puncture occurred as a byproduct of a deeper phenomenon that could be considered fractured internal containment. As such, puncture was a symptomatic expression for a ruptured mind that enabled destructive forces in the young man's personality to gain an upper hand in dominating his psyche. Loss of emotional communication is but one possible consequence of this process. When this happens, however, it renders the boy or young man incapable of describing and speaking about what it feels like inside himself. Problems then arise in identifying feelings, in perceiving them, reflecting on them, and in holding on to them. A positive meaning behind this symptom of puncture may be that the patient is trying to break in or break through his own house to create an opening for something helpful to come inside, reducing his alienation.

The imagery in these cases expressed some of the pain associated with feeling alienated and wanting desperately to break out of it. Gustav Bovensiepen, a Jungian analyst, articulates that aggressive imagery can point toward the emergence of symbolization for harsh, even traumatic parts of experience.[21] He uses Bion's concept of turning beta into alpha elements to describe how this process unfolds. *Beta elements* refer to concrete sensory impressions and unprocessed emotional data that we may want to rid ourselves of because they can feel bad; *alpha elements* are the transformed pieces that alpha function makes available for symbolic processes such as dreaming. Bovensiepen's case example, based on medical trauma that a nine-year-old boy suffered early in life, shows how violent and destructive images are created as part of a comic-book game played between the analyst and his young patient. Such images have therapeutic utility and could be conceived as indicating a dawn, or even a restoration, of the alpha function, converting raw beta elements into metabolized pieces of psychic experience.

In this chapter's case examples, alpha function may have existed in a proto-form, which is vivid, visual, and not easily linked to language. If so, then it is critical to take up images verbally for transformation to proceed. As my patients and I discussed them, we needed to get at the bodily pain that the puncture caused. The images offered an entry into this material, and the focus quickly shifted to body-based anxieties and fears. Mishaps of puncture seemed to encompass a view of body image that could be mutilated or misshapen.

There are many ways to understand this impulse to break something. Jung writes about the trickster archetype – that the "most alarming characteristic is his unconsciousness . . . that his body is not a unity, and his two hands fight each other."[22] This idea captures poignantly the struggle of these young men caught between alienation and a desire for someone to see their suffering. The images of

Edward's hands touching his groin but not telling me why, of Anthony describing what he felt when he cut himself, and of Tom breaking car windows while high – they each reveal someone in the grip of a harmful trickster who undermines self-regulation, initiative, and longings for a more positive identity. This trickster is not playful and growth-oriented in testing limits to experiment with possible ways of developing. Instead, he is reminiscent of what Donald Kalsched describes as an inner "daimon" that persecutes a psyche seeking to move outside its influence and power.[23] As a result, a person so affected ends up even lonelier and further traumatized, which is a recipe for alienation.

A psychoanalytic understanding of breaking or puncture and the associated images in these young men's minds might look at ego functioning and problems of containment. For example, as I summarize in Chapter 2, Didier Anzieu theorizes a containing function called "the skin ego" that arises in part from the skin-to-skin contact of a mother's holding her baby when she encircles him in her arms.[24] The skin thus becomes our first container for distress and sensations, as well as a place of soothing, pleasure, and arousal. Anzieu's work builds on Esther Bick's groundbreaking contribution about the skin in early object relations.[25]

To understand one aspect of the skin ego, Anzieu uses a metaphor of a kernel and a shell, the kernel representing instinctual impulses and the shell a container. When this container fails us:

> An instinctual excitation that is diffuse, constant, scattered, non-localizable, nonidentifiable, unquenchable, results when the psychical topography consists of a kernel without a shell; the individual seeks a substitute in physical pain or psychical anxiety: he wraps himself in suffering.[26]

The three cases discussed here show a manifestation of this failure of containing, which would occur from a break in the skin ego, with the psyche becoming over-stimulated, losing a protective shell, and replacing it with an envelope of pain and suffering. For Anthony and Tom, this led to situations of bodily harm; whereas for Edward, it took the form of hallucinations. Perhaps the monstrous images they each reported in representing these experiences were the beginnings of a repair for a lost containing function. Importantly, each young man shared that nighttime was troublesome. Edward and Tom both reported recurring nightmares, and Anthony spoke of dream fragments with Kafkaesque images and scenes. Thinking of theory here, I would hypothesize impairment in Bion's alpha function, leading to a condition in which the remains of the day cannot be adequately dreamed about at night. Anzieu might say that the skin ego is torn in a way that it can't be used as a screen for dreaming.

Lost for words

Loss of words that signify and express emotional meanings suggests something specific about the toll on the psyche of these young men. Bion writes, "I think that what the patient feels is the nearest thing to a fact – as I ordinarily understand it – that he is ever likely to experience."[27] Regardless of how we conceptualize it, a loss of communicative ability frequently brings intense bodily preoccupations that often are self-destructive. In such an alienated state, breaking and causing a real puncture might be signs of internal and relational brokenness. Additionally, loss of a feeling vocabulary is an actual social and interpersonal impairment, which is somewhat ironic given these young men's preoccupations with strength and power. Emotional intelligence is required for deeper satisfaction at work and in relationships.

Puncturing is an act of breaking through a barrier, opening separate spaces. Through this perforation, entry is gained to another closed and often protected space. From a sexual standpoint, it is akin to penetration. Edward's situation most clearly resembled this aspect of puncture with his tale of the broken condom. One could also imagine here some of Edward's oedipal dilemma in identifying with a weakened father who seemed lost in a cloud of marijuana – that penetration could be problematic, unsure, hazy.

Literally, puncture connotes piercing, crossing, and violation. We can see in Anthony's compulsion to cut how this violation served both to punish himself for being weak and to feed omnipotence about an imagined ability to withstand pain. Symbolically, a puncture that breaks through can also mean crossing into new territory, and in that manner, puncture can also allude to a later adolescent process of moving into adulthood. This meaning has more of an initiatory context that represents crossing a threshold, and in many ways, this reflected the experience of Tom, who failed at his attempt to launch into more independent living and had to return home.

In ordinary everyday use, we speak of getting to the point, cutting someone off, sharpening an argument, trimming our expectations, carving out an exception, breaking through the nonsense, and puncturing someone's dreams or pride. Puncture seems to represent clarity in expression as well as a discriminating mind that can categorize and create order based on observable differences. Along these lines, puncture could be viewed as an aspect of thinking itself, one that moves right into the core of a subject, separates overlapping and indistinguishable parts, and makes them available for new thoughts to emerge.

Our thoughts are not the same as our language. Steven Pinker, a Harvard psychologist, notes the following:

> The idea that thought is the same as language is an example of what can be called a conventional absurdity. . . . We have all had the experience of uttering or writing a sentence, then stopping and realizing that it wasn't exactly what we mean to say. To have that feeling, there has to be a "what we meant to say" that is different from what we said.[28]

In this sense, language is a behavior that depends on internal access and cognitive skill to express what we mean. Pinker believes that words are symbols. A word's "power comes from the fact that every member of a linguistic community uses it interchangeably in speaking and understanding."[29] Think about this: if the interior of our minds, our "houses," is missing these symbols, if they're hidden there from us, then we will not be able to use language to communicate meaningfully. We cannot participate in the behavioral levels of language, which include not only sharing, telling, and explaining, but also lying, gossiping, and joking.

For Edward, Anthony, and Tom, a frightening loss of language occurred. At the onset of their therapies, they were not able to communicate how they felt, which emotions stormed inside them, and even how these feelings might be named. Feeling words, as symbols, were not accessible, because there was a defensive split isolating feelings within the unconscious. These young men were thus in states of profound alienation, in which disturbing parts of their existence had been broken off and hidden beyond verbal expression. They were, in a sense, isolated as much within themselves as outside. They used the containing aspects of their therapeutic relationships with me to learn an emotional vocabulary to speak about their suffering. There were probably hundreds of repeated moments of my asking, "What's that like, what's that feeling right there?" before feeling words became useful to them. In this endeavor, my hope was that they each felt not only more contained but also less alienated.

The German philosopher and essayist Johann Gottfried Herder, who lived and worked mainly in the later 18th century, wrote a treatise on human language about the origins of language.[30] In his work, he proposes that language emerges only when human nature has a capacity for containing the totality of its experience. He defines this totality as referring to a unity of feeling and thinking, of receiving and doing. Herder argues that an exclusion of one or the other degrades our capacity to communicate through language. He views language above all as naturally incorporating the many paradoxes of human existence. When we lose this capacity to express all that our existence encompasses, we lose our humanity. We become alienated.

Notes

1   D. Mitchell, *Black Swan Green*, New York, Random House, 2007, p. 26.
2   W. R. Bion, *Learning from Experience*, Lanham, MD, Rowman & Littlefield, 1962.
3   Dictionary.com. Online, available: <www.dictionary.com/browse/adultescent>.
4   D. W. Winnicott, "Struggling through the doldrums" (1963), in C. Winnicott, R. Shepherd, and M. Davis (eds.), *Deprivation and Delinquency*, pp. 124–33, London and New York, Tavistock Publications, 1984.
5   D. Meltzer, "The Kleinian expansion of Freud's metapsychology," *International Journal of Psychoanalysis*, 1981, vol. 62, pp. 177–85; A. Alvarez, *Live Company: Psychoanalytic Psychotherapy with Autistic, Borderline, Deprived and Abused Children*, London and New York, Routledge, 1992; A. Ferro, *The Bi-Personal Field: Experiences in Child Analysis*, London and New York, Routledge, 1999; and A. Ferro, *Mind Works: Technique and Creativity in Psychoanalysis*, East Sussex, and New York, Routledge, 2009; J. S. Grotstein, *Who Is the Dreamer Who Dreams the Dream?* Hillsdale, NJ, The Analytic Press, 2000; J. L. Mitrani, "Taking the transference: Some technical

implications in three papers by Bion," *International Journal of Psychoanalysis*, 2001, vol. 82, pp. 1085–104; T. H. Ogden, *Rediscovering Psychoanalysis: Thinking and Dreaming, Learning and Forgetting*, East Sussex, and New York, Routledge, 2009.

6 D. Meltzer, *Sexual States of Mind*, Perthshire, Scotland, Clunie Press, 1973; R. Anderson, "Suicidal behaviour and its meaning in adolescence," in R. Anderson and A. Dartington (eds.), *Facing it Out: Clinical Perspectives on Adolescent Disturbance*, New York, Routledge, 1998.

7 E. Erikson, *Identity: Youth and Crisis*, New York, W. W. Norton & Company, 1968.

8 S. Freud, *The Psychopathology of Everyday Life*, London, Penguin, 1901/2002, p. 183.

9 P. Casement, *Learning from the Patient*, New York, Guilford, 1991.

10 This was an unusual word for Edward to use. *Prick* can mean "to pierce" as well as being a vulgar term for an obnoxious man. This dual sense may have been an unconscious condensation of how he felt, judging himself to have been a prick for pricking her.

11 *Wuss* is American slang for a "weakling."

12 C. G. Jung, "On the psychology of the unconscious" (1917/1943), *Two Essays on Analytical Psychology, CW* 7, 1969, p. 40, ¶54.

13 G. Straker, "Signing with a scar: Understanding self-harm," *Psychoanalytic Dialogues*, 2006, vol. 16, no. 1, pp. 93–112.

14 *Diagnostic and Statistical Manual of Mental Disorders*, 5th Edition, (DSM 5), Arlington, VA, American Psychiatric Association, 2013.

15 H. Segal, *Introduction to the Work of Melanie Klein*, New York, Basic Books, 1974, p. 83.

16 Oakes Children's Center is in San Francisco, California, and was founded in 1963 by a group of parents.

17 A. Alvarez, "A new look at the concept of unconscious phantasy with Bion and child development in mind: Links between the dynamic form of unconscious phantasy, and walking and thinking in three child cases," paper presented as part of the Child Development Program of the San Francisco Psychoanalytic Institute and Society, April 5, 1997, in San Francisco, California.

18 R. Tyminski and P. Goel, "Outcome-based evaluation of day treatment for children with pervasive developmental disorders," Unpublished manuscript, 2000.

19 G. J. Taylor, D. Ryan, and R. M. Bagby, "Toward the development of a new self-report alexithymia scale," *Psychotherapy and Psychosomatics*, 1985, vol. 44, no, 4, pp. 191–9; P. E. Sifneos, "The prevalence of 'alexithymic' characteristics in psychosomatic patients," *Psychotherapy and Psychosomatics*, 1973, vol. 22, no. 2, pp. 255–62.

20 W. R. Bion, "Attacks on linking," *International Journal of Psychoanalysis*, 1959, vol. 40, 308–15. See also Bion, *Learning from Experience*; and Meltzer, "The Kleinian expansion of Freud's metapsychology"; Alvarez, *Live Company*; Ferro, *The Bi-Personal Field* and *Mind Works;* Grotstein, *Who Is the Dreamer Who Dreams the Dream?*; Mitrani, "Taking the transference"; and Ogden, *Rediscovering Psychoanalysis*.

21 G. Bovensiepen, "Symbolic attitude and reverie: Problems of symbolization in children and adolescents," *Journal of Analytical Psychology*, 2002, vol. 47, no. 2, pp. 241–57.

22 Jung, "On the psychology of the trickster figure" (1954), *The Archetypes and the Collective Unconscious, CW* 9i, 1968, p. 263, ¶472.

23 D. Kalsched, *The Inner World of Trauma: Archetypal Defenses of the Personal Spirit*, London and New York, Routledge, 1996.

24 D. Anzieu, "Fonctions du moi-peau," *L'Information Psychiatrique*, 1984, vol. 60, pp. 869–75; *The Skin Ego*, trans. C. Turner, New Haven and London, Yale University Press, 1989; "The film of the dream," in S. Flanders (ed.), *The Dream Discourse Today*, London, Routledge, 1993.

25 E. Bick, "The experience of the skin in early object relations," *International Journal of Psychoanalysis*, 1968, vol. 49, no. 2 and 3, pp. 558–66.

26 Anzieu, "Fonctions du moi-peau," p. 873; and *The Skin Ego*, p. 102.

27 W. R. Bion, *The Italian Seminars*, London, Karnac, 2005, p. 7.
28 S. Pinker, *The Language Instinct: How the Mind Creates Language*, New York, Harper, 1994, p. 47.
29 Ibid., p. 145.
30 J. G. Herder, *Abhandlung über den Ursprung der Sprache*, Stuttgart, Reclam, 2001 (original work published 1966).

Chapter 5

Alienation and identity
Immigration, race, and ethnicity

> You're hidden right out in the open – that is, you would be if only you realized it.
>
> —Ralph Ellison, *Invisible Man*[1]

I was on a flight from London to San Francisco when the woman sitting next to me, a psychologist with an Iranian background now living in the United States, asked me what kind of person or situation she should have in mind if she were to make a referral to me. I thought for a minute about my current practice and then considered the many patients I've worked with over thirty-five years. I realized that most of them fell into two sometimes overlapping categories: those with ethnic minority backgrounds and those who were either immigrants themselves or children of immigrants. I eventually answered that she might think of a person who was either dealing with differences compared to mainstream American society or living some aspect of an immigration story. The latter is partly my story, too, because my grandparents on one side were immigrants to the United States coming from Austria-Hungary and Russia; on the other side, my great-grandparents traced back to Ireland. My spouse is also an immigrant.

This chapter will explore clinical stories of alienation and identity as they relate to immigration, race, and ethnicity. I will neither provide an overview of the complicated history of these topics in the United States, nor will I offer a synopsis of various socially critical perspectives on acculturation, assimilation, stigma, race, and discrimination. There are many highly competent academic scholars in psychology, sociology, social work, political science, economics, and law who better tackle these subjects from positions that examine historical influences, comprehensive research into marginalization, and theorizing about exclusion and inclusion. What I offer here is based on my experiences as an analyst and psychotherapist having worked with many patients who have expanded my horizons to appreciate the myriad dimensions of human suffering, trauma, adaptation, and resilience that stem from feeling cast aside, alienated, and scapegoated because of their perceived differences.

The kinds of alienation I see in this clinical material, however, derive from social forces beyond an individual's control or influence. Invisibility typically happens when the majority chooses not to see or acknowledge a person's differences. When a person is basically unseen, then that person's relationship to social reality comes into question. Many immigrants and ethnic minorities encounter this invisibility. Additionally, they may feel inferior because they do not measure up to desirable cultural norms. Such perceptions express judgments about worth, power, and relevance. They can lead to internalizing a sense of being a misfit who won't fit in beyond a certain level of acceptability and achievement.

Those who feel invisible or who have been labeled misfits often have stories about misperceptions, not being looked at, and powerlessness. These stories speak to the difficulty of claiming an identity that comes from within rather than one being imposed from outside. Sometimes, out of frustration and desperation, young men and boys in these circumstances will do whatever they can to gain attention, even if it is negative. They appear as time bombs or explosive and volatile volcanos. The boy or young man in this situation draws to himself projections of someone threatening and dangerous, and often these projections are accurate. But too frequently, these are misattributions that force an identity onto him: troublemaker, delinquent, criminal. I think of this as *scapegoating*, when a boy or man is defined as unwanted and faces the prospect of being cast out of his social group.

This downward-spiraling process is accelerated when a person chooses to embrace and act out a negative identity. The monster is a version of this. This destructive identity is not just an identification with an aggressor, turning the once-experienced powerlessness into wrath, but also a turning away from the healthy internal self in reckless defiance of what seems good, safe, and creative. A monster frightens and wields power over our fears when he terrorizes us, so we feel helpless and weak. Like someone invisible or a misfit, a monster is always alienated, although extremely so. And he is usually determined not to remain invisible.

In the 1960s, Erik Erikson wrote about identity formation, providing a framework for viewing adolescence and early adulthood from this perspective. Erikson conceived of the lifespan as consisting of eight stages beginning after birth, with each one of these stages forming a building block in human development:[2]

- Trust versus mistrust
- Autonomy versus shame-doubt
- Initiative versus guilt
- Industry versus inferiority
- Identity versus identity confusion
- Intimacy versus isolation
- Generativity versus stagnation
- Integrity versus despair

Identity is the task for adolescence and early adulthood, and it includes finding a life direction, coming to terms with social roles, defining a persona, and deepening friendships. *Persona* is a Jungian concept referring to the social mask that we need at work and in public. One of the key social and psychological roles that adolescents tussle with pertains to masculinity (or femininity). Erikson credits Jung for having seen the internal aspect of this struggle with his idea of *anima* (or *animus*), the contrasexual piece within that corresponds to the other gender in us. He notes that when young men strive to exclude this from their identity, they express a fear of feeling feminized, "making a shell of mannishness out of what is left."[3] Erikson's view about the fear of the feminine in the male psyche is consistent with my clinical observations, as I discuss in Chapter 3.

Erikson gives us a springboard to think about identity, especially now when online presentations offer multiple platforms for playing with it – and lying about it. He wonders if our sense of identity is truly conscious, a question that we might find peculiar given the dramatic and affected poses many take in cyberspace. Online identities make use of hyperbole and often appear operatic. Many could argue that identity is now exceedingly conscious, but Erikson might ask, Is it? Self-conscious is not the same as conscious; self-consciousness encompasses an anxiety about how others see us, perhaps not buying who we believe we are because they see through to something deeper we may be unsure of in ourselves. Instead, Erikson speaks of identity meaning well-being, being at home in our bodies, having direction, and not opting for pretense.[4] Identity confusion comes from not being able to resolve these multiple and simultaneous demands on a developing mind. One fairly common example today arises when a young man says, "I can't decide what I want for myself. There are so many options, so many decisions – how would I know?" When faced with the appearance of too many choices, like in a supermarket aisle with a hundred brands of cereal, how would you know which is really best for you? Having to choose among these overfilled shelves can intimidate a person, sometimes revealing a fear of making the wrong choice, a mistake looming, and the sought-after ideal not grasped. Confusion spreads like an infection, and a person cannot decide what he wants.

Identification is a complex process of taking in from others important lived experiences, making room for them in our psyches, and giving preference among them in forming an idea of who we want to be. This internal prioritization is shaped consciously and unconsciously by our ideals, aspirations, social perceptions, educational opportunities, socioeconomic status, extended and nuclear families, and intergenerational dynamics. Identification happens at the border of self and other, interior and exterior, person and society. Identity grows out of identifications, but it not merely the sum of them. In healthy development, it is important to identify with benevolent figures who can become internal resources for us moving forward. Identification can, however, occasionally be a defense that imposes an apparent identity on us, creating self-negation as if the psyche had been colonized.

Identity confusion

One of the more gripping examples of this problematic form of identification negating a boy's own identity occurred when I worked at Oakes Children's Center, a school for children with severe emotional disturbances.[5] Carlos was a ten-year-old Latino boy who came to the center mostly because he was floundering everywhere else. He had been diagnosed with mild to moderate mental retardation. Carlos also showed exceptionally poor social judgment by getting in the middle of fights with other boys. As a result, he was frequently injured, although he almost always had no stake in these altercations.

He presented as a lethargic, dull child, dragging himself along the halls or on the recess yard. He slurred his words and was difficult to understand. I supervised his therapist, who reported being sleepy and bored. He found Carlos a challenge to engage. He reported that Carlos spent most of the play therapy sessions either staring out the window or arranging dolls on a table, though they still lay flat and had no purpose. Whenever his therapist tried to play with him and the dolls, Carlos withdrew to stand by the window. His therapist said in his supervision meetings with me that he often felt hopeless with Carlos and could barely understand him when he muttered something.

When Carlos was six years old, his father died and Carlos went to live in foster care. His father was an immigrant and had struggled to find work. Carlos supposedly did not know his mother, who had been addicted to opiates and lived in a different city, never having shown an interest in her son.

Something in Carlos baffled me. I observed him in his classroom, which operated as a therapeutic milieu, and saw moments when he seemed more attentive and curious. However, whenever a teacher noticed him, he withdrew and became his typical dulled and confused self. One day, I followed him out to recess, and he was walking into the wall like a drunk. He was clumsy, had poor muscle tone, and sometimes tripped and fell, so I had thought his walking into the wall was another aspect of his sensory-motor problems.

On the play yard, he stood apart from the other children on the periphery of a game. They were playing basketball, and he was near a play structure some distance away. Suddenly, one of the boys threw the basketball hard into the air. It flew toward Carlos. He whirled around without hesitation and caught it, a difficult move for anyone, and he clearly said, "Out." The ball was, indeed, out of bounds. He appeared focused and awake. I thought, Who is this boy and where has he been hiding?

I reread Carlos's chart to see if there was anything else I might discover about his earlier development. His father's death was noted to be from cancer. I suggested his therapist see if he could find out what kind of cancer it had been. After calling social services, the therapist learned that it was stomach cancer. We knew from Carlos's chart that there was a family member in a nearby city who occasionally saw Carlos on holidays. I suggested the therapist phone this relative and try to find out more about Carlos's father. It might seem odd that we knew so little about him, but this was not unusual for several legal and bureaucratic reasons when children came to the center through social services. Sometimes parts of a child's record were sealed, missing, or just undocumented.

We discovered that Carlos's father had been an alcoholic. Carlos's dullness, confusion, slurred speech, and stumbling now seemed to possibly be about something else, an identification with a lost parent at a precious moment in Carlos's life. In supervision, I suggested that Carlos's therapist begin to talk with Carlos about his father in a gentle and nonintrusive way. He told Carlos that he felt Carlos looked out the window perhaps in hopes of finding or seeing a man like his father. He suggested, too, that the dolls lying flat on the table represented how Carlos felt about losing his father – knocked down and with nowhere to go. Carlos listened to these repeated interpretations, making eye contact with his therapist and sometimes nodding. The therapist next said he'd like to work on a memory book with Carlos, a book about his father. Carlos seemed interested. The therapist obtained a few photos from the relative he'd been in touch with, and Carlos looked at them with sadness, holding them like precious gems in his hands. This process occurred over several months.

During this time, Carlos began to speak louder and without slurring his words. He started to join in games at recess and was physically rather agile. He didn't stumble. He was more focused in his classes, and his teachers began to feel he was learning, at a slow pace, but learning nonetheless. We all could see Carlos's turnaround. This example, which I summarize here, shows the potent effects of losing a parent at this age. Identification can be a way of keeping that parent alive inside the child. It can also crowd the child's own psyche, complicating his development because too much energy and space is devoted to holding on to the lost parent. Even the child's body becomes a living memorial to the dead parent. We might not usually consider identification to be a defense, and even in Carlos's case, it is not entirely clear it had only that function. It did, however, seem to be a route to bypass his alienation, loss, and profound aloneness after his father died. It was the best he could do.

When identification interferes with psychological and cognitive growth and when it operates to distance a boy from his feelings, then I conceptualize this as defensive. Carlos acted and moved like a drunken man – perhaps like the father he unconsciously remembered, although consciously had not yet come to terms with losing. The consequences for Carlos's identity were extreme because he didn't know how to let go of his father or make sense of how his father had died. His love continued, and as an act of devotion, he embodied this father in the only ways he knew – by seeming to become him. It is worth noting the cultural dislocation that Carlos and his father experienced as contributing to both their stories. Culture, like an extended family, holds us with language, community, myths, art, music, and traditional roles. Carlos's father himself likely suffered a degree of alienation, not finding a job and drinking too much to deal with his frustrations. Although this is speculative in Carlos's situation, a father who is adrift can feel that much harder for a child to hold onto. The gaps may be what stand out, and a child then might imitate such a parent to make up for what feels missing.

Negative identity

Returning to Erikson, I find it important to consider not only his concept of identity confusion in the context of immigration, race, and ethnicity, but also his ideas about a negative identity. He defines *negative identity* as when "the loss of a sense of identity is expressed in a scornful and snobbish hostility toward the roles offered" by family, school, and community.[6] Some of this posturing can be playful, when the skater boy, videogamer, or Goth dude tells me how boring everyone else seems and how their group is the only one with credibility. This rebelliousness is mostly welcome in adolescence. Winnicott refers to an aspect of it as "the antisocial tendency" that he believes is an attempt to get the environment to pay attention.[7] He finds that it becomes problematic when unaddressed, in which case it can escalate and assume greater proportions within the developing personality.

Erikson comments that a negative identity usually has "been presented to [young men] as most undesirable or dangerous and yet also as most real."[8] He finds that a young man seeking extremes does so in part to feel something about himself, to locate a kind of realness – authenticity – that otherwise seems blocked and unavailable. I certainly see this clinically in thrill-seeking and risk-taking behaviors that sometimes lead to accidents and injuries. Here, realness stems both from an experience of subjective intensity and from the reaction of the environment, which typically is disapproving or condemning. The telos in a negative identity, therefore, gives a young man a sense of this realness, as well as a feeling of mastery when other positive alternatives don't seem accessible.

Erikson explains that many young men "would rather be nobody or somebody totally bad . . . than be not-quite-somebody."[9] This urge for a total answer can be idealistic, utopian, paranoid, or tyrannical. We have only to think about the young men drawn to terrorist groups like ISIS, as I mention in Chapter 1, or to drug gangs, or the many young men committing mass shootings to see the dark side of this totality as a powerful psychological force. Erikson finds this weakness – looking for a "totalistic" solution – in all of us and that it appears especially when there are developmental strains and when "reintegration into a relative 'wholeness' seems impossible."[10] The apparent appeal of totality is that it circumvents conflict and the need to reconcile opposing points of view, ambivalence, and contrasting feelings we may have.

Jung sees our ability to hold opposites, when we might feel emotionally stretched to a point of confusion or distress, as a condition potentially ushering in new psychological growth.[11] He defines a human psychological tendency to experience these opposites as *enantiodromia*, meaning "running counter to": "I use the term enantiodromia for the emergence of the unconscious opposite in the course of time."[12] The totalistic trend in our psyches suppresses a capacity to perceive opposites and to allow for feelings about them to emerge. A conscious identification with one position splits off the other, forcing it to remain unconscious. The split-off piece is, in effect, dissociated, but it can sometimes intrude unexpectedly. For example, idealism readily turns to persecution when thwarted, or compulsive precision frequently leads to a mess of some kind. In fairytales, a similar process often happens, as when an ugly frog later turns into a handsome prince.

Negative identity can be viewed as a stance refusing to accept the inevitability of these opposites in adult life. Stigma can also be a factor in limiting a young man's options, however. Being "totally bad" may seem like the only way to rebel against social oppression. When a young man is alienated by dealing with the real effects of marginalization, such as those of limited opportunities and discrimination based on race or immigration, then a negative identity may be not only a way to rebel against this repressive order, but also a way to claim what feels devalued and scorned by others. An idea of appreciating opposites or opposing points of view may then seem a luxury to someone in this situation. Importantly, most young men of color and most young men from immigrant families manage this transition of settling into an adult identity when they are supported by their families, mentors, schools, and communities.

Invisible

In Chapter 2, Zack appeared as a 19-year-old young man playing a clinical version of hide-and-seek with me. He was good at hiding. Zack spent a lot of his spare time online surfing imageboards and using social media, where ironically his avatar or profile picture was either blank or a cartoon figure. He once said to me, "Online, nobody knows you."

Zack was born in the United States, the second child of immigrants from an Asian country. He didn't like to speak much about his parents' origins, and he told me they also did not tell him much about their lives before they came to the U.S. His mother sometimes visited the city where she had grown up, but Zack had never accompanied her there. It was as if there was a hard stop to investigating this immigration story, a secret past that he claimed not to be interested in, perhaps complying with his mother's desire not to talk about it. Zack's parents had divorced when he was four years old, and he had little contact with either his father or older sister. Perhaps his isolation from them was another hard stop in his mind, which he felt he couldn't cross.

I often asked Zack how he saw himself as a young Asian man, and he found my curiosity about this baffling. He asked, "Why would you be interested in that?" Although he grew up in a highly diverse city with a large Asian population, he had chosen a college in a part of the country that is not ethnically diverse. He also had elected to attend a high school that was less diverse than most others in the city.

I explained that I was curious because I felt identity was made up of many strands, including where our parents came from as well as how we develop our attitudes about culture and ethnicity into an understanding of who we are.

He spoke about widespread perceptions of "the good Asian" in his high school and at his college. I asked him to describe what he meant. He related a list of virtues, such as intelligent, polite, hardworking, and conscientious, but he also rolled his eyes. I noticed and said that he had a feeling about what he was telling me, and he replied that he disliked this stereotype because he thought it demeaning, like "being put in a box." He mentioned that these were good traits, but they also implied a person who was compliant and had less power than others.

I asked if he ever felt this way about himself, and he agreed, adding that he didn't like that he might conform to a stereotype and wished he could change that. He noted this was one reason he didn't like to post photos of himself on social media. "I'd rather they not see I'm Asian." Here again, I felt a hard stop, this time coming from him about his identity. He seemed to be telling me he had limited options to show who he was. He indicated that this step was too complicated and being invisible was preferable.

At the start of one of his sessions, I saw Zack looking at my name on the door as he came in. I shared that he seemed curious, and he asked, "Is your name Russian?"

I smiled and said that my Polish grandparents never got used to that question.

He knew some of the history: "Oh, I can see why if your country was always getting carved up, you might not like being mistaken for one of the people with the knives."

His metaphor made me think about histories that get cut out because parents might not want to own them and pass them on to their children. I said something like this to Zack, and he told me he'd recently asked his mother about where she'd grown up. He said she seemed uncomfortable, but he persisted. He'd never met her parents – his grandparents – because her father had died, although her mother was still alive. Zack had only seen photos of her, and he now asked his mother to tell him stories about her. This felt like an important shift in his trying to claim an aspect of himself – it's difficult to show what we don't even know exists.

We talked some, too, about how Zack felt speaking with me, a white man with an unusual last name. He welcomed my questions and said that most of the doctors he'd had were white, although he noticed that this was changing. For example, the physician he saw for his antidepressant medication was Middle Eastern, and Zack liked him. "He has a funnier name than yours."

I affirmed that he could see differences and think about them, which felt important if he was to have a narrative about himself that included his differences. I am summarizing here what was a months-long process, but it was an important therapeutic piece of this young man's being seen and learning to show more of himself.

Immigration is a complicated topic in most Western countries. In the United States, as of 2013, over 40 million people are foreign-born, comprising 13% of the population.[13] People immigrate and leave their homelands for many reasons. Many models of immigration reflect economic factors such as pressures in the labor force, materialism, and established migrant communities in the destination country.[14] During recent years, large numbers of immigrants to the United States have been people of color from Asia, Africa, and Central and South America, with over 400,000 settling here each year.[15] However, researchers have found that since the terrorist attacks of September 11, 2001, "there has been a substantial increase in xenophobia against all foreigners."[16] This virulent xenophobia has been growing. During and since the 2016 election cycle, when this topic became a divisive strategy to gain political advantage among certain voters, there has been more explicit hostility in the United States toward immigration and immigrants. Many immigrants now report more anxiety, depression, and other mental health problems subsequent to these blatant threats to their communities and cultures.

Salman Akhtar, a psychoanalyst born in India and practicing and teaching in the United States, comments on the difference between "living" and "living in someplace" as representative of the strain many immigrants feel upon resettling.[17] Whereas "living" assumes a felt continuity with one's environment and society, "living in someplace" refers to a different experience, when a person is instead aware of a gap in that relationship. Psychologically, this gap can lead to a strain related to a sense of dislocation. Akhtar finds that immigrants adapt through various means, such as repudiation (the change is minimal to nonexistent), return (planning on going back), replication (re-creating the homeland here), reunion (idealization and nostalgia of homeland), and reparation (identification with treasured aspects of homeland).[18] Zack's parents apparently were caught in repudiation of their homeland and conveyed this attitude to their son. Perhaps, repudiation as a coping strategy can make "living" seem a more accessible description as opposed to feeling the conflicts of "living in someplace" because repudiation tends to keep the gap in experience within the unconscious.

Noisy misfit

Trauma can also accompany an immigrant's tale, especially for refugees. Jungians have developed an idea that between the personal unconscious containing our repressed developmental and family experiences and the collective unconscious containing the archetypes, there is a cultural unconscious that stores myths, stereotypes, traditions, rituals, and linguistic characteristics.[19] This layer of the unconscious is home then to what we would call cultural complexes that define a level of group dynamics and social organization. Samuel Kimbles outlines five components to cultural complexes: 1) they function both within groups and within the individual mind to represent the group; 2) they are autonomous, meaning we can have little conscious control of them; 3) they organize group interactions; 4) they facilitate an individual's relations to the group; and 5) they provide a sense of belonging and identity.[20] These complexes often encompass tendencies to exclude, to stereotype, and to discriminate, and are usually based on historical patterns within a culture.

Kimbles explores the idea of phantoms operating as secrets that transmit intergenerational trauma. They are like complexes with powerful imagery, and they include trauma, the collective shadow, and social suffering.[21] The *collective shadow* is a culture's dark side, or what it wants to expel or disavow. Social suffering originates in the blatant misuse of power when it is cruelly wielded by authority structures over those who have little or no power. Kimbles's discussion of phantoms is a useful way to conceptualize cultural effects on an individual psyche that is caught in historical waves of oppression and tyranny. Citing Samantha Power, he notes six genocides in the 20th century: the Armenians in 1915, the

Jews during World War II, the Cambodians in the 1970s, the Kurds in the 1990s, parts of the Kosovar population in the 1980s and 90s, and Rwanda in 1994.[22]

Lee was a ten-year-old boy when I met him as a new student at Oakes Children's Center. Although I am disguising elements of his background, I believe it is relevant to note that his parents were survivors of the Khmer Rouge Killing Fields in the late 1970s when more than a million Cambodians were killed by a brutal regime. Lee's parents escaped to a refugee camp in a Southeast Asian country where they stayed for several years. Lee was born during that time. The family resettled in the United States after that. Lee lived with his mother and three younger siblings. Because of a severe mental illness, Lee's father lived in a group care home apart from the family. Lee was fluent in English by the time of his enrollment, although his parents had not yet mastered this new language.

Lee came to the center after a stay on a children's psychiatric unit where he had been hospitalized for bizarre behaviors, such as poking others, talking in a nonsensical way no one could understand, facial grimacing, and auditory hallucinations. He took medication to control his psychotic symptoms and saw a staff therapist two or three times a week for psychodynamic psychotherapy. I supervised Lee's treatment for five years, met with his family often (with translators helping), and occasionally met with Lee when his troubles caused conflicts with other children at the center.

Lee could be quite noisy. He spoke loudly and fast. He interrupted and didn't seem to care about waiting for answers or replies from others. This behavior gradually got better but never quite disappeared. Lee took up basketball, playing at school with gusto, and later joining a community league. He developed an idea that he might become a groundbreaking Asian player in the NBA. Staff at the center encouraged his play because it gave him an outlet for being loud in a sport, although they also emphasized having fun rather than fostering a goal that might have been unrealistic for Lee. He didn't exactly give up on this ambition, however, which we understood as his jumping into his new culture and being a hero in it. Lee knew relatively little about Cambodia – only that there had been "a big war" and that he wasn't born there. This lack of knowledge, similar to Zack's, may further illustrate Akhtar's idea about repudiation to cope with immigration strains, but it also demonstrates a secretive aspect of a phantom haunting Lee and his family. Phantoms, as Kimbles emphasizes, are often secrets that families choose not to discuss but that nevertheless feel present.

Lee's hallucinations may have been an attempt to listen to this phantom and find out the secrets. In an early session with his therapist, Lee told her that he sometimes saw things.[23] She empathically told him he could choose whether he wanted to tell her more, and he went on to explain that he saw ghosts in his room at night and even a decapitated woman in the bathroom. His therapist suggested ways he could deal with his worry about whether these visions were real, and this calmed Lee. Now as I write about this, Lee's ghosts seem a family phantom transmitted from the terrible experiences his father had during the massacres in his country.

Lee's parents did not want to talk about what had happened back then. His father suffered severe post-traumatic stress with psychotic symptoms, and his mother indicated she preferred to keep silent about those memories. A year later, in a family session, Lee mentioned his fears of ghosts and dead bodies coming back to life. After Lee left the room so the therapist could speak privately with his parents, his father revealed he'd been left for dead in a mass grave that he crawled out of and escaped. He lived for a while in a jungle and later walked a long distance to cross the border to a refugee camp.

Lee didn't consciously know of his father's agonizing experience, but he seemed to be holding psychologically some part of it with his fears of ghosts and reanimated dead bodies. Lee's ghosts were signs of intergenerational phantoms, as Kimbles describes them, secret and unspoken. Lee's father said he could not imagine telling his son or his other children what he had gone through, and his reticence seemed to represent a level of a cultural complex about shame and survival. Lee's father wanted to protect his son from an image of his father as beaten and dying.

When Lee was a teenager, he was caught shoplifting, a behavior that many adolescents engage in and that I discuss in a previous book.[24] His stealing seemed partly a result of adolescent impulsivity and a sense of emotional deprivation that he conveyed about what he could rightly have. In discussing the difficult emotions behind this incident, he complained that his parents kept their distance, didn't show up for his basketball games, and rarely talked with him. Lee's protest was actually positive, another hidden dimension of stealing not always seen, because he wanted something he didn't yet know how best to ask for – more emotional contact with his mother and father. In a subsequent family session, Lee asked his father about life in Cambodia and wanted to know why they never talked about it. His father began crying, but with encouragement, he began to tell his son about his earlier life there. Eventually, he also told Lee about the war and disclosed in summary form some of the awful suffering he had experienced. Lee was quite interested in all of what his father had to say, and he seemed relieved that finally they could talk about the past. He was ready to listen to his father's painful story.

Haydee Faimberg writes about intergenerational aspects of trauma and asks, "How can the transmission of a history which at least partially does not belong to the patient's life . . . be explained?"[25] She hypothesizes that a part of the parent's psyche intrudes unconsciously into the child's and there becomes a burden to carry without the child knowing why. In addition, the parent, suspecting the child does hold this unwanted part of his or her psyche and to protect him- or herself from contact with that, actively distances from the child. Such a parent may view his or her child negatively, fearing that the child will potentially bring to light what the parent does not want to see. Faimberg notes that three generations are usually involved in this process of alienation.

None of Lee's grandparents survived the war. His parents were left with their own unresolved mourning of their parents and with survivor guilt or, perhaps more accurately, survivor shame. In Lee's case, following what Faimberg describes,

Lee, with his complaints about ghosts, would have represented a painful reminder for his parents about Cambodia and what they lost there. Their unspoken distance and effective silence communicated a confusing message to him, but in their minds, he seemed to belong elsewhere, not with them. Faimberg, describing her patient, writes, "He had become what each of them [parents] had not accepted in their respective histories."[26]

Lee's ghosts and visions of dismembered bodies seemed to belong elsewhere. Although there were many reasons for his emotional problems, his parents' losses and their traumatic suffering haunted the whole family, and Lee absorbed a lot of their pain psychically. He had a difficult time knowing himself and feeling what he wanted because the ghosts took up too much room in the house of his mind. Fortunately, over years of psychotherapeutic intervention, he freed himself from some of this intruded parental heaviness, became more interested in his future, and aspired to go to college.

The volcano

Many years ago, I bought a toy volcano that contained a spring mechanism for launching two plastic lava balls into the air. This toy was quite popular with boys, not so much with girls. They loved hurtling the lava balls out and often screamed excitedly: "Wow, look how high that went!" "That one hit you!" It was certainly not diagnostic, but such play with this volcano often pointed to a boy's issues with expressing anger. Somewhat like Goldilocks in the fairytale, many cannot find the "just right" place for anger. Either it is too big – explosive – or it is too small – tightly bottled inside. When the volcano came out, I often found myself wondering what or whom the boy was angry at and what he felt he hadn't been able to express "just right."

Angelo was eight years old and at the end of third grade when I first met him. He was a multiracial boy, half African American, part white, and part Native American, with a sturdy and muscular frame, big for his age. He lived mostly with his maternal grandparents and spent several weekends a month with his mother. His father had abandoned the family when Angelo was two years old, and his mother was overwhelmed by caring for him and working full time. Her mother stepped in to help. Angelo had furious tantrums at home and at school, had been suspended many times, and was enuretic at night. His pediatrician had tried several remedies (bell-and-pad, medication, behavioral plan) to treat the enuresis, although none had worked for Angelo.

Angelo's grandparents and mother described a history of his angry outbursts arising even before his father's departure. His mother reported he had a bad temper "just like his father." His grandmother remarked that he was "sensitive" and had "a short fuse." They felt he was quick to escalate and slow to soothe. His grandmother showed more patience for his problems and was openly affectionate with him. Angelo's mother, at times, seemed more like an older sister than his mother. She was frustrated with his needs as a child, competed for attention with him, and often said she wished he would just "grow up." His grandfather was a solid presence who encouraged Angelo to help out during afterschool hours with his part-time business repairing bicycles. He believed teaching Angelo manual skills would contribute to his development.

Angelo struggled in school with a learning disorder that made reading and writing difficult. He received extra services from a specialist on a weekly basis, but otherwise participated in all the activities of his classroom. His third-grade teacher was fond of him and told me he could be an appealing child. However, she also noted that many children were afraid of him and kept their distance.

During one of my initial sessions with Angelo, he came into the office and said he was thirsty. I gave him a cup and he returned with it filled to the top and sloshing over the brim. Thinking some about his enuresis, I commented how full the cup was and asked if he'd noticed. He looked surprised and said no, he hadn't. I suggested that a full cup might spill and make for another problem. He laughed nervously and got some markers from the cupboard to draw a picture. He began drawing a volcano with red lava spilling down the sides. He was dissatisfied with a line, began to erase it too vigorously, and the paper slid into the cup knocking it over. Water spread over the table top and onto his drawing. He looked at me with an expression of great fear that within seconds turned to a scowl of anger. I said that we could clean it up together, and he relaxed hearing me say this, although he remarked, "I ruined it."

In this important series of interactions, I learned quite a bit about Angelo. He appeared to have some difficulty anticipating a situation that could become more problematic. He was somewhat rigid in not adjusting to neutral observations from someone trying to help him. A pressure to self-correct made a problem worse. Symbolically, both the volcano and the overflowing cup pointed to a container that would not hold, much like a mind that cannot expand or be flexible. His immediate reaction of fear seemed to indicate a broken expectation that felt crushing, but it soon fed into anger at not controlling his environment. At the beginning of a treatment, such a meaningful set of exchanges can communicate a figurative map about where we are headed, and it seemed promising that Angelo was letting me see these emotional contours in his psyche.

Angelo soon discovered the toy volcano, which became a regular play feature during the first year of his psychotherapy. He like launching the lava balls, trying to hit various action figures he positioned around the volcano. Who would be killed and who would survive? At first, he stated that my role was to watch. He didn't want me to say anything – only while he played with the volcano, because we conversed during board and card games. His need to control me here was how he could let me get to know the part of him that exploded and spilled. I would usually agree to his terms, although noting my predicament when he was done – that I had ideas I'd like to share with him but had to stay quiet. I soon introduced a feeling chart with faces and, by pointing to it, showed him while he played with the volcano that I felt confused, lonely, or frustrated. Angelo smiled whenever I did this and seemed to take in that feelings were important parts of our relating.

After a couple months of this play, he announced that I could talk while he used the volcano. He warned me, however, not to say "things about feelings." I again agreed, with the addition that I'd still use the feeling chart when I wanted to explain with a picture what I saw. I became a commentator on various scenes of massacres of soldiers and animals. The volcano was unpredictable and savage. Angelo generally enjoyed my remarks, although he'd withdraw if I relied on the feeling chart too much. I said that he felt safer when the feelings weren't coming up between us and that he backed off if I brought them in too much. I felt it important to label his withdrawal and to offer an understanding for why he did it.

After he'd been in therapy for six months, he invited me to play with him when he used the volcano. This was an important shift because it introduced direct conflict between us. We were always on opposing sides. Under his direction, my team suffered immense losses, and I told him how lousy this felt week after week. My team was constantly destroyed. He now let me speak more about feelings – my own only – and introduce an idea of how it felt having no hope and no options to win or survive. Angelo listened when I offered these statements, and he now told me to shut up less frequently. He was in fourth grade and doing a little better at school. His grandparents felt encouraged, and Angelo's enuresis, which had been occurring nightly at the start of therapy, was infrequent.

Angelo's fourth-grade teacher was strict, told me she felt he was "a time bomb," and asked me to come observe him in class before the annual review of his educational plan toward the end of the school year. Angelo's desk was situated slightly apart from the other students who were in small groups at tables around the room. Although an ethnically diverse school, there were fewer African American students in attendance, and Angelo was the only student with an African American background in his class. He seemed distracted and was staring out a window. I went over to him and asked if he would show me what he was working on. It was a vocabulary worksheet with so many erasures that he'd torn the paper. I encouraged him to ask for another, and he said, "Good idea." He had become more open to such suggestions, and he was less preoccupied with feelings of having spoiled what he was doing. There appeared to be some movement in a positive direction away from his unconsciously viewing himself so much like a volcano spilling onto what was around him and ruining it. But his teacher's remark about the time bomb made me aware of how others might feel he was threatening and would want distance from him. The position of his desk to the side and apart seemed an obvious reminder of this.

Around this time, Angelo's mother began dating a white man involved in law enforcement. He repeated to her messages about discipline and firmness when she sought his advice about Angelo. Although his emphasis on consistency made some sense, his "hard knocks" philosophy about boys struck me as not what Angelo needed, since he already had to contend with enough hard knocks in his young life. Following a weekend spent with his mother and her boyfriend, he came into an appointment with me visibly upset. I asked what had happened, and he ignored me. He played with some wooden blocks and looked at some dragon cards he collected. I was getting the cold shoulder, and I said as much. I reflected to him that he seemed angry and I was in the dark about why – could he tell me anything? I tried to coax him with questions about home, school, and his weekend.

Angelo crumpled a piece of paper and threw it my way. I bent over to pick it up, and at this moment, he threw one of the wood blocks at me. It hit my glasses hard enough to knock them from my face. I was startled and then angry. Probably with more of a raised voice than I would have wanted in this situation, I told him that he had gone too far and that I expected him to use his words when he was angry, not throw things at me. He looked surprised, scowled, and then his eyes welled up with tears. He had never cried in session before.

I put my glasses back on, sat down near him, and realized he was flooded beyond any ability to express why he was upset. I told him I was all right, that I had been angry for a bit, but now was worried about him. Tears streamed down his cheeks. I acknowledged that he couldn't speak right now and that he was sad about something, perhaps my reaction to his throwing the block at me. He shook his head no, which surprised me because I had not expected him to be able to com-municate at this point. I asked if he wanted to write down why he was upset, and he nodded. I gave him a piece of paper and a pencil, and he wrote in tiny letters, "My mom." I told him I appreciated his letting me know and added that we were still friends. He stopped crying, sighed, and as he left, said "See you next time." This was unusual, and it seemed to express his anxiety about reparation and his hope about my still being there for him after this incident.

I learned shortly after this session from his grandmother that Angelo had returned home from the weekend with his mother subdued. She wondered if he was coming down with a cold. But she found out from Angelo's mother that she had told him she wanted him to spend the entire summer with her and her boy-friend at their place outside the city. His mother had sprung this on Angelo, and she'd not discussed it with her mother, who still was Angelo's primary caregiver. Angelo's grandmother argued with her daughter, who eventually agreed to a more limited time of two weeks.

Angelo's ambush of me was a reversal, common in child psychotherapy, of how he had felt impinged on by his mother, and so he let me know by turning the tables on me. Angelo's relationship with his mother showed varying degrees of such impingement, from her competing with him to her denying his child-like needs and wishing instead he'd grow up. He experienced these intrusions as attacks when he felt aggressed upon and not able to defend himself. His identi-fying with a volcano appeared to represent the only release he felt open to him, namely evacuating what had been forced on him.

Angelo's identity within a multiracial family was complex and somewhat unformed. He didn't know his biological father and was told stories that his father was an irresponsible alcoholic. Although his grandfather offered important male contact and bonding, his availability was confined mostly to wanting to teach Angelo how to work with his hands. He wasn't interested in how Angelo did in school, and he seemed to believe his grandson would not do well educationally.

In a way, what was on offer in terms of identity for Angelo had something of a negative cast to it. Perhaps the telos of the volcano was trying to break out of these limitations.

Could Angelo's eruption in my office when he hit me with a block have represented a racial aspect of our relationship? I felt this was more than likely, because here I was, another white person in authority trying in his eyes to get him to do what he refused to do, talk about how he might have felt and make sense of his emotions. Sometimes, refusal is the beginning of asserting an identity. I wouldn't have said it this way to Angelo, but I did mention some of what I saw during my visit to his school. I said that I noticed there didn't seem to be many African American boys, and that I imagined he might find that strange, even hard in finding others like him he would want to know better. He responded to my bringing this up by saying he wished he attended ABC School, one with a larger African American presence among its student body and faculty. He described this school as cool and exciting. I told him this aspiration made sense to me because one way we learn about ourselves is by finding friends like us to share with and learn from.

After this interaction, he teased me, affectionately, about my lack of knowledge about rap music and rap artists. He'd brought up these artists and their albums many times, and I'd usually ask him to tell me more, but he would struggle with my request. Around this time, I suggested we could listen to them, and he liked this idea. He began bringing to session a portable CD player his mother had gotten for him and he'd play songs he liked for me. In one session, while we were listening to an angry rant, he turned to me and said, "I need you." I was surprised because he'd never said anything this personal or touching during our work over almost three years. I had known him best through his anger and fear, and this expression of need was new. In retrospect, I feel it had to do with our opening a window on the differences he experienced at school and with me, including his racial identity.

I continued to work with Angelo for another year, and we had many family sessions that emphasized a theme of inclusion. I supported their effort to do activities together, and his mother's boyfriend occasionally participated in these sessions. I repeated a message that it was important for Angelo's development to feel he belonged somewhere. I pointed to his interest in music and encouraged them to find a way to take advantage of this. Angelo joined a dance group that taught hip hop and break dancing, and he became interested in attending a school for the arts for high school. In my mind, these family sessions, as well as his finding social interests to pursue, helped to begin forming a positive identity based on what he wanted and what he could choose. He continued to have emotional struggles, and even though his "short fuse" got a bit longer, it was still present. He ended his therapy around the time of entering high school.

C. Jama Adams writes, "Psychoanalysis pays relatively little attention to the social forces that promulgate and enforce models of normality, dominance, and otherness and that facilitate and inhibit the attempts of individuals to love, work, and pursue whatever goals they cherish."[27] He writes about these forces as shaping powerful projections of deviance and danger – meant to keep distance and exclude those felt to be "other" in ways the majority prefers not to see, to accept, and to interact with. In describing clinical work with young African American men coming from lower socioeconomic strata, he finds there is resistance to considering vulnerable aspects of the self because this kind of attention brings emotional pain and feelings of hopelessness.[28] Psychologically, there can be a struggle for identity when labels stigmatize and create conditions in which subjectivity itself comes to be equated with suffering. Some of Angelo's protests were to claim an identity, to refuse what he felt was being imposed on him, even if he did this through anger and aggression. Developmentally, this is akin to what Winnicott describes when a young child or infant appears to lash out in part to express the creation of his own subjective experience in a clash between reality and psyche.[29] In a clinical setting, nonverbal exchanges like passing notes, playing, and listening to music may assist in providing a safe environment for exploring what's inside us. These forms of communication helped Angelo to open the door to his house.

Racism and identity

As I am discussing how race and ethnicity pertain to issues of identity and alienation in clinical practice, I believe it important to note the devastating reality of racism in the United States. According to the NAACP, one in twenty-one black men in this country are behind bars, and 60% of all prisoners are African American and Hispanic.[30] Michelle Alexander notes, "We have not ended racial caste in America: we have merely redesigned it."[31] The so-called war on drugs has become the latest installment of this oppression. She carefully documents that despite the fact that all races and ethnicities tend to use and sell illegal drugs at comparable rates, the United States has imprisoned more African American men than South Africa at the height of apartheid.[32]

This system of social control actively targets the African American population. It is not at all covert, although it relies on continued social projections about deviance, danger, and crime as represented in fears of "otherness" threatening the majority. It is a form of social control based on creating alienation within and between groups. The individual psychological impacts are vast and rob a large segment of our society from equitable chances at economic opportunities, education, and social development. Alexander concludes toward the end of her book,

> It is fair to say that we have witnessed an evolution in the United States from a racial caste system based entirely in exploitation (slavery), to one based largely on subordination (Jim Crow), to one defined by marginalization (mass incarceration).[33]

This marginalization translates into social isolation, which is associated at an individual level with deep alienation. Those affected have to grapple with various identity problems such as identity confusion, identity loss, and negative identity.

"You're just like your father."

When we first met, Nicolas was a thirty-year-old man, an immigrant to the United States from a South American country. He had moved to this country for his university studies and remained after graduating. An only child, his parents divorced when he was six years old. His father cheated on his mother and was involved in illegal activities. Nicolas's mother had recently died after a short illness. The last time Nicolas saw her, months prior to her death, she had told him, "You're just like your father," a remark that he said felt like a knife to the gut. He felt remorseful that she eventually died without his seeing her a final time.

The country where he grew up had a violent history of coups, corruption, machismo, and militarism. Nicolas's father had been in the military before Nicolas was born but left after a scandal that Nicolas only later learned about from his mother when he was a teenager. In his first dream, Nicolas reported *that he saw his mother who asked how he was doing. He told her he was trying to get his life together, and she replied that honesty will help him.* He woke up crying. As this was his first dream, we discussed mostly his feeling of being shaken up. Nicolas felt his mother was trying to share an opinion about how he needed to change. He had a long line of girlfriends whom he usually cheated on and left after a few months. He'd even had a short marriage, but left that too, although he said this was because they were doing "too many drugs" together. He had been reluctant to keep his appointment with me, but then this dream motivated him to come in. When I asked about honesty, Nicolas described himself as a chronic liar, that he felt he was "a total fraud." I wondered if his dream communicated something about his father, although he was not in it: Nicolas described his father also as a liar who cheated on others to make money. From a Jungian perspective, Nicolas's dream may have symbolized his initial attitude about psychotherapy, that he was afraid about confronting problem areas in his psyche, sad at losing his mother, and ambivalent about trusting someone to help him. It seemed to suggest that an aspect of his mother complex saw through to a truth about himself he didn't want to yet face.

Nicolas's next dream, soon thereafter, confirmed his apprehensions about himself. He reported that *a young black boy was chasing him with a gun wanting Nicolas to give him something. Nicolas hit the boy, eventually pulled out a gun, and began shooting the boy who wouldn't die.* He said he woke up sweating and angry. Nicolas recalled, when he was a child, his father had owned several guns, as had his stepfather. He said that he had learned how to shoot from his stepfather. Nicolas related this dream to guilt he felt about his mother. He regretted not being there when she died, and this circumstance angered him. He had not been expecting her to pass so quickly. He was surprised that these feelings had lasted and not gone away. I didn't make any interpretation at this point about his dream, although it seemed to represent Nicolas in a state of panic and alienation from his own shadow – what he feared most in himself and what he perceived unconsciously as other. The young boy chasing him was insistent and demanding attention, but Nicolas wanted to get rid of him. Nicolas was probably afraid of what I might make of this part of himself. The father appeared to be associated to this dream, with the memories of guns that both his biological father and stepfather had. The dream alluded to a violent transaction. Importantly, in the session after this one, Nicolas told me he'd lied to me about his skills with guns, that he had exaggerated to impress me. I acknowledged his concern for our connection, because he'd told me lying was a problem for him and here it was happening between us.

Lying was an ongoing theme for Nicolas in our work. Alessandra Lemma discusses lying as having different psychological functions, examining differences between lying for self-preservation and lying for sadistic control.[34] Self-preservative needs may reflect wishes to impress someone or to create distance from a person, fearing too much of that person's attention. Sadistic lying, in contrast, is aimed at attacking the truth to express contempt or triumph over someone. My work with Nicolas showed elements of both forms of lying. At times, he used his lies to push me and others away from him because he felt we might otherwise intrude too far into his subjective reality. We were unwelcome guests barging into his house. He also used lies to manipulate others and to feel superior, because they couldn't tell they were being duped – stupid guests who didn't recognize what they were being shown was fake.

I'll discuss some of my work with Nicolas here in the context of cultural complexes and then return to his case in Chapters 8 and 10. The cultural context for Nicolas's lying appeared related to growing up in a country where corruption was rampant. Both his parents had participated in this system to support themselves. Further, they lied within their family and denied him access to truths about the family history. Lying was perhaps a social and cultural necessity to protect from tyrannical intrusion and to secure economic advantages.

A tendency to confuse his listener showed up in how Nicolas spoke. He could be evasive, use language to obfuscate, and cloak what he really meant. I inquired why he did these things; was he conscious of wanting to hide?

He was surprised I'd noticed and said that he liked being mysterious. This both protected him from someone knowing too much about him and gave him a feeling of "invincibility." In this latter way, Nicolas identified with being a liar, a negative identity, but one that expressed an inflated sense of himself regarding everyone else. Confirming this, he told me he enjoyed reading books about the role of power in relationships. When I asked where he thought he learned to hide so well, he appeared stumped. He noted "everyone did it" and then added that his parents didn't let him know them. He explained how upset he was learning of his mother's death, because he would have gone to visit her if he had known that she was in critical condition. She didn't tell him. He said that he felt he had turned into a person who avoided confrontations because he didn't know how to show more of himself or ask someone to do that. From the way he described his early years, I began to understand his background as a boy who felt admonished to be silent, not entirely helpless but definitely shut down around voicing his needs. In his mind, needs implied weakness, and feeling powerful through lies seemed a better alternative.

He described himself as arrogant and "walled in," impenetrable, and like his father and other men he knew from his childhood and adolescence. Nicolas continued to dream about his mother and would awaken crying. He was disturbed by these dreams, and I mentioned that he was grieving someone he wished he had known better. He agreed with this idea and felt angry that his father was so distant from him now. I wondered what he might want from his father, and he found this a difficult question. He said he didn't want to appear vulnerable to his father. Thinking of our relationship, I asked how he felt sharing these parts of his experience with me. He said it caused him anxiety, especially fear that I was secretly judging him and forming negative opinions that he'd never know about. I mentioned how I might seem like one of his parents or men in his country, holding back, deceptive, and not forthcoming, and he initially disputed this idea but later returned to it with an affirmative association. He said he always felt his father was a fake, yet when he thought about me, he said, "You're not fake. I don't know what you are, but you're not that." He worried then that he was showing vulnerability in telling me this and added, "The weak are taken advantage of." This attitude not only described Nicolas's family dynamics when as a child he felt silenced, but also captured aspects of the social climate of the country he grew up in, when the military took thousands away and they simply disappeared.

In a situation like that, pretense becomes a means for survival, and it can inflate into feeling powerful through a clever façade and hiding behind it. The cultural impact of tyranny usually invades the personal realm so thoroughly that a certain kind of paranoia is required to navigate social and intimate relationships. Florian Henckel von Donnersmarck's *The Lives of Others*, a 2006 German film about life in East Germany, captures this pervasive intrusion – all typewriters were registered with the state – and portrays the hypervigilance, desperation for privacy, and suspicions that permeated East German society.[35] Even after finding social and political freedom, citizens adapted slowly because a tyrannical presence lingered within their psyches.

Nicolas made an interesting remark that he was born guilty, and I asked how that was possible. Nicolas explained he came to believe as a child that he was expected to make sacrifices, that needs were undesirable, and that punishment was a regular part of life. Interestingly, Nicolas connected these beliefs to his mother tongue, Spanish. He said he felt able to separate from those beliefs by forging a new identity in English when he had moved to the United States. "I could become a different person." He reported that before this, he felt Spanish was his mother's language and that she used it to exert power over him. His Spanish-speaking identity had been colonized by his mother, and he wanted little to do with it. He now found that he had lost some fluency in Spanish and said that he dreamed mostly in English. I asked what he saw when he looked at the Spanish-speaking part of himself, and he said, "a black box" that was scary. This claustrophobic image conveyed a dark, hidden space, jail-like, that could leave Nicolas diminished and trapped. I wondered about the cultural and social representations of this black box in the context of a military dictatorship, dangerous secrets, and many lies.

Nicolas used his immigration experience to separate from what he described as many obstacles in his personal development when he lived in his home country. Many family dynamics seemed linked to collective aspects of corruption and persecution. His parents didn't share much of their inner worlds with him, and as a boy, he described long periods of loneliness and confusion. His adolescence did not lead to a sense of becoming someone, an identity he could reach for and begin to work on. His immigration instead seemed to be an opportunity for him to experiment with who he wanted to be. A launch into becoming a person. As he tried on different poses – womanizer, prankster, artist – he was prolonged in his search for identity. His lying, which appeared to come from developmental experiences of his parents' deceptions and hiding, burdened him psychologically because he avoided meaningful contact with people who might see him and give him truthful emotional feedback. Perhaps they might find a demanding and angry young boy. How can someone who has lived in hiding find a use for the mirroring of another to reflect what's been unseen for so long? This is a relational dilemma for men like Nicolas. He struggled to see himself in anyone, to let them inside, and the few friends he had couldn't get beyond his cloak of mystery.

Adult identity comes to involve mourning who we once were and who we believed we would turn out to be. We must find a balance somewhere between the regret of lived experiences and the disappointment of our idealized expectations. This process includes developmentally appropriate suffering, letting go, and coming to terms with limitations. Immigration can sidetrack this experience when it is viewed as a workaround solution to bypass mourning, rather than a continued working through of identity. A workaround can lead to further alienation. Nicolas had some of this belief in seeing moving from his homeland as an escape. The trouble, of course, was that he still brought his psyche with him – it was the same psyche he had when he left, and it didn't magically regenerate into something different. This escape fantasy is a bit different from Akhtar's idea of repudiation; it is more like hoping to sever the cord and forget the past.

I found Nicolas's ideas about language compelling. He did describe a freedom that many might find in adopting a new language – a freedom to rediscover themselves, perhaps unencumbered by habitual expressions of language and all its ways of defining a self. Language communicates to others who the self is. Sophie Walsh suggests that we have transference to language and that acquiring a new language often reorients our object relationships in positive ways.[36] A new language can feel like a rebirth. For Nicolas, it may well have been the case that using English gave him distance from his Spanish-speaking self and allowed him some degree of separating from his past. Yet the boy of his homeland was still chasing him, and Nicolas continued to lie in English.

Building on the discussion in this chapter, in the next one, I turn to consider the monster as a type of extreme negative identity usually bent on destruction. This character represents what can happen with apocalyptic inflation within a psyche. Many of these monsters nowadays commit murder as vengeful glory, although creating mayhem, for example, through hacking that disrupts social contracts, is another expression of compensating for alienation through omnipotent, destructive fantasy.

Notes

1 R. Ellison, *Invisible Man*, New York, Vintage Books, 1980, p. 154.
2 E. Erikson, *Identity, Youth and Crisis*, New York, Norton & Company, 1969, p. 94.
3 Ibid., p. 59.
4 Ibid., p. 165.
5 Founded in 1963 in San Francisco, Oakes specialized in the treatment of children with autism spectrum disorders.
6 Erikson, *Identity, Youth and Crisis*, pp. 172–3.
7 D. W. Winnicott, "The antisocial tendency" (1956), in *Delinquency and Deprivation*, pp. 103–12, Abingion, Routledge, 1984/2012.
8 Erikson, *Identity, Youth and Crisis*, p. 174.
9 Ibid., p. 176.
10 Ibid., p. 176.
11 C. G. Jung, "The alchemical view of the union of opposites," in *Mysterium Coniunctionis, CW* 14, 1963, pp. 457–69; and "The opposites," in *Mysterium Coniunctionis, CW* 14, 1963, pp. 3–6.
12 C. W. Jung, "Definitions," in *Psychological Types, CW* 6, 1971, pp. 425–6.
13 F. Dews, "What percentage of the U.S. population of foreign born?" October 13, 2013, Brookings Now. Available: <www.brookings.edu/blog/brookings-now/2013/10/03/what-percentage-of-u-s-population-is-foreign-born/> (accessed March 14, 2017).
14 U. Segal, D. Elliott, and N. S. Mayadas, *Immigration Worldwide: Policies, Practices, and Trends*, Oxford, Oxford University Press, 2010, pp. 20–1.
15 Ibid., p. 31.
16 Ibid., p. 44.
17 S. Akhtar, *Immigration and Acculturation: Mourning, Adaptation and the Next Generation*, New York, Jason Aronson, 2011, p. 9.
18 Ibid., pp. 12–17.
19 J. Henderson, "The cultural unconscious," in *Shadow and Self: Selected Papers in Analytical Psychology*, Wilmette, IL, Chiron, 1990.
20 S. Kimbles, *Phantom Narratives: The Unseen Contributions of Culture to Psyche*, Lanham, MD, Rowman & Littlefield, 2014, p. 103.
21 Ibid., p. 46.
22 Ibid., p. 71.
23 Lee's therapist at Oakes was Amy Huerta. I supervised her psychotherapy with Lee and am using this clinical material from process notes she presented to me during supervision. She gave me permission to use her notes for teaching, lectures, and research, and I'd like to acknowledge my gratitude to her for this.
24 R. Tyminski, *The Psychology of Theft and Loss: Stolen and Fleeced*, New York, Routledge, 2014, pp. 84–98.
25 H. Faimberg, "The telescoping of generations," *Contemporary Psychoanalysis*, 1988, vol. 24, no. 1, pp. 99–118. Quote is from p. 104.
26 Ibid., p. 112.
27 C. Jama Adams, "Psychotherapy with poor African American men: Challenges around the construction of masculinity," in B. Reiss and R. Grossmark (eds.), *Heterosexual Masculinities: Contemporary Perspectives from Psychoanalytic Gender Therapy*, pp. 163–87, New York, Routledge, 2009, p. 163.

28 Ibid., p. 180.
29 D. W. Winnicott, "Transitional objects and transitional phenomena," *The International Journal of Psychoanalysis*, 1953, vol. 34, pp. 89–97; and "Hate in the counter-transference," *International Journal of Psychoanalysis*, 1949, vol. 30, pp. 69–74.
30 NAACP, NAACP Game Changer Fact Sheet: Public Safety and Criminal Justice, 2011. Online, available: <action.naacp.org/page/-/resources/Criminal_Justice_Fact_Sheet.pdf> (accessed March 21, 2017).
31 Michelle Alexander, *The New Jim Crow: Mass Incarceration in the Age of Colorblindness*, New York, The New Press, 2012.
32 Ibid., p. 6.
33 Ibid., p. 219.
34 A. Lemma, "The many faces of lying," *International Journal of Psychoanalysis*, 2005, vol. 86, no. 3, pp. 737–53.
35 F. H. von Donnersmarck, *The Lives of Others* (*Das Leben der Anderen*), Wiedemann & Berg, Bayerischer Rundfunk, Arte, and Creado, 2006. Distributed in the United States by Sony Pictures.
36 S. D. Walsh, 2014. "The bilingual therapist and transference to language: Language use in therapy and its relationship to object relational context," *Psychoanalytic Dialogues*, 2014, vol. 24, no. 1, pp. 56–71.

Chapter 6

Alienated monsters cut loose

My person was hideous and my stature gigantic. What did this mean? Who was I? What was I? Whence did I come? What was my destination? These questions continually recurred, but I was unable to resolve them.

—Mary Shelly, *Frankenstein or the Modern Prometheus*[1]

There are some boys, male adolescents, and young men who develop a self-image of themselves beyond what I'd simply call negative. They actually see themselves as monsters, scary to others and frightening to themselves, too. My patient Anthony from Chapter 4, for instance, viewed himself as a gargoyle, and he didn't mean the kind seen on cathedrals and other large buildings. As a boy and teenager, he read graphic novels in which many of main characters were gargoyles, and he began to think of himself as like them. This fantasy eventually took hold in a deep way, and Anthony drew his own comics with himself as a powerful gargoyle character. In engaging with various demonic forces, gargoyle characters in graphic novels often combine superhuman strength, magic, and an ability to fly; sometimes they are also demonic. When Anthony spoke of his fascination with them, I could see traces of a younger boy who feared what he might become. Anthony did often verbalize that he considered himself "a freak."

Monsters

Monsters frequently represent an embodiment of alienation by physically bringing horror into the real world. They express an outcast sense of being quite beyond the perimeters of civilized society, and they threaten to terrorize it with their rage and destructiveness. Mary Shelley's story about a fabricated creature made of dead bodies, who comes to life as a monster, originates in her book that was written in 1818. In it, she provides the details for a creation myth that mesmerizes Victor Frankenstein and compels him to construct a living demon. This still amazing, eerie tale shows a struggle between resurrection and death – a struggle that is part of Mary Shelley's personal history as well. Her own mother died of an infection soon after Mary's birth in 1797. This painful echo of death after birth returned at

Mary's first pregnancy, when she lost a child born prematurely in 1815. In 1816, her son William was born, and he, too, would perish a few years later. The idea for Frankenstein came to her during the summer of 1816, after William's birth, and she would finish it in 1817.

Important for delving into this story is the recognition that Victor Franken-stein – the driven, possessed, and maniacal protagonist – is a young man in his late teens and early twenties for most of the creation part of the tale. He thus represents elements of what can go wrong when a young man becomes inflated psychologi-cally with ideas that take on a shimmer of crusade, conquest, and self-righteous domination. My patient Anthony showed aspects of this psychic infection when he spoke about his plans for developing a super-computer with artificial intelli-gence. He was a talented young man, and listening to him speak about this topic, I occasionally wondered whether he might, indeed, be capable of something like this. My speculation may have also reflected concern for what appeared mon-strous to me about him – that he might bring terrifying things from another realm into my relatively safe world.

Mary Shelley describes her inspiration for the novel as follows:

> I saw – with eyes shut, but acute mental vision – I saw the pale student [Vic-tor] of unhallowed arts kneeling beside the thing he had put together. I saw the hideous phantasm of a man stretched out, and then, on the working of some powerful engine, show signs of life and stir. [2]

She clearly imagined a primal relationship between the pale student and the mon-ster, a psychological connection that modern film versions pay less attention to when the monster is merely demonized and eventually has to be eradicated.[3] This splitting apart of the two has led to the creature now being popularly referred to as *Frankenstein*, as if the demonic intentions of Victor reside fully in his creation, leaving us to think of Victor as a misguided genius. Shelley's intent in pairing the two may, however, reveal an important linkage that they cannot be so easily sepa-rated. They may belong together as parts of a whole that encircles mania, creative impulse, rebirth, death, and destruction. These factors often appear dramatically in the ideas and behaviors of young men who feel monstrous.

Victor is a grave robber and also a thief stealing secrets from nature about life itself. His thieving is power-driven – its purpose to exalt himself – and is a kind of stealing often motivated by status, inflation of self, and narcissism.[4] As he con-ducts his experiments, he believes he has discovered the secret to life, and over-estimating his capabilities, he doesn't notice his own increasing alienation from his teachers, fellow students, and family. Later, upon seeing what he has done, he remarks, "How can I describe my emotions at this catastrophe, or how delineate the wretch whom with such infinite pains and care I had endeavored to form?"[5] He is shocked that his creation is beautiful and ugly, intoxicating and repulsive. He betrays a glimmer of awareness that trouble may come, because he feels dif-ferently from how he had imagined, not simply ecstatic but disgusted when "the beauty of the dream vanished."[6] Many thieves often revel in getting away with it, only later to face a series of unintended consequences that spoil their fantasy.

The Creature teaches us something about severe alienation that turns to destructiveness. Confronting Frankenstein about his loneliness, he laments, "I was benevolent; my soul glowed with love and humanity; but am I not alone, miserably alone?"[7] He adds that other humans "spurn and hate" him. He describes here a nearly unbearable feeling of not belonging anywhere, a kind of isolation ripe for an agony that reinforces strong negative beliefs about an outcast self and the world in which he lives. The Creature is repulsed when he realizes how he looks to others:

> how was I terrified, when I viewed myself in a transparent pool! At first I started back, unable to believe that it was indeed I who was reflected back in the mirror; and when I became fully convinced that I was in reality the monster that I am, I was filled with the bitterest sensations of despondence and mortification.[8]

His repulsion reflects a type of expression that I have heard many young men in the throes of existential alienation voice about their appearance. Anthony avoided looking into mirrors, leaving his hair uncombed, because what he saw disgusted him. "I look creepy." To me, he was a disheveled, sloppy young man, but not an unhandsome one, although he felt otherwise. Tom, the manic patient from Chapter 4, was obsessed with his weight, measuring each pound of variation from day to day. He longed for "six-pack" abdominal muscles that he felt would change how he felt about himself. I have heard numerous times, from boys and men, about those desirable abs, which seem to embody a visible definition of powerful masculinity. Luke, who I mentioned in Chapter 1 and who you'll learn more about in the next chapter, constantly checked his appearance in mirrors, finding evidence that he was a "walking skeleton" who everyone would despise. Each of these men saw in their physical appearance some proof of being a freak. Like the Creature, they were mortified by how they believed others saw them.

Where do such beliefs and "dire" emotions lead?[9] Charles Stewart shows through various publicly known cases, such as the Columbine High School shooters Eric Harris and Dylan Klebold, who in 1999 murdered thirteen people on campus, how such emotions snowball into violent enactments.[10] He believes that social isolation reinforces intense loneliness, which in turn leads to a poor self-image and further isolation. As this cycle continues, it eventually produces such painful emotions that they can no longer be contained and, instead, compel a person to act out. The Creature would be another example of someone similarly isolated who snowballs in his alienation toward violence and destruction. The Creature's articulate narrative, constructed by Shelley to voice her own familiarity with death and loss, makes us as readers look at the source of his rage. "I will revenge my injuries . . . cause fear . . . swear[ing] inextinguishable hatred."[11] He warns us how his alienation will be inflicted on others to cause misery. This model of a traumatized psyche is well known, the victim becoming the aggressor when his suffering finds no other outlet. Shelley adds to this psychological understanding through the duo of Victor and the Creature, who portray a manic creation-despairing destruction sequence. What brings them together is their mutual alienation.

The Creature shows which emotions can become dire: shame, humiliation, rage, and contempt. This combination of negative affects can easily become unbearable. A person caught in them – and absent any containing presence – may seek the only release that appears to offer an end, namely violence and destruction. I suggest that these emotions are at the core of severe alienation when a self-image of being a monster or freak takes over. Shame and humiliation might be considered developmental antecedents that arise from childhood and adolescent experiences of being shunned, banished, and ridiculed. Certainly not everyone goes down this path, and likewise, shame and humiliation are universal human emotions, part of us all. For some, however, if shame and humiliation are coupled with repeated experiences of rage and contempt without someone else to help out, then a dangerous pattern may be primed for igniting destructively. Rage and contempt may be understandable reactions to shame and humiliation, but when the former emotions lead to steady persecutory fantasies with outcomes of revenge, a boy may incorporate whatever bizarre things he imagines he needs into his fantasy life to feel extremely powerful. Monsters are almost always strong in some way.

Anthony often shared with me his contempt for coworkers and for women. He turned on them for small slights and conjured malevolent fantasies of revenge. His stealing of women's underwear was an enactment of one of these fantasies, in which he saw himself as a victor over a humiliated woman. Perhaps, Shelley intuitively gave Frankenstein the first name Victor to remind us he is a young man with contempt for nature's limits. Because Anthony worked in medical research, he had access to controlled and dangerous substances, including pathogens. He sometimes imagined unleashing one of these on someone who he felt had offended him. I had to draw a firm line with him about dwelling on these fantasies, because I sometimes felt concerned that he might hurt someone. I told him I had a duty to warn anyone if I concluded he might act on his ideas, although he always denied any intention to do so. I would discuss with him what he imagined he would gain, what would happen if he were caught, and how would others feel about him when they found out? These questions were appeals to empathy, and in Anthony's case, there was just enough nurturance from his mother and others in his childhood that he had a slender foundation of empathy to refer to. He stated that it mattered to him that he cared about others and that he didn't want to hurt anyone, although his reasoning sounded like what a grade-school boy might say when prompted for reasons not to pick unprovoked fights. Still, this basic empathy probably made a difference to him.

A self-image of being a monster seems to grow, in part, out of severe alienation. The Creature, toward the end of Shelley's important novel, anguishes, "I, the miserable and the abandoned, am an abortion, to be spurned at, kicked, and trampled on."[12] Here, he expresses an idea that there can be no growth, no positive development toward something better. Abortion, as used in metaphor, implies a psyche that is not allowed to come into being, a house that simply explodes outward into pieces. Under the weight of shame, humiliation, rage, and contempt, all that remains is to hurt others in any way possible.

Edna O'Shaughnessy writes about a psychotherapy case of a twelve-year-old boy who consciously identified with the Creature (though calling him "Frankenstein" in the sort of misattribution I referred to earlier).[13] She explains how this boy turned his alienation into a fantasy of being a powerful and scary monster, and how he rationalized his isolation as a willful and contemptuous rejection of what was ordinary. This was also true of my patient Anthony, who would often remark, "Normal is so boring." O'Shaughnessy's patient based his fantasy on the 1931 film of the story, and she felt he was using it to supersede any sense of true limits by engaging in "an act of self-creation."[14] She notes throughout this discussion that her patient's contempt for her and for others was observable and potent. One of her main points is that the boy chose a monstrous identity as an alternative to being psychotic. Quoting Freud from 1911, when he wrote about the paranoid Dr. Schreber, she writes, "The delusional formation which we take to be the pathological product, is in reality an attempt at recovery."[15] This important recognition helps us see that even severe alienation grasps for identity, and when it is elusive, madness looms. Jung, too, saw the delusions of psychotic patients as meaningful attempts at self-healing and expressions of subjectivity.[16] In a disturbing way, taking on a monster identity averts falling into the dissolution of psychosis, and this is something that appeared accurate in Anthony's case as well.

Running wild

Monsters on the loose seem to be everywhere in zombie films and in other popular media, including social media and graphic novels, especially those with themes of apocalypse.[17] The year 2000 brought fears of computer meltdown with warnings of a Y2K bug disabling all our electronic devices. Apocalyptic symbolism is prevalent today from political discourse to terrorist imagery, from explanations of economic distress to artistic forms. The word *apocalypse* originally meant the disclosure of knowledge, an uncovering or lifting of the veil. Calypsis, the opposite, means covering up, hiding, and concealing. Calypso was a nymph and daughter of Atlas in Greek mythology, and in Homer's *Odyssey*, she seduces Odysseus and keeps him captive on her island for seven years.[18] Calypso effectively deceives him and keeps his true purpose hidden from him, namely returning home. Apocalypse, conversely, would signify a revealing of truth and meaning.

Now, however, when we hear the word *apocalypse*, we tend to think of an end-of-time scenario, which comes to us mainly from the Bible's Book of Revelation, although *revealing* is still part of the word's broader meaning.[19] It is also here that we meet the four horsemen of the apocalypse who bring devastation in the procession to the Final Judgment. "And I saw, and behold a white horse:

and he that sat on him had a bow; and a crown was given unto him: and he went forth conquering, and to conquer."[20] This first horseman is believed to represent with his bow and arrow both conquest and plague. Psychologically, this symbolism signifies triumph and then a deadness following it. Such deadness occurs in psychic states of emptiness and desolation. The conquest is empty, a manic inflation with little substance that brings exhaustion. Psychic infection – plague – overcomes a person in this state, piercing him to the core of his being with emptiness.

The next horse that St. John recounts in his vision is red with a horseman carrying a sword.[21] This red horse with its rider represents war, violence, and killing. From a psychological perspective, this figure perpetrates aggression, lives it out, and inflicts pain on others, perhaps like the Columbine High School shooters and other mass murderers.

The third horse is black, and its rider holds a set of scales used in measurement. He is thought to represent famine and greed, when appetites spin out of control. On the one hand, this figure could represent emotional deprivation viewed as kind of internal famine. On the other hand, he evokes an idea of craving, in which appetites cannot be curtailed, and these weigh a person down with self-destructive urges. Moderation and balance are felt to be impossible.

St. John sees a fourth horse, a pale horse, and "his name that sat on him was Death, and Hell followed with him."[22] This rider is commonly depicted as carrying a scythe like the Grim Reaper. Both Joseph M. W. Turner (c. 1825) and William Blake (c. 1800) illustrated this rider. He would seem to denote the final end, dying and dissolution. This horseman conveys mortality. Yet he may also symbolize the quest for meaning, the search for faith and spiritual enlightenment. The pale horse reminds us that our time is limited and that individuation entails giving this finality a shape and meaning in our psyches. How do we choose to respond to that ultimate task?

Apocalyptic art is spread across centuries of Western visual media. The iconography of such art is typically based on apocalyptic manuscripts that refer to the Book of Revelation and often proliferate before or after a millennial date, such as 500 CE, 1000 CE, and 1500 CE.[23] Natasha O'Hear, in her book on this subject, notes that artists use various approaches to show the coming apocalypse, including metaphorical, decoding, symbolic, and psychological. In the 13th, 14th, and 15th centuries, these texts and art were often anti-Semitic in advancing propaganda about the alleged struggles of the Catholic Church.[24] During this period, Jews were stigmatized, massacred at times, and expelled from several countries.

These apocalyptic images that artists draw almost always depict a vision of a final war for justice and vengeance fought between powers for good and evil. O'Hear notes that many illustrated apocalyptic cycles begin with John of Patmos, the St. John of the Book of Revelation, asleep and in a position seeming to be "at odds" with the angel's instructions to record what he sees.[25] It sounds as if he is dreaming. Apocalyptic images usually depict a mingling of three realms: heavenly, earthly, and demonic. They portend a sort of prediction of imminent doom.

Figure 6.1 The Four Horsemen of the Apocalypse, 1498, Albrecht Dürer (1471–1528)
Source: © Trustees of the British Museum

Albrecht Dürer's woodcut illustration of the Four Riders shows in dramatic form the terror that they bring forth. Done in 1498, right before 1500, he shows them spurred on by an angel and trampling over miserable victims. Some believe he made his apocalypse series after an apocalyptic dream that he had.[26] Erwin Panofsky, a scholar of Dürer, writes, "Like Leonardo's *Last Supper*, Dürer's *Apocalypse* belongs among what may be called the inescapable works of art."[27] He notes that Dürer's illustrations of the apocalypse were copied extensively and their influence was far reaching. His description "inescapable" tells us as viewers that there is something archetypal here that reaches deep into our psyches to capture and hold our attention. Might our attraction to this illustration be about how it portrays destructiveness?

These four riders can also show us something about the male psyche in states of extreme alienation. The end of time of apocalypse certainly is a hopeless place with no outlook forward. Many young men now play violent video games, blowing up the world or fighting a war in animated post-apocalyptic settings. I asked one fourteen-year-old boy in my practice what he enjoyed about playing these games, and he replied, "Simple, I play to destroy!" He's also a boy who likes watching *YouTube* videos about making your own weapons. Although he's never indicated he would use anything like this, he seems drawn to violent content, which may put him at some future risk for acting out. Fortunately, he is in therapy.

The American Psychological Association recently issued a report from a task force assessing violent video games.[28]

> Consistent with the literature that we reviewed, we found that violent video game exposure was associated with: an increased composite aggression score; increased aggressive behavior; increased aggressive cognitions; increased aggressive affect, increased desensitization, and decreased empathy; and increased physiological arousal.[29]

Their conclusions are based on a meta-analysis of thirty-one articles published since 2009 on this subject. There is much debate about how harmful these violent games might be, and those who support the video-game industry consistently claim that there is no causal link between such games and violence. The authors of this report are careful to note that there is no proof of causation to endorse an idea that these games lead to criminal behavior or delinquency.

Nonetheless, these are troubling findings. For example, the study's authors note, "The link between violent video game exposure and aggressive behavior is one of the most studied and best established," and that these behaviors include "hitting, pushing, and fighting."[30] Physiological effects include increases in heart rate and blood pressure. This information is not insignificant at a time when many boys and young men, as I mentioned in Chapter 1, are not performing well academically when compared to girls and young women. Another example of this gender disparity would be the skew in ADHD diagnosis toward boys, with one recent study showing over 80% of the total are boys.[31] Boys and young men addicted to their online activities are at risk for social and cognitive impairments. Many now tell me that because of Google, it is no longer necessary to memorize, learn cursive, or understand math facts. "I'll just Google it."

Another key finding of the APA task force was that there was "no support for positive outcomes after violent video game exposure."[32] This statement flies against claims that video games help in various ways with attention, motor coordination, and memory. The finding of decreased empathy after playing violent video games is alarming; we have to wonder about the cumulative effects from playing these games and about temporary effects that may become permanent from repeated exposure. Loss of empathy creates all kinds of relational problems, including an inability to be intimate, delayed social skills, impairment in resolving conflict, and lack of cooperative understanding needed in families and at work. This empathy deficit can be difficult to remediate in either individual or group psychotherapy, and it can lead to resistance for getting psychological intervention at all. The four riders are neither empathic figures, nor are they thinking ones. They are simply sent to avenge and destroy. I refer to these figures of the four riders in what Jung might characterize as an archetype to understand a kind of destructive impulse. The four riders hurt others in carrying out an omnipotent doomsday scenario, leaving us with no hope in this world (the only hope being in the afterlife). They may, in this limited context, help to illustrate – and reveal – what happens in extreme alienation when a boy or young man feels driven to act like one of them.

Red horse

Changing the order in the Book of Revelation, I'll begin this discussion with the red horse, its rider carrying a sword, and believed to signify killing and overt destruction. In the United States, the list of mass shootings is dismally long and a national tragedy. A selected few of these massacres include: Blacksburg, Virginia, 2007 (by Seung-Hui Cho, age 23); Tucson, Arizona, 2011 (by Jared Loughner, age 22); Sandy Hook, Connecticut, 2012 (by Adam Lanza, age 20); Aurora, Colorado, 2012 (by James Holmes, age 24); Washington, DC, 2013 (by Aaron Alexis, age 34); Charleston, South Carolina, 2015 (by Dylann Roof, age 21); Roseburg, Oregon, 2015 (by Chris Harper Mercer, age 26); Orlando, Florida, 2016 (by Omar Mateen, age 29); Las Vegas, Nevada (by Stephen Paddock, age 64); Sutherland Springs, Texas, 2017 (by Devin Patrick Kelley, age 26); Parkland, Florida, 2018 (by Nikolas Cruz, age 19); Santa Fe, Texas, 2018 (by Dimitrios Pagourtzis, age 17).[33] All men, and mostly in their twenties. Two of these horrifying assaults by men in their twenties were among the deadliest in U.S. history, those at Virginia Tech University (thirty-two victims) and at the Pulse nightclub in Orlando (forty-nine victims). Loosely regulated gun ownership laws in the United States are partly to blame for this public health epidemic, which threatens our civil fabric.

Europe, with tighter gun control laws, has had its share of tragedies like these, although many there have been associated with domestic terrorism. But not all.

In July 2016, an eighteen-year-old young man, a student in Munich, went on a rampage that left nine dead before he killed himself. His name was Ali David Sonboly. He was being treated for depression, had a copy of Peter Langman's book *Why Kids Kill: Inside the Minds of School Shooters*,[34] and was an avid player of the first-person-shooter video game *Counterstrike*.[35]

Sonboly apparently felt proud to have the same birthday (April 20) as Adolf Hitler. He was born in Germany and was of Iranian descent, although he was said to have taken inspiration for his shooting from the Norwegian right-wing extremist Anders Behring Breivik.[36] Behring Breivik was responsible for killing seventy-seven people in Norway five years previous, on the same day that Sonboly made his attack.

When Sonboly played *Counterstrike*, he often offended other players, especially by using xenophobic hate language. He criticized Turks, Arabs, and Jews online in chat rooms and posted under the user-name "Hate."[37] He was allegedly bullied at his school. Seven of his victims were teenagers, three ethnic Albanians and three Turkish.[38] Sonboly hacked a young woman's Facebook account to lure others into a shopping center in Munich where he went on his killing spree. He may have taken some of what he learned about shooting through playing *Counterstrike* into his horrific actions in Munich. But he also learned to shoot during gun-range lessons with his father.[39]

Sonboly purchased his weapon, a Glock pistol, through the Darknet and researched not only Behring Breivik but also Tim Kretschmer, a seventeen-year-old who killed fifteen people in and around a school in Winnenden, Germany, before taking his own life.[40] This premeditation reveals something about Sonboly's sense of being like these other shooters, perhaps identifying with them and wanting to emulate them. The Darknet is usually accessed with a browser like Tor, providing anonymity, to view hidden services such as the sale of guns and drugs. Sonboly's planning may have gone on for as much as a year because he visited Winnenden and took pictures there.[41] This timeline intersects with another important point in his young life, when he was hospitalized for psychiatric reasons in a Munich hospital.[42] After the shooting, police detectives found psychotropic medications in the family's apartment.

What are we to make from this outline of such a disturbing tragedy? Psychiatric disturbance seems a feature in so many of these attacks, although often there have been significant interventions. In Sonboly's case, treatment seemed to have overlapped with his descent into more violent preoccupations, such as planning his attack and visiting Winnenden. Psychiatric resources are frequently limited, and they cannot ultimately deter someone who is highly motivated to violence.

Likewise, Sonboly's violent videogaming cannot be seen as predictive of his violent behavior, although it might have provided too much stimulation for a fragile mind that could not otherwise contain his aggressive impulses. The videogaming industry would certainly push back against attempts to regulate it more stringently, other than through parental advisories and muted warnings about content. In 2011, the U.S. Supreme Court ruled in a case regulating sales of violent video games to minors that research evidence did not yet support claims of harm caused to minors.[43] Of interest, though, is the fact that so many of these shooters have compulsively played violent video games, similar to what investigators discovered about Sonboly's involvement in the game *Counterstrike*. Although violent video-game exposure may not yet be causally associated with violent and criminal behaviors in the real world, it is difficult to ignore that the crime in Munich might have had some undetermined link to the shooter's having gotten carried away by what happened in cyberspace. A fragile ego can quickly lose its bearing, as many clinicians know from their practices.

As discussed in Chapter 5, a further psychological consideration is the notion of negative identity, as developed by Erikson, for adolescents who are casting about for an identity. Sometimes, they settle on rebellion, violence, and drug abuse as ways to patch together a brutal and monstrous identity to express their alienation. In these shooting incidents, young men are heartless about whom they target for their violence, often preying on those who are obviously vulnerable. As with Frankenstein's creature, children are not safe from such young men. There has to be a tipping point for someone like Sonboly, when alienation cannot break free from an escalating cycle of shame, humiliation, contempt, and rage. When this combination erupts, a person in its grips has to find real targets, no longer just virtual ones. The tipping point, of course, is largely unknown in Sonboly's case because we have no psychiatric or biographical data. That is a limitation of my discussion here: these ideas are speculative because there are no clinical observations on which I can ground them. Still, we might ask, "Why is it that we rarely learn of a young mass shooter, in highly developed countries, who has *not played* violent video games?"

The rider of the red horse suggests someone who wants to kill others. Perhaps some of this willful destruction is just pure sadism. Alienation in this situation leads to revenge that locates targets and cruelly hurts them. An eleven-year-old boy whom I discussed in my earlier book on stealing showed aspects of this sadism.[44] TJ taunted his classmates, provoked fights, and manipulated boys whom he thought were weak. He stole from teachers, and when caught, he was defiant, once writing, "I AM NOT SORRY." TJ came from a divorced family. His parents seemed frustrated with him but could rarely agree on an approach to take for his delinquent behaviors because they openly despised one another. Although materially he was well cared for, he was a pawn in their mutual contempt. In their counseling sessions, they seized control from therapists to turn against one another, complaining and arguing.

TJ escalated over the time he was at the day treatment center where I worked as director. He brought crack cocaine to school one day, having allegedly obtained the "rocks" from someone in his neighborhood. His parents denied any drug abuse. TJ was only caught with these "rocks" when he attempted to sneak into the kitchen. He may have been planning to use them to poison someone's lunch. On another occasion, he feigned being hurt by a mishap on the play yard. A teacher sympathetically bent closer to him to console him, and he abruptly turned and punched him in the face. This teacher had to go to an emergency room for stitches where TJ's punch had lacerated his face. The school attempted a long list of behavioral interventions, consequences, parental meetings, and consultation with the agencies that had placed TJ at the center. Nothing worked to improve his behavior.

There followed a too-long process of securing a residential school placement for TJ. He clearly needed twenty-four-hour care and staff supervision in a more restrictive setting. Several years later, I received a phone call about TJ. He was a young man by then and had been arrested after a horrifying incident in a city park. He had bludgeoned a homeless man and nearly killed him. The caller was from a legal team assigned for his defense, and she told me that TJ had admitted his guilt saying, "I'm not sorry." She also mentioned that he had several tattoos, one of which spelled out the word *revenge*. TJ's identification as a monster and brutal outsider began early in his life – and continued without much exposure to video games, since these events occurred before they became wildly popular. The profound sadness of his case has often reminded me of our professional limits, what we can and cannot accomplish as analysts, psychotherapists, teachers, social workers, and childcare advocates. How can we turn around someone bent on rampage? I can only imagine the alienation he must have felt – he and I had many interactions during his time at the center. I recall many times asking myself, "What's inside that makes him so angry?" and always feeling a bit frightened.

White horse

This part of the apocalyptic grouping is especially complex because the rider wears a crown and carries a bow and arrow. An obvious interpretation has been conquest, but others suggest evil and plague or pestilence. A psychological explanation that combines these attributes could allude to seeking false victories that infect us. Examples could include sex, drugs, and money, which offer enticements of conquest and power. Frequently, these turn out to be empty and insubstantial. However, this rider may help us understand when alienation leads either to compulsive behaviors or to addictions. These can seem like infections – hard to treat and prone to relapse – though also potentially destructive.

I introduced Luke in Chapter 1; he was a thirty-five-year-old gay man suffering from panic attacks and using cocaine during episodic drug binges. Luke would often be provocative when describing his binges to me. For example, he'd tell me these weren't such a big problem because he limited himself to five or six a year. He asserted that this relative infrequency meant he was not an addict. He'd also watch carefully how I responded when he spoke about the ecstatic feeling he got when using. For example, he might say, "I don't really know anything like it; there's nothing to compare," and then ask, "You probably have no idea what I'm talking about?" When I urged him to explain, he'd tell me he believed I was somewhat naïve about drugs and he "just knew" I had never used cocaine. When I asked how he would know that, he'd resort to various explanations ranging from "you don't look the type" (something about my appearance) to "you'd agree with me if you had" (something about my inexperience). I was split off in his mind into a category of nonuser who wouldn't get it. This split put me into a position of "raining on his parade" when I questioned the effects on his health and his psyche. I was viewed as spoiling his good times. He stated that I wasn't really in a place to advise him because I'd not known the ecstasy he described. For him, this ecstasy was numinous and bestowed a golden crown on him at the height of pleasure.

I interpreted to Luke that he put me in an awkward relationship around his drug use: either I could keep quiet and seem to condone it, or I could speak up out of ignorance, which made me unpersuasive to him. He oftentimes became angry with me for this interpretation, arguing that it seemed "unfair" for me to express this dilemma because "you're just a clinician in a white coat." (I never wear a white medical coat to my office.) He seemed to be saying that the drug made him feel powerful and that power meant he could subvert my authority. I became, in his view of me, a dry, almost sterile cliché of a healthcare professional. I usually felt alienated in these discussions and wondered if he also felt the same way.

After one of these exchanges, Luke brought in a dream. *He heard a professional man saying that the land needed work. A Native American woman agreed, and she added that the earth was too hard. She said no one can dig in it if it stayed this hard. She looked sad.* Luke told me that this dream made him feel very sad, although he didn't understand why. He said the professional man seemed to be trying to get him to look at something. I asked him what he saw when he looked at the land and the hard earth from the dream. Luke's eyes became teary, and he brought up cocaine. He mentioned how it looks like white sand, but that when it's sold as crack, it's a hard rock. I noted that he seemed sad thinking about his cocaine use, and that, in this dream, there wasn't any reason to be ecstatic. He nodded, replying that it made him worry he was beyond help – like the land, too hard, in his dream. This shift felt significant to me because Luke seemed to take off the crown of his cocaine-induced ecstasy and to have a budding idea about its harmful consequences.

Another example of a false conquest linked to compulsion and addiction comes from my patient George, a twenty-nine-year-old gay man, who avidly used various websites and apps to hook up sexually with other men. George had tested negative for HIV. He explained to me his screening procedure when he met another man for sex, a procedure he felt made him practically risk-free for any infection. When they chatted online before meeting, George would ask a potential sex partner questions about sexually transmitted infections (STIs), as well as about his HIV status. Anything affirmative would end the chat. When George let someone get to "phase 2" – in person, he would scan the other man for signs of any observable physical symptoms. If he saw anything that looked suspicious, he'd leave. Nonetheless, even when his procedure reached "stage 3," George assumed the other man "was probably lying," and he practiced "safer sex" during these encounters.[45] George liked his sexual freedom and thought a relationship would only tie him down.

He reported that he felt exhilarated after each sexual encounter. "It's a little like getting high." George assured me that he stayed within the bounds of safer sex, which, for him, included the use of condoms for anal intercourse but otherwise allowed for unprotected oral sex. His background around his homosexuality was characterized by punitive and cruel judgments. George's parents had reacted harshly when he came out to them in his late teens. They openly rejected him and refused to pay for his college education. Only recently had they resumed phone and email contact when his mother came down with a serious illness. George, at this time, hadn't seen them in nine years. His parents explained that they were coming to town and wanted to meet with him. George was unsure about this meeting, because he still felt great resentment and alienation from them. He believed they had only begrudgingly resumed contact with him because of his mother's illness. I encouraged George to pay attention to his feelings and to see what he might decide if he didn't feel pressured to give in to what they wanted. From what he'd told me about how deeply he felt rejected by them, I was concerned he would agree to something that might afterward overwhelm him with his own punitive judgments – in a way of identifying with the aggressors.

There was a brief meeting at a coffeehouse that was cordial and seemingly inconsequential. His parents reportedly did not criticize him or express any disapproval about his sexual orientation, but George felt angry that they never apologized for their past behaviors. Around this time, George's employer assigned him to a worksite in another state. As this appeared to be temporary, I suggested to George that we continue to work together by phone. He declined and, in a dismissive tone, told me he wanted a break from therapy. I indicated my surprise, wondering whether this sudden decision had to do with hard feelings that came up around seeing his parents. He denied any linkage. I remarked that I was feeling shut out, and perhaps this was similar to how George had felt his parents treated him. He nodded and said he could understand why I'd say this, however, his mind was made up – like the king has spoken. Now, I did feel quite alienated from him, dismissed, and wondered what had happened, not really knowing.

Months later, George phoned me saying he was back in town and asked if we could meet. When he came for his appointment and I saw him in the waiting area, I immediately felt he was sick. George told me that while he'd been living in this other city, he "went wild," meaning he had numerous unprotected sexual encounters. Before I could ask anything, he blurted out, "And now I have HIV." I was stunned and upset.

George resumed psychotherapy with me, and trying to make sense of his contracting HIV, he explained that he'd been feeling "invincible" when he moved away. He consciously believed he could take whatever risks he wanted because of his screening system and that he was somehow protected from harm. George was not delusional, but I thought he was unconsciously reacting to the impact of cruel parental rejection, newly resurrected, and to his fear of closeness with me. By leaving when he had and refusing my continued help, he rejected me. This distancing may have also enacted a rejection of the unconscious part of him that hurt so much and was associated with his therapy. His defensive belief in being invincible, like wearing a crown while riding through his sexual conquests, put him in obvious danger. His state of mind before and after his infection expressed a double-edged form of alienation – initially, that he was not at risk like other gay men, and later, that once he had contracted HIV, he was now "destined to be sick and alone." George's story about HIV is not uncommon.

In clinical situations when I felt alienated from Luke and George, I wondered how best to convey it in a way that they could hear. This is a paradox about communicating a message about the very thing that obstructs communication. We were, at times, alienated, especially in addressing their harmful actions, and they were not open then to hearing me speak about this feeling because of their own difficulties with alienated states. Their denial of feeling dependent on me – preferring not to take the royal crown off – impeded my access to their house. With each of them, I often noted, somewhat like a broken record, their pushing me away, not wanting to listen to me, and being afraid of feeling close to me. I looked for ways to bring up when we were alienated from each other. Luke's dream about the land opened space between us to take up his addiction. George became more vulnerable in therapy only after he got HIV. He fortunately responded well to antiviral medication and began to use his psychotherapy in a deeper way.

Black horse

The rider of the black horse carries scales used for weighing, and these are believed to refer to scarcity and famine, when, for instance, grain supplies dwindled. The psychological correlates would likely be hunger, starvation, and deprivation. Appetites are not satisfied, and emotions such as envy and anger increase in the face of frustration. We often try to push such intense emotions like these far from consciousness. Charles Dickens describes real deprivation in *Oliver Twist:*

> Be that as it may, however, it was his ninth birth-day; and he was keeping it in the coal-cellar with a select party of two other young gentlemen, who, after participating with him in a sound threshing, had been locked up for atrociously presuming to be hungry.[46]

Hunger is punished and locked in a deep and dirty place. This symbolism applies to how many of us react to a craving by choosing to make it unconscious because it seems "dirty."

A male psyche in such a state of deprivation can find it relatively easy to relegate emotional needs and feelings of dependence to the coal cellar of the unconscious. The film *The Social Network* shows this dynamic at work in how it portrays the rupture of the friendship between its two main characters, Mark and Eduardo.[47] Greed and competition ruin this friendship in a story of ruthless ambition that sacrifices the dependence of human relationships. The character Mark betrays his friend Eduardo in an underhanded takeover of their firm that reduces Eduardo's ownership to less than 1% . Signing the documents, Eduardo is too trusting, perhaps naïve to a degree, and misreads Mark because he believes in him, believes in their company as a viable partnership growing out of a friendship. In this film, he gets taken, and Mark assents to this theft and betrayal. A climactic scene near the end comes during a legal deposition, when dueling attorneys question the two of them about their prior agreements. Mark appears stony, obstinate, and unmovable. Eduardo is angry and hurt, not quite able to grasp what has happened. With his back turned, Eduardo answers that he didn't understand he was being taken advantage of. He admits his stupidity, and then turning to Mark, says, "I was your only friend. You had one friend."

Although it is a bit unclear why Mark behaves this way, viewers are left to infer that he judged a better deal would occur by ditching Eduardo. And he may have wanted revenge for Eduardo's earlier freezing of the firm's accounts in order to assert power against what he saw as Mark's drifting away from him. It's not hard to see Eduardo as the victim and Mark as the snake in this drama. But their story may also show something deeper about what happens when male friends become alienated because of competition driven by greed. Certainly, in these last scenes, the contempt they feel for one another appears evident, even as the dialogue revolves around legalities of ownership, stock shares, and money. Deprivation and emotional hunger may lead to a kind of alienation that easily turns into greed and contempt in a drive to have power and to exercise it.

Jake was a ten-year-old boy, an only child, who came to see me for an explosive temper. His parents felt he shut down easily and wouldn't communicate about his feelings or what upset him. Jake wore sunglasses during his sessions the first several weeks we met, even though there was no obvious need for them – his eyesight was fine, and my office was not overly bright. The emotional need, however, was for distance and control. The sunglasses were a shield. Jake had no friends at school and usually got into heated arguments with his cousins who lived nearby. Sometimes these disputes became physical, and Jake would throw things at his cousins. Jake liked the toy volcano (recall Angelo from Chapter 5) in my office, and he frequently wanted to demonstrate that he could make the lava balls fly higher into the air than anyone else. When I asked him early on to draw me a picture of himself, Jake drew a stick figure with a control pad that steered a large wrecking ball dangling from a chain. Symbolically, his rage was massive, loosely contained, and he felt an intense need to control others, with a threat of damage if necessary.

Jake's mother was often frustrated by his volatile moods, and she feared his anger. She reported one episode when she told him no more video games, and he threw a night table down the staircase, while she stood helpless at the foot of the stairs. He frequently acted cruelly toward her. She said she was surprised when she had given birth to a son, since she'd been hoping for a daughter. She grew up with sisters, and she often felt she didn't understand boys. Because she was afraid of what he might do to her, she may have emotionally put distance between herself and Jake. Jake's father was more engaged with his son, and he readily accepted advice about spending more time with him. He also agreed to set limits with Jake for the times when Jake was openly mean toward his mother. Jake seemed able to accept these limits better from his father. As a couple, they appeared affectionate and supportive of one another, but there were inevitable tensions about how to respond to Jake. Father felt mother could show him more affection, and mother believed that father didn't get the extent of Jake's cruelty.

Jake played in a greedy way during his sessions with me. It wasn't enough to simply win. He had to "demolish" and humiliate me with lopsided victories that left me poor and weak. Playing board games, he hoarded money, sometimes stealing from the bank, and devising his own rules to accumulate more than the game allowed. We would often be in a situation where the bank had run out of the largest bills, and Jake insisted we make additional ones that were even greater in value. He rarely tolerated losing, and when I set limits on how far rules could be modified, he would become sullen and withdraw. I'd comment on his anger at me, and he'd often reply, "You're just crazy to say that." During games when his luck was bad, and he was losing, he would often throw money, tokens, and other game pieces at me. When I told him to stop this because it felt mean, he smiled and said, "So?"

Jake was a therapeutic challenge, in part, because I felt his greed came from a place of intense emotional deprivation and, in part, because I tried to empathize with his emptiness and hunger but found this was not easy. Winnicott describes what he calls an antisocial tendency in which "the child is looking for something, somewhere, and failing to find it seeks it elsewhere."[48] Jake's greedy hoarding and stealing were, I thought, signs of his searching for nurturance and tenderness, which he had felt deprived of very early in his life. Jake's mother acknowledged that she had "outsourced" his early care to relatives and to a nanny because she had been disappointed in having a boy to raise. Later on in his psychotherapy, Jake was caught shoplifting in an electronics store. This incident reminded me of his ongoing antisocial tendency with a demand for love, for which, of course, the stolen items were poor and fully inadequate substitutes.

Jake expressed his contempt of people too easily. This emotional response alienated him from his peers and extended family, although as he got a bit older, in middle school, he reported connecting with other boys who were equally mean, sarcastic, and derisive. They would text one another about "epic fails" when others did things they felt were stupid and inferior. He related to me like this, as a failure, and I found myself having to be consciously less warm toward Jake because he regarded my warmth as weakness and a sign of stupidity. I often took a few minutes before his sessions to steel myself by rehearsing a sort of detached neutrality that Jake might respect. Anne Alvarez writes about treating children who can be contemptuous of us: "This implies not evading the full bleakness and horror of the patient's impulses, nor the inadequacy and foolishness of their internal objects and of ourselves in the transference."[49] I take her observation to mean that signs of softness will be gleefully trodden on and trampled over, a bit like one of the victims of the riders of the apocalypse. Jake could gloat and acknowledged he liked seeing me lose. When I would add, "Because you feel I hurt inside," he'd respond, "Losers should hurt. It's not my problem."

Alvarez also remarks that we "need to be alert to the tiniest flickerings of faith and hope that *are* there."[50] She reminds us, as child and adolescent psychotherapists, that growth is unpredictable. We have to remain open to it and look for signs that small or even miniscule change can happen. Winnicott, too, commented that an analyst's despair and impatience could undermine psychotherapeutic work when he or she feels a case is hopeless. Patients like Jake are exquisitely sensitive to being perceived as having losses, and even when these might be admitted, they tend to deny having any feelings about them. This circumstance is at least a twofold problem – admitting a loss and recognizing a feeling about it – that is covered through entrenched defenses of denial and manic control. Jake would not take me seriously whenever he felt I was soft or tender. Two incidents bear out the degree of his contempt for what he saw as my vulnerability.

During a heated phase of his work, when he'd been caught shoplifting, he came in one day rolling his eyes and shaking his hands in a goofy way. When I asked what was the matter, he mumbled nonsense. Jake had seen a boy with autism leave my office recently, and my mind went to recollecting this scene. I asked if he was making fun of people with autism, and he instantly flared at me, "They're stupid, so what!" I tried to remain calm, but my temper probably showed a little, and I remarked, "They have a disability; their brains develop differently; and you somehow find that funny. When I think of you talking this way, I find myself miles away from you. There's a big gap separating us now." Jake shook his head, accused me of "crazy talk," but then momentarily looked sad. I didn't say anything right then, waiting until later in the session, when I mentioned that we were far apart earlier and now maybe not quite so much. I explained that when two people are too far apart, they can hardly expect to work together on anything. For once, Jake did not reply sarcastically, and he let these comments stand. If anything, he appeared surprised – for a few seconds. Here, I did find a way to speak to our alienation that he could let himself hear.

I'll mention one other incident when Jake's contempt was aimed directly at me. He came in for his session speaking with a lisp; he did not have a speech disorder, nor do I. He spoke with a high-pitched, effeminate voice, clearly caricaturing a stereotype of a gay man. He gesticulated dramatically for flamboyant emphasis. I asked why he was talking and acting like this. He continued in a lisp telling me he thought he sounded smart.

After a few more questions on my part that led nowhere, I then said something like, "You are trying to mock a gay man, and it seems intended to make me react. I don't know if you believe I'm gay and are trying to push me away, or if you believe I'm straight and are trying to push me away. Either way, you want to find out just how much I'll be put off by your mockery."

Jake continued to use the lisp, saying I misunderstood – he just liked speaking this way because he sounded "so smart."

I changed tack and suggested if he liked speaking with a lisp, then perhaps he might consider how others would react in public to hearing him.

He stopped lisping and asked, "What do you mean?"

I explained that there were at least two groups, and possibly many more, who would be offended. Could he think why?

"You mean gays?"

I said yes, and he replied that they'd know he was joking. I responded that not all of them would, and he wasn't considering others who would be offended.

He looked stumped and said aggressively, "Who else?" I remarked that people with speech disorders would not take kindly to being mocked like this. He frowned before saying, "Oh, them." He hadn't even considered "them."

Jake had very limited empathy, as these two episodes show. I believe, however, his main intent was to aggravate and upset me. He had noticed a change when I became less warm in our interactions, although he denied this meant anything to him. I suspected he worried I had given up having any feeling for him, and he now was attempting to provoke me, as he could with his mother by cruelly needling her. Jake was not a boy who, at this point, would even understand an interpretation linking how he was with me to anyone in his family. He was not psychologically oriented to bring these details up from his coal cellar – yet. Both examples illustrate how deeply alienated he was, and how off-putting he could be – reinforcing the alienation and further isolating him. His contempt was an expression of his emotional deprivation and his belief that he needed no one. He was an empty boy, meaning that close, reciprocal relationships were not something he consciously valued.

Dark Triad

Jake certainly had psychopathic components to how he related to people. His lack of empathy, his emotional deadness, his narcissistic beliefs of superiority and avoidance of closeness, and his manipulating peers pointed toward incipient psychopathy. Research has identified three aversive personality factors: Machiavellianism, narcissism, and psychopathy. These are sometimes referred to as the "Dark Triad" because "all three entail socially malevolent character with behavior tendencies toward self-promotion, emotional coldness, duplicity, and aggressiveness."[51] In their study, Delroy Paulhus and Kevin Williams find "males scored significantly higher on all three of the Dark Triad."[52]

They argue that the three constructs are not equivalent and only one trait of the "Big Five" (these five are long-accepted research variables in personality studies: agreeableness, conscientiousness, openness, neuroticism, and extraversion) shows commonality across the triad, namely low agreeableness.[53] Some of the differences they find include Machiavellians being more reality-based and narcissists being more self-deceptive; they also report higher nonverbal IQs for Machiavellianism and psychopathy, raising the possibility that those with these traits are not able to clearly communicate needs and desires, and they might thus rely on "malevolent interpersonal strategies."[54] The latter is important given the clinical presentations discussed in Chapter 4, examples where young men struggled with communicating their painful emotional states. If accurate, this skewing of nonverbal IQ scores would possibly account for an inherent tendency toward alienation based on some cognitive differences interfering with verbalization of internal states and feelings.

There is debate about whether the three constructs of the Dark Triad are separable. Sharon Jakobwitz and Vincent Egan contend that they overlap, although their finding is based on a small sample.[55] Gregory Carter, Ann Campbell, Stephen Muncer, and Katherine Carter report, however, that they do function as separate scales as well as a single construct in a nonstudent population, but that they do not function separately in a student sample.[56] They report that student men score higher on the composite Dark Triad scale than student women, perhaps because of consistently higher scores on the psychopathy items.[57]

The Dark Triad posits a modern and contemporary typology that serves as a counterpoint to the archetypal configuration I propose based on the four riders of the apocalypse. It would be too speculative to suggest specific correlations between components of the Dark Triad and any single rider, but some of the research findings, such as higher male prevalence, are noteworthy for consideration. The Dark Triad may have certain diagnostic value. In contrast, an archetypal exploration of the four riders of the apocalypse suggests plausible symbolic and affective representations for why young men act out in states of extreme alienation when they are 1) seeking brutal revenge, 2) caught in addictive cycles, and 3) expressing contempt out of internal deadness.

In the next chapter, I will look at the fourth horse, the pale horse, whose rider brings death. Using this figure, I will examine alienation that leads to dissolution, a consequence that occurs in bad accidents, overdoses, suicides, and severe depression.

Notes

1 M. Shelley, *Frankenstein or the Modern Prometheus* (1818), London, Penguin Books, 1992, p. 131.
2 Ibid., p. 9.
3 *Frankenstein*, screenplay F. E. Faragoh and G. Fort, based on the play by P. Webling, based on the novel by M. Shelley, *Frankenstein or the Modern Prometheus*, 1818; directed by James Whale; produced by Universal Pictures, 1931.
4 R. Tyminski, *The Psychology of Theft and Loss: Stolen and Fleeced*, London, Routledge, 2014.
5 Shelley, *Frankenstein*, p. 58.
6 Ibid.
7 Ibid., p. 103.
8 Ibid., p. 116.
9 C. T. Stewart, *Dire Emotions and Lethal Behaviors: Eclipse of the Life Instinct*, Hove, Routledge, 2007.
10 Ibid., pp. 125–52.

11 Shelley, *Frankenstein*, p. 148.
12 Ibid., p. 224.
13 E. O'Shaughnessy, "A projective identification with Frankenstein: Some questions about psychic limits," in E. Hargreaves and A. Varchevker (eds.), *In Pursuit of Psychic Change: The Betty Joseph Workshop*, pp. 168–180, Hove, Routledge, 2004.
14 Ibid., p. 173.
15 Ibid., p. 178.
16 C. G. Jung, "The psychology of dementia praecox" (1907), *The Psychogenesis of Mental Disease, CW* 3, 1982.
17 *The Walking Dead*, created by F. Darabont, produced by American Movie Classics and Circle of Confusion, 2010–2017. R. Kirkman, *The Walking Dead: Compendium One*, Berkeley, CA, Image Comics, 2009.
18 T. Gantz, *Early Greek Myth*, Baltimore, Johns Hopkins University Press, 1993, p. 705.
19 "The revelation of St. John the Divine," The Bible, King James Version, Oxford, Oxford University Press, 1997, pp. 299–319.
20 Ibid., Rev. 6:2.
21 Ibid., Rev. 6:4.
22 Ibid., Rev. 6:8.
23 N. F. H. O'Hear, *Contrasting Images of the Book of Revelation in Late Medieval and Early Modern Art: A Case Study in Visual Exegesis*, Oxford, Oxford University Press, 2011.
24 Ibid., p. 21.
25 Ibid., p. 29.
26 Ibid., p. 147.
27 E. Panofsky, *The Life and Art of Albrecht Dürer* (1943), Princeton, NJ, Princeton University Press, 2005.
28 S. L. Calvert, M. Appelbaum, K. A. Dodge, S. Graham, G. G. Nagayama Hall, S. Hamby, L. G. Fasig-Caldwell, M. Citkowicz, D. P. Galloway, and L. V. Hedges, "The American psychological association task force assessment of violent video games: Science in the service of public interest," *American Psychologist*, 2017, vol. 72, no. 2, pp. 126–43.
29 Ibid., p. 126.
30 Ibid., p. 133.
31 Epidemiology: Gender, ADHD Institute. Online, available: <adhd-institute.com/burden-of-adhd/epidemiology/gender/> (accessed April 27, 2017).
32 Calvert et al., "The American psychological association task force assessment of violent video games," p. 139.
33 J. Turkewitz, "Mass shootings in the U.S.," *The New York Times*, June 12, 2016.
34 P. Langman, *Why Kids Kill: Inside the Minds of School Shooters*, New York, St. Martin's Press, 2010.
35 P. Faigle and L. Caspari, "AMOK im Kopf," *Zeit Online*, July 23, 2016. Translated by author.
36 M. Wehner, "Amokläufer von München war Rechtsextremist," *Frankfurter Allgemeine*, July 27, 2016. Translated by author.
37 P. Hell, J. Lutteroth, and C. Neumann, "Münchner Amokläufer David S," *Spiegel Online*, July 24, 2016.
38 Julie-Anne Barnes, "All so young: Bloodshed in the streets as a teenager obsessed with killing guns down his peers," *Daily Record & Sunday Mail*, July 24, 2016, pp. 2–3.
39 "Amokläufer von München machte vor der Tat mit seinem Vater Schießübungen," *FOCUS*, August 5, 2016.
40 "Amokschütze von München besorgte sich Waffe im Darknet," *Süddeutsche Zeitung*, July 24, 2016.

41 "Amokschütze plante die Tat seit einem Jahr," *Spiegel Online*, July 24, 2016.
42 Ibid.
43 "Are violent video games associated with more civic behaviors among youth?" APA Journals, Article Spotlight, August 15, 2016. Online, available: <www.apa.org/pubs/highlights/spotlight/issue-72.aspx>. Summary of C. J. Ferguson and J. Colwell, "A meaner, more callous digital world for youth? The relationship between violent digital games, motivation, bullying, and civic behavior among children," *Psychology of Popular Media Culture*, 2016, available: <http://dx.doi.org/10.1037/ppm0000128>.
44 Tyminski, *The Psychology of Theft and Loss*, pp. 70–1.
45 "Safer sex" includes sexual activities that are thought to reduce risks of infection but not eliminate them. See "Safer Sex," Poz. Online, available: <www.poz.com/basics/hiv-basics/safer-sex>.
46 C. Dickens, *Oliver Twist*, Mineola, NY, Dover Publications, 2002, p. 5.
47 *The Social Network*, screenplay by A. Sorkin, directed by D. Fincher, produced by Scott Rudin, Dana Brunetti, Michael De Luca, and Ceán Chaffin, for Columbia Pictures and Relativity Media, 2010.
48 D. W. Winnicott, "The antisocial tendency," in C. Winnicott, R. Shepherd, and M. Davis (eds.), *Deprivation and Delinquency*, pp. 120–31. London, Tavistock Publications, 1984, p. 125.
49 A. Alvarez, *The Thinking Heart: Three Levels of Psychoanalytic Therapy with Disturbed Children*, London, Routledge, 2012, p. 100.
50 Ibid., italics in original.
51 D. L. Paulhus and K. M. Williams, "The dark triad of personality: Narcissism, Machiavellianism, and psychopathy," *Journal of Research in Personality*, 2002, vol. 36, no. 6, pp. 556–63, available: <https://doi.org/10.1016/S0092-6566(02)00505-6>. Quote from p. 557.
52 Ibid., p. 559.
53 Ibid., p. 560.
54 Ibid., p. 561.
55 S. Jakobwitz and V. Egan, "The dark triad and normal personality traits," *Personality and Individual Differences*, 2006, vol. 40, no. 2, pp. 331–9, available: <https://doi.org/10.1016/j.paid.2005.07.006>.
56 G. L. Carter, A. C. Campbell, S. Muncer, and K. A. Carter, "A Mokken analysis of the Dark Triad 'Dirty Dozen': Sex and age differences in scale structures, and issues with individual items," *Personality and Individual Differences*, 2015, vol. 83 (September), pp. 185–91, available: <https://doi.org/10.1016/j.paid.2015.04.012>.
57 Ibid., p. 190.

Chapter 7

Accidents that become catastrophes

To be, or not to be, that is the question:
Whether 'tis nobler in the mind to suffer
The slings and arrows of outrageous fortune,
Or to take Arms against a Sea of troubles,
And by opposing end them: to die, to sleep
No more; and by a sleep, to say we end
The heartache, and the thousand natural shocks
That flesh is heir to?

William Shakespeare, *Hamlet*, Act III, scene 1[1]

Alex was sixteen years old when he first came to see me for therapy. He had been depressed, brooding, and sullen, and he refused to tell his parents why. Increasingly socially isolated, Alex had started spending hours in his bedroom in the dark, with the lights out and windows covered. A breakup with a girlfriend had ended badly for him. She hacked his social media accounts and spread false stories about his involvement with other girls. Many of his friends deserted him, and he quit the basketball team, even though he had shown himself to be a skillful player. Alex eventually told me that he felt crushed by what his ex-girlfriend had done, and he collapsed, having no will to defend himself or to fight back against rumors and lies about his disreputable behaviors. Alex was adopted at age 4, and he came to his adopted family through the foster care system because he had been physically abused by his parents.

Alex's depression obviously had immediate antecedents in what had happened with the breakup and his girlfriend's revenge. Yet, it also likely brought back to him feelings and memories of his earlier abandonment. When he described what his girlfriend had done to him, he said, "She dumped me, and that wasn't enough. She had to beat me when I was down." He spoke at length about their relationship "drama," which entailed numerous turbulent breakups and reunions. He also seemed surprised by how hard he had taken the final separation: "You'd think I'd have been prepared by everything we'd been through."

I mentioned to Alex that feeling dumped and not able to fight back were difficult feelings and that often they reverberated with earlier events in our lives.

Alex nodded. He thought more about this and then replied that he was angry his parents had "dumped" him. In his therapy with me, Alex worked through his depression and opened up about the horrible incidents of abuse that his stepfather had inflicted on him, including being burned, strangled, and nearly drowned. I reinforced to Alex how brave he had been, that he was a survivor, and that telling me his story was important. I saw both the abused child and the resilient one; this fragile dynamic appeared to have been activated by the recent breakup, when he withdrew into darkness and couldn't locate any strength in himself.

Alex had a good memory, which served to construct a useful narrative about what he had been through as a child with his abusive parents. His stepfather had gone to prison for what he had done to Alex, and since then, Alex had only sporadic contact with his mother. He felt love for her and wished that he could help her turn her life around, but I cautioned Alex that he could hardly be her hero, no matter how much the young boy in him wanted to rescue her.

Alex loved his adoptive parents, although he challenged them in fits of rebellion that they experienced as startling and destabilizing. I worked with his parents to help them understand the normative part of Alex's rebellion and to see when he needed limits to rein in his own aggression. Within his psyche, there was a heated struggle between the boy who'd been a victim and the young man who wanted to avenge him. Alex's adoptive parents were thankfully understanding of this dilemma and did not react punitively when he tested their patience and authority.

The fate of the boy who could have been killed stayed on my mind throughout my work with Alex. After his first weekend trip away with another young man – Alex was now 18 – he came into his session smiling and asked me if I could guess why. I said no but could see that he was excited to tell me. "I got a tattoo!" Before I could say a word, he pulled down the collar of his t-shirt to show me a tattoo over his heart of the Grim Reaper.

I was shocked. There he was – like a rider of the pale horse – in a robe with a scythe. I stuttered, "Do you realize what that is?"

Alex laughed, "Yeah, it's the reaper guy. It's cool. It's like my heart is protected by him now." What I felt to be a sign of his murderous stepfather getting too close, Alex saw as a shield of protection.

I shared with Alex my concern about the image, remarking that it reminded me of all the close calls he'd had when he was a young boy. I continued by saying that I felt worried because he seemed to embrace being scared out of his wits by turning those awful memories into a badge of courage. He took in what I said and didn't argue, although he focused more on the fact of his getting a tattoo rather than what it symbolized. The Pew Research Center documents the increased popularity of tattoos among Millennials – those born from the early 1980s to the early 2000s – with nearly 40% sporting a tattoo and half of those having more than one.[2] In addition, nearly one-quarter, or 25%, have a body piercing that is not on the ear.[3] Interestingly, prisoners with tattoos have a 42% greater likelihood of being re-incarcerated for violent crime within three years after their release.[4]

Alessandra Lemma discusses the psychoanalytic meanings of body modifications such as claiming identity and protest, and she notes,

> Body modification, per se, is not the province of a group of people who are very different to the rest of 'us'. We are all dependent upon the gaze of the other . . . these practices most likely provide solutions to universal anxieties.[5]

She points to an archetypal underpinning for the attraction of these body modifications. She also emphasizes the importance of seeing and looking as interpersonal and social processes that shape who we are in relation to one another. During a panel discussing aspects of Lemma's ideas about body modification and tattooing, I mentioned the Jungian concept of initiation, which often involves some visible change to our bodies.[6]

Jung writes,

> Initiation ceremonies have the purpose of effecting the separation from the parents . . . There must be no more longing glances at childhood . . . A simple parting from the parents is not sufficient; there must be a drastic ceremony that looks very like sacrifice.[7]

Tattoos are a visible way for a young man to mark an event in time, when what has come before is behind him and when what is ahead of him is unknown. Such marking of time, often exposed for others to see and look at, can require an act that feels like sacrifice. Tattooing occurs with some pain, submitting to the hand of the tattoo artist. This sacrificial element invokes a giving up of parts of prior identity as the body is marked with a new sign or symbol. These changes during an initiation are both physical and psychological.

Two weeks after Alex got his tattoo of the Grim Reaper, he was in a car accident that totaled his vehicle. He was not high or drunk, just an inattentive young driver who crashed into a truck that had stopped in front of him. Fortunately, no one was hurt, and Alex was mostly upset about what he'd done to his first car. He admitted responsibility, although he mixed his acknowledgement with much grumbling about heavy traffic and slow drivers. I asked him if he could think of any other reasons why he might have had this accident. My intuition about his tattoo was on my mind, and I felt unsure how best to bring it up. Alex told me no, then said, "You got something on your mind, I bet."

I nodded, agreeing that he'd read me correctly. Thinking about his tattoo as a shield, I commented that it felt almost like irony that soon after getting a Grim Reaper tattoo, which he thought would protect him, he got into this bad accident.

Alex replied, "Slam, Rob, irony! That's harsh but true."

Alex went on to say that it felt harsh because his idea about protection was "busted," but he wondered if he hadn't "needed" that. I understood him to be saying that he recognized he'd been inflated about the tattoo, and now he felt a reality check corrected for some of that. Alex reviewed the accident many times with me;

he wanted to understand why his mind had "tricked" him into distraction. This effort on his part felt promising as it suggested he could see that his unconscious was tripping him up. His attitude about the tattoo changed after the accident. He still liked it but remarked, "It's just ink – I can't rely on ink."

Although I chose not to bring up his early history in relation to this tattoo of the Grim Reaper, I thought about it for a long time. I believed that Alex's tattoo was a symbolic marker of his early survival and that his fears of survival were activated anew around finishing high school and separating from his adoptive family. After this accident, we spent many sessions discussing his worries about being on his own as well as planning together what he would need. This combination of encouraging him to express his feelings and hashing out plans worked well with Alex because he could be open to both. Not every young man in psychotherapy is.

The pale horse

The rider of the pale horse brings death and dissolution: "Hell followed with him."[8] They march together and kill through the sword, through hunger, and through "the beasts of the earth."[9] The color of this horse is usually translated as pale or ashen, indicating the color of a corpse. For this reason, this figure seems to be a metaphor of death, mortality, and our reactions in face of them. We can be oblivious, as Alex was, but then work at gaining understanding, which he did after his accident. Oftentimes, recognition of these life limits comes painfully, with a retreat into despair, as Erik Erikson cautions in writing about mature stages of the life cycle. "Despair expresses the feeling that the time is now short, too short for the attempt to start another life and to try out alternate roads to integrity."[10] The way he sees it, integrity is what helps us not to fear death and to avoid despair, although despair can strike at nearly any stage of life.

Integrity entails not only that we give meaning to how we choose to live, but also that we appreciate the creation of meaning. Jung discusses this quest for a purposeful life in terms of our engaging with mystery.

> It is important to have a secret, a premonition of things unknown. It fills life with something impersonal, a *numinosum*. A man who has never experienced that has missed something important. He must sense that he lives in a world which in some respects is mysterious . . . inexplicable.[11]

For Jung, a numinous thing inspires awe and reminds us of something far greater than ourselves. Susan Rowland writes, "Jung's numinous proves liminal, a quality denoting disputed regions between consciousness and unconsciousness, the conceivable and the unknowable."[12] This ability to find meaning in spite of what we do not know is a challenge that our mortality forces upon us. William James, in his famous work on religious experiences, notes, "The essence of religious experiences, the thing by which we must finally judge them, must be that element or quality in them which we can meet nowhere else."[13] He regards this region of existence as where most of our ideals come from and that it holds us more inti-mately than the visible world.[14] He is also careful to describe religion as "only one of many ways of reaching unity."[15]

I feel it important not to overemphasize a specific religious tradition, but rather to focus on an internal capability for regarding what is ineffable and awe-inspiring around us. Recognition of the numinous is a bit like Panofsky's calling Dürer's *Four Horsemen* "inescapable," and many great works of art, music, and literature strike us as so. Dreams can, too. This capability allows us to regard mysteries that we cannot decipher, yet are drawn to consider for long periods of time. In contrast, the pale rider spreads despair and meaninglessness, which are the psychologically lethal effects of the hell accompanying him.

This horseman stands as a sign of our apocalyptic tendencies when a self-destructive side of fate might appear to have the upper hand, when foolish impulse leads to self-harm, and when the search for meaning is severely compromised. John Bowlby, an original attachment theorist, writes that when a child cannot expect his mother's return, despair sets in:

> The longing for mother's return does not diminish, but the hope for its being realized fades. Ultimately the noisy restless demands cease: he becomes apa-thetic and withdrawn, a despair broken only perhaps by an intermittent and monotonous wail. He is in a state of unutterable misery.[16]

This "unutterable misery" belongs to the psychological territory of the archetypal pale rider when catastrophes intrude on the security of being and hope feels lost.

I write about Jack in my previous book.[17] There, his story shows how under-handed distribution of private text messages constitutes a new form of the pur-loined letter when information is stolen and used for revenge or exploitation. His girlfriend at that time assaulted him with a broken bottle, barely missing his spinal cord, an injury that could have paralyzed him. They ended up in court, where she pled guilty, and part of her sentence forbade her from texting Jack or coming near him.

When we first met, which was after the incident I just described, Jack was sev-enteen years old, charismatic, extraverted, and addicted to alcohol and marijuana. For months, I insisted that he receive substance abuse treatment, and I referred him to different inpatient and outpatient programs. He would typically initiate a phone call or look at a program's website, but then he'd find fault with some aspect of what the program offered that made it not right for him. I pointed out his pattern of avoidance, and Jack agreed. I was surprised he didn't argue with me about this observation, but he seemed to understand there was a problem and eventually committed himself to working on his addiction through a twelve-step program while continuing his psychotherapy with me. As he got sober, he con-fided that he liked me and that he had been afraid of losing our relationship, either by having to go somewhere else like a rehab facility or by, as he put it, "your throwing me out for not listening to you and lying" about his addiction. Jack was

Figure 7.1 The Fall of Anarchy, c. 1833–4, Joseph Mallord William Turner (1775–1851)
Source: © Tate, London 2017

aware of his frequent lying as a protective mechanism when he felt threatened by what could be possible humiliation.

We worked together for over two years. Jack started college, continued with his 12-step program, and even became a sponsor for a peer in that group. His parents noticed a turnaround, and tensions within the family decreased noticeably since they no longer argued about his drug use. Jack came in to session one day telling me that he had planned a road trip to Oregon to attend a large outdoor concert. A young man, who was a friend through college, was going with him. Jack planned to drive, and he suddenly said to me, "I'm not going to tell my parents." I asked why not, and he replied that, because the car belonged to one of them, they would disapprove and not allow him to take it. I wondered what he did plan on telling them, if anything. He responded that he'd make up something about writing a paper for one of his courses and being out of touch until he finished.

We sat in silence for a bit, and then he smirked at me. "What?" He said it as an accusation. I sighed, "Sounds familiar, doesn't it, your making something up?" He became angry; he told me I was being too hard on him, because he believed he deserved this bit of fun with the road trip to the concert. Why couldn't I see that?

I waited for a couple minutes, thinking about addiction and the role of lying – that one harmful behavior may change while another less harmful one still seems like a good option. I mentioned to Jack that perhaps he didn't have to lie about the road trip – that he was now sharp enough to make a direct case to his parents. I said maybe they wouldn't approve, but how did he know? He was struck by this question; he considered that he was planning to lie based on something he didn't know, which he thought was actually peculiar.

Jack reconsidered and told his parents that he wanted to go on this road trip to the concert. They did argue some about whether it was a good idea, but most of the heated discussion centered on his not planning well for it. With their help, he got new tires and a tune-up for the car, found a hotel room, and mapped a route with his friend. He seemed proud that he had decided to do what felt hard and persisted by engaging with his parents, even if it meant they argued.

A week later I got a phone call I'll never forget. It was from Jack's uncle. I barely understood what he was telling me and felt overwhelmed by denial, telling myself it wasn't true. Tears running down my face, I had to call back minutes later to hear it again. On the way home after the concert, Jack's car had been hit by a large truck making an illegal turn on the highway. Jack's car was crushed; he and his friend were dead. In the following investigation, it was determined that the truck driver was completely at fault. There was no evidence that any drugs were involved. Jack was twenty years old.

I met for many weeks with Jack's parents. Their grief was deep and heavy. We cried together as we spoke about him, his many difficulties, his numerous appealing traits, and his turnaround. They were grateful for that. His mother said to me, "You gave him back to us" – which wasn't true because Jack did most of the hard work by digging into himself, although I understood her appreciation that he had relied on me for that. She was voicing that they had felt worried for so long about losing him to despair and that his addiction would consume him. That the pale rider would take him. Instead, an accident took him, and Jack's story came to be about resisting the pale rider, even as he appeared to have the advantage. Jack, however, became a young man looking for meaning, rather than one concluding there wasn't any. Jack reminded me that the psyche surprises even in our darkest times. When he first came to see me, he had reached a kind of inflection point in his life where addiction was about to trap him – but it didn't. He taught me to respect not knowing if, when, or how this might happen to someone. We really don't know whether the pale rider will swoop in or not.

Males and especially young men are vulnerable to these accidents. 71% of all motor vehicle deaths in 2015 were males.[18] Moreover, 97% of truck driver deaths, 85% of bicyclist deaths, and 91% of motorcyclist deaths were males.[19] The gender divide is greatest for those aged twenty to twenty-nine, and these statistics are also true when presented as fatal crashes per 100 million miles driven. The number of deaths due to firearms is six times higher for males than females.[20] Deaths by suicide are 3.5 times higher for males than females, and in 2014, the age group most affected was forty-five to sixty-four.[21] Deaths by drug poisoning or overdose show a similar trend, which is further troubling because it continues to rise. 63% of these deaths in 2015 were males.[22] These overdoses, whether accidental or intentional, are increasing the mortality rate for young white adults.[23] The rider of the pale horse is nearby, even when these deaths are accidental. An epidemic of despair and meaninglessness seems afoot when reading through these statistics about men and trying to make sense of them.

Anne Case and Angus Deaton have researched the effects of an increase in mortality among white Americans and concluded that nearly 100,000 deaths could have been avoided if mortality rates from 1998 had held constant.[24] This increase is primarily from drug and alcohol overdoses, suicide, and chronic liver diseases.[25] Furthermore, those with the least educational level were most at risk. They speculate that this increase stems from addictions, particularly opioid addiction, and that this epidemic will not be easily reversed. By comparison, they note that mortality rates in Europe continue to fall for those with low educational attainment.[26] In their more recent work, they tentatively name these mortality causes the "deaths of despair."[27] Despair is the emotion accompanying the pale rider.

The grasp of despair

In Chapter 6, I discussed the rider of the white horse in association with compulsion and addiction. In that section, I mentioned that experiences of false victories could lead to feelings of ecstasy and conquest. The omnipotence felt in these episodes is usually fleeting, and once deflated, the person sinks into emptiness. Over time, however, this pattern can lead to despair when alienation effectively encapsulates someone into an unreachable shell. This despair would be more characteristic, I suggest, of the pale rider. In addictions, after a long period of active abuse of a substance, an incident can occur that shifts the psychic locus from denial, externalization, and excuse-making into collapse and darkness like an abyss. This is the pale rider's territory, and most addictions seem to head in this direction. Case and Deaton's studies illustrate the lethality of this trend.

I mentioned Luke in Chapter 6 when discussing his belief drugs brought him to ecstasy, a numinous link attached to the intoxication that many addicts report as being beyond words, powerful and intensely pleasurable. During the course of Luke's analysis, a shift occurred that disoriented him considerably when his cocaine-induced odysseys began to lose their glow. For example, he reported a dream to me in which *he was young and constantly defecating into a toilet. He tried to stop, but couldn't, and when he looked at the feces, they were contaminated with worms.* He spoke about his revulsion, worrying that he had created such a large mess of his life that it was beyond any hope of salvaging it. He sunk into despair. He told me that the dream made him face his addiction: "I've accumulated all this shit from years of drug binges." I asked about his young age in the dream; he thought it referred to his having started experimenting with various drugs as a teenager. In that sense, the dream was, for him, autobiographical, from when he started taking "shit" to his current situation as an adult.

Around this time, Luke went on a seriously harmful drug binge. He used cocaine over a week, at the end of which he was delusional and hallucinating. He had canceled his appointments that week and did not return any of my calls. When he came in the next week, he looked like he'd been trampled on, gaunt, with an ashen face and slumped shoulders. The pale rider had him in his grasp.

As we talked through what had happened, I felt upset and helpless, as if I were watching him self-destruct. He told me details of how he ingested the drug, about his not sleeping or eating, and about his eventual paranoia that he was being watched. He complained that he couldn't get to the ecstatic state, no matter how he much of the drug he took, and he said that this had never happened before. I noticed that I got angry when he suggested that *this* was the problem. I felt it important to tell him something about my experience. I knew that Luke's parents had been too permissive and too absent during his development, and right now, I believed I had to assert something different to him. In his mind, this arm's length approach to family relations meant that no one really wanted to get more involved.

I told Luke that his binges affected me, and he looked surprised. He asked how I was affected, and I continued that when I saw him this way, I felt angry at how he was hurting himself and our work, and that I felt he was trying to convince me he was hopeless. I added that he seemed in these binges to undo any sense that he might make progress with me. He listened, almost captivated, as though wanting to hear more. I wondered how he felt hearing what I'd said, and he replied that he felt ashamed, which at first made me question what I'd been saying, but then it felt right; shame implied concern for what he'd done. Luke needed to feel more concern for himself, and shame indicated a recognition of that omission.

He noted that he had been imagining that I had few feelings for him, perhaps recapitulating a fear about his own parents. He said, "I guess I put you in a white lab coat, but maybe that's not been true." He cried when remarking that now the coat was gone he could see me as a man who cared for him. He seemed to be commenting on a defensive projection that he had of me in order to keep me at a distance. Luke's description also reminded me of how an analyst's or psycho-therapist's apparent neutrality could be misinterpreted as permission or collusion. He told me he knew intellectually that I didn't approve of his drug use, but he hadn't thought about it upsetting me or making me angry. He explained a kind of alienation that he reinforced through beliefs that others were too busy or too preoccupied to want more from him. His withdrawal when he binged seemed to represent this rigid, closed system with no human contacts.

Soon after these interactions, Luke decided with my guidance to start an inpatient rehab program. He continued his sessions with me during his substance abuse treatment and afterward, when he committed to attending a twelve-step program. Adopting some of the new language about addiction that he learned, he referred to our talking through his weeklong binge as when he "hit rock bottom." He expressed relief that I'd been direct about my feelings rather than offering him advice, opinions, or ideas. He said, "Later, I realized that I liked that you got upset – that meant I got through to you."

Despair often arises when we feel completely alone and alienated. It can lead us down a path where the slings and arrows of fortune seem too much to bear, and then we might choose to die to end the heartache. This is a desolate place where we no longer find meaning because there seems to be nothing other than our own suffering. The pale rider travels easily across this terrain.

To die and to sleep no more

I met Tim when he was admitted to an inpatient psychiatric unit where I was working as a therapist. Tim was eighteen at the time. He had made a dramatic suicide attempt that was both shocking and unique. Tim had had dental surgery performed to realign his jaw, and afterward, his upper and lower jaws were wired together while they healed. To get nourishment, he had to drink various shakes with nutrients in them. His parents resided in another part of the state, and he lived in an apartment in the city with roommates since he attended a local college. After the surgery, he went home to his apartment, where over a period of days he became more and more psychotic. He heard voices demanding that he sacrifice himself to save the earth, essentially a kind of mythical renewal theme about paying homage to nature through a blood sacrifice.

Tim went naked into a forest outside the city, where he believed the voices had directed him to go to locate a large redwood tree by which he was to die. Tim had no weapon or pills to do this. Instead, he decided to rip off the wiring on his jaws and to lie by the tree until he died. He apparently believed that he would now starve without food. When I asked Tim how he had thought this would happen, he replied that he'd simply wither until his remains became part of the tree. This describes a fantasy – or delusion – of sacrifice uniting him with Mother Earth, through which he would disappear and be enveloped by her. In a way I didn't recognize at the time, this reunion fantasy also incorporates aspects of the story of Narcissus as told by Ovid, when he cannot separate from his reflection in a pond of water. Narcissus's parents were water creatures, and this myth may represent problems with identity, separation and self-absorption.[28] I discuss this topic in Chapter 3. I would learn that Tim had many problems freeing himself from his parents' hold on him. In this regard, Tim fantasized that suicide would allow a separation from them that he could not otherwise achieve. His sense of identity was quite fragile.

Tim was a tall, thin young man, gaunt in appearance, and often disheveled and wearing dirty clothes. I was his therapist during his stay on the unit. I met with him daily and with his parents frequently during the week. Tim's mother did not believe that he could handle living on his own, and she wanted him to move in with her. Although she may have been accurate, he did not want to do this. She made emotional demands on him, confusing what she needed with what he needed. During family sessions, she often interrupted him and tried to finish his sentences. She glared at me when I explained that this was not helpful. After the sessions, she would apologize in a sticky way, acting too sweet and implying that

I'd hurt her feelings. At these moments, I understood why Tim would want distance from her. One reason was her intrusion into his mind when she attempted to say what he thought, and another was her domination of his emotional life. I later learned that Tim's mother had lost a child from a prior marriage and that this child had died from a genetic disorder that interfered with her metabolism. Perhaps Tim's mother had never recovered from this loss and felt a manic sense of guilt that fueled her interference into his psyche.

Tim's father was an academic who came across as cerebral and overbearing. He browbeat Tim in their discussions until Tim became quiet. I commented that this pattern of interacting was undermining Tim's sense of self. Tim's father became irritated with me, but then he asked how he could change this. He cared about his son and did not want him to suffer more. Tim's parents did not seem emotionally engaged with one another, and Tim's problems seemed to be part of what kept them together. From a family systems' perspective, Tim was the *identified patient* kept in a double bind of mixed messages about "grow up, don't grow up" that seemed to form what contact there was within the family. Tim told me that he liked these family therapy sessions because he felt freer during them. He made good progress during his hospital stay, began taking antipsychotic medications, and had his jaws repaired. He stayed on the unit for a long time until his jaws had healed and the wiring could safely be removed, because there was an obvious concern for his safety, that he might repeat what he'd done before.

After his stay in the hospital, he continued to work with me while he also attended a psychiatric day treatment program to give him structure and further therapeutic care. Tim told me several dreams during the course of our work together. He reported a recurring childhood dream. Recurring dreams are of therapeutic interest because they usually indicate a deep place in the psyche wanting attention, like a chronic wound that remains troublesome. In Tim's childhood dream, he *had a toy robot that grew when he pressed a button on it. But it didn't stop growing until it was 6 feet tall. Tim ran into another room to get help but no one paid attention to him. He went back and hid behind a couch.* Tim told me the robot was male and humanoid. At the time, I thought this was a story about himself and his fears about his development. Tim was a little over 6 feet tall. In thinking about his dream now, I am struck by Tim's isolation and lack of human contact that seemed to turn him into a freak – he was afraid of what he would become. Robots are unnatural, automatic and mechanical, and have no will of their own. There was despair in this dream – Tim's despair about his future – and I often felt helpless and alone when trying to simply be with him and these painful feelings. I now partially understand why his mother felt such an urge to fix him.

One of my approaches with Tim was to look for spots where I could encourage his initiative so he could feel himself to be effective and independent. For example, he considered resuming his studies but doubted he could handle four classes. I wondered if he might try one? He wasn't sure because he quickly became discouraged when things didn't go his way. In another dream that showed this process, Tim *was talking with a friend his age when a boy came and snatched a book from Tim. Tim chased him and tried to get the book back, but the boy's grip was too tight. Tim slipped into a ditch and found himself surrounded by barbed wire and unable to move.* The friend was someone whom Tim knew from school, and the dream suggested that a younger part of Tim – the boy in the dream – wasn't going to let him advance in his life, the book symbolizing learning that became impossible, out of Tim's reach. It was promising that Tim ran and tried to get what he wanted, but the outcome was dismal, the image of him being trapped and, once more, despairing. This is the symbolic realm of the pale rider in which we are emotionally paralyzed by a sense of impending catastrophe.

During the time that we worked together, Tim slowly made gains. He found a part-time job doing work with his hands that he enjoyed. He continued to attend his day treatment program and had graduated to a reduced frequency of three days per week. He told his mother that he didn't want her involved any more in his life, a message that infuriated her. When she tried to ingratiate herself back into his good graces, he saw what she was doing and told her "no more sweet talk."

I had worked with Tim for almost a year when our work was suddenly – and I thought temporarily – interrupted. My grandmother had died, and I had to travel out of town for a week. I explained to Tim that someone was covering for me, and we would resume his sessions when I came back. We reviewed a detailed plan for how he would contact my stand-in to set up an appointment, how he could also call the hospital clinic at any time he felt it was urgent to talk with someone, and how he could call his father as well, if he needed to. With Tim's permission, I had phoned his parents to let them know that I had to be away for a brief time.

We reviewed a scenario for what steps he might take if he felt unsafe during this week. He joked with me, something unusual for him, that he had no plans to see a dentist any time soon. I also asked Tim if he had any questions about why I was leaving, something I'd not done with my other patients. In the back of my mind, I was worried but couldn't consciously explain why. He asked me, "Will you be okay?" and I told him yes. I then asked, "Are you going to be okay?" and he nodded yes. Perhaps I misunderstood something here. This plan for my absence had seemed fairly solid, yet this break would be longer than any previously. At the time, I thought that my worry for him was related to that detail.

On the weekend before my return, however, Tim went into the woods again. He brought a knife and slit his arms, not across, but parallel to the veins. People bleed out faster this way.

The pale rider almost got Tim. Park rangers discovered him, and he was rushed to the emergency room. I saw him that week in the hospital with his arms bandaged. Weak, he told me that he couldn't explain what had happened. I felt awful and held his hand for a minute until he dozed off. After Tim was medically stable, he was transferred back to the psychiatric unit where a different clinician took over his case and advised Tim's parents that electroshock therapy (ECT) was indicated in situations of chronic suicidality. For clinical and humanitarian reasons, I opposed this intervention but was overruled since it had been his second serious suicide attempt within less than a year. I no longer worked on the inpatient unit, and his therapist on the ward believed that Tim's depression had become intractable and warranted ECT. His parents also supported this decision. Tim agreed, although his state of mind at this time was quite disoriented, and he seemed overwhelmed by the idea.

I saw Tim a few more times, including after the course of ECT. Part of the rationale for ECT is that it can help reset the brain's neuropathways. One possible side effect is retrograde amnesia, in which a person struggles to remember events before the treatment. Tim had this side effect, and although he remembered our work together and even his dreams, he couldn't recall that I'd gone away and that he'd gone into the woods again. Seeing his forgetful state of mind, I found myself feeling sad and discouraged.

Tim's case shows the devastating effects of despair in a young person's life, when depression becomes so deep that it's a trap, with seemingly no future to move toward. Tim's childhood dream of becoming a robot underscored that his problems went back a long way in his life and that his development seemed characterized by a confusing split between emotional neglect for who he really was (no one paid attention) and intrusive parenting that overrode his developing a cohesive sense of self (instead, being programmed like a robot). One of these would have been problematic enough, but both combined put Tim at extreme risk for trying to find dangerous solutions to separate psychologically. Suicide as a kind of sacrifice seemed to be one way out of his painful dilemma.

Tim's wish to merge with Mother Earth showed a potent spiritual impulse in him as well. He seemed to be searching for something greater than himself, to join with something that was not part of his family. His intense longing for separation and meaning got confused with sacrifice. He certainly is not alone in this desire to find meaning and to be initiated into something greater than a self that is dependent only on family. Many young men struggle with this same longing, and if their pain about not finding another possibility becomes too great, then despair and the pale rider may come dangerously close.

Aaron Swartz, a young prodigy at computer programming, may have exhibited a similar longing before taking his life at age twenty-six.[29] In a *New Yorker* article, Larissa MacFarquhar refers to a friend of Swartz who told her that he wanted to save humanity, as shown by an unpublished essay titled "How to Save the World, Part 1."[30] Yet this yearning to accomplish a personal quest also came from a young man who wrote that "my existence is an imposition on the planet."[31] I believe that such disparate expressions capture an emotional polarity about being tossed between a wish for meaning and reactions to its absence. Despair usually arises when we feel there is no meaning to be found, yet we may also struggle with how to construct meaning in a world that so often defies it. Tim sought to resolve this tension through some fantasy/delusion about nature, where he tried to escape from his family's problems with separation. But he couldn't get away from questions like, "Who am I after all, and what do I have to contribute to others?" Swartz, too, in spite of his considerable successes, seemed to grapple with a search for meaning in a world beyond the achievements of ego. Of course, events around his suicide were complicated by his prosecution at the time for wire fraud and theft of information via a computer.[32] The point here may be that looking for meaning, something we do every day, also makes us aware of not finding it and feeling alienated. That usually hurts.

Jung's intuition of the Zeitgeist's pale rider

Following his break with Freud in 1913, Jung went through a period of deep alienation, and he struggled with despair during this time. "After the break with Freud, all my friends and acquaintances dropped away. My book was declared to be rubbish; I was a mystic, and that settled the matter."[33] He often referred to this time as a period of "disorientation," and it led to his active imaginations that resulted in *The Red Book*. In his introduction to that work by Jung, Sonu Shamdasani notes, "In the years directly preceding the outbreak of war, apocalyptic imagery was widespread in European arts and literature."[34]

In October 1913, Jung had a vision.

> I saw a monstrous flood covering all the northern and low-lying lands between the North Sea and the Alps . . . a frightful catastrophe was in progress. I saw the mighty yellow waves, the floating rubble of civilization, and the drowned bodies of uncounted thousands. Then the whole sea turned to blood.[35]

Here Jung described himself in a state of severe alienation, when he did not even consider a possibility of war, but his strong intuitive reflex was picking up something in the collective unconscious and disturbing him. The pale rider represents both death and dissolution, much as in Jung's vision in which water overcomes everything. Even the vision's yellow waves are evocative of the pale rider – in Greek, the horse's color is often described as greenish-yellow, the color of many a corpse, but translated as pale.

In the spring and early summer of 1914, Jung reported a dream that recurred three times. "In the middle of the summer an Arctic cold wave descended and froze the land to ice. . . . All living green things were killed by the frost."[36] The third dream ends differently, with Jung picking grapes with healing juices from a tree and handing them to a crowd. WWI broke out at the end of July. He felt these dreams were "fateful" and began exploring his personal fantasies to try to understand his unconscious at greater depth.

Jung's dreams, somewhat different from his vision, depict an icy desolation that hints at severe depression and profound anxiety over what is to come. Would he find purpose in living? Or would the green of life go out of him too? These dreams speak of despair with the frozen landscape robbed of vitality and growth. Only in the final dream of the sequence does there appear a hopeful sign suggestive of resolving this crisis. He had to turn into himself – the tree, which he saw as symbolizing that – to heal and be able to reach outward again. In some sense, this third dream suggests Jung's model of following an inner path to individuate and to discover what is hidden within ourselves.

Terrorism and the pale rider

Although the many young men – and sometimes women – who commit terrorist acts might seem from outward appearances to resemble the red rider of apocalypse bent on killing and revenge, I feel it appropriate to mention terrorism in association with the pale rider. Terrorism is largely intended to frighten us, to dishearten us, and to sow despair into the lives of those affected by such acts. It may, therefore, be appropriate to consider in regard to terrorism that the pale rider follows the red rider. Most people surviving a terrorist act suffer significant trauma from this experience.

John Horgan remarks that psychological research into terrorist activity is relatively sparse and that there is no research showing an explicit pathway into terrorism.[37] He notes terrorism's appeal for those who feel disenfranchised and turn to violence as a way to exert control. The major psychological factor that many describe is alienation that fuels rage. Clark McCauley and Sophia Moskalenko, citing work by Bartlett and others, comment that this alienation is grounded in feeling excluded, distrusting authority, hating government policy, and being cut off from a local community.[38] They emphasize the importance of a person's emotional life to understand the process of radicalization. Thus, alienation alone is not enough; it has to lead to rage tipping into violence, perhaps with an impulse to inflict despair on others.

Arie Kruglanski and his co-authors find that experiences of loss of "significance" can lead to someone taking on extremist ideologies, and they cite earlier research that the " 'composite terrorist' is a single male in his early 20s."[39] Their definition of significance is close to what an analyst or psychotherapist would term the meaning that we find in valuing personal identity and its connection to a community, something deeper than status or prestige. Analytically speaking, these object relations form a web or network holding our internal world as much as our outer one. When they fray, alienation frequently creeps in to our psyche. McCauley also notes the role of humiliation in this process, when a loss of status or power is experienced as subjugation and wounding.[40] He cites Stern who writes that "repeated, small humiliations . . . add up to a feeling of nearly unbearable despair."[41] It seems that experiences of humiliation, rage, and despair are aspects of an emotional constellation that may contribute to terrorist acts.

On November 13, 2013, the American band, Eagles of Death Metal, were playing at the Bataclan concert hall in Paris. Three armed gunmen opened fire on the crowd and eventually killed ninety people in what was one of a series of apparently coordinated attacks that night by terrorists throughout Paris.[42] The three Bataclan terrorists, having grown up in France, identified as jihadists affiliated with ISIS and were all in their twenties: Omar Ismaïl Mostefai, Samy Amimour, and Foued Mohamed Aggad.[43] Two blew themselves up and the third was shot dead by tactical police forces. All three had traveled to Syria.[44] Aggad and Mostefai had taken hostages on the second floor before their deaths.

The Bataclan terrorists grew up in France, yet they attacked French society. One hypothesis for their violence would be that it was the outcome of deep alienation and exclusion that they experienced as outsiders looking in on something they felt they could never join. Inherent in this idea, the negative affects of humiliation and shame would be pivotal in later shaping emotions of contempt and rage that nurtured fantasies of revenge and retaliation against the insiders. "Home-grown" terrorists now confront Western societies with confusing questions about social equity, acculturation, and fairness of opportunities. When the latter seem in short supply, then a young man may struggle with identity. He may feel adopting a negative identity, as Erikson discusses, is his only option, and he may choose to take it to an extreme of monstrosity to feel empowered. Such radicalization can also include young men who join extremist groups that traffic in hate speech and authoritarian ideologies.

In searching the literature on what we know about terrorists, I came across one piece of research that describes terrorists "in their own words."[45] Jerrold Post, Ehud Sprinzak, and Laurita Denny report that in analyzing the backgrounds of these thirty-five Middle Eastern interview subjects, there were a mix of hero figures from their boyhoods, including religious men and revolutionary activists. The importance of the hero in child and adolescent development is largely that he provides a fantasy object for ambition and purpose. The hero character can be an anchor in a boy's mind for striving to improve his skills and to grow in unique directions. If the hero identification becomes inflated, however, it can lead to problems with realistic understanding of one's capacities and limitations.

These authors state that peer influence weighed heavily in recruitment to terrorist organizations and groups. This finding is consistent with more recent research that shows recruitment occurring through social media platforms and contacts with known peers who have been radicalized. Joining a cause offers an apparent sense of belonging to something larger than oneself and it can mask significant identity problems. Alienation is likely a major factor in this process because the accompanying isolation, lack of purpose, and identity confusion would combine to augment psychosocial difficulties in later adolescence and early adulthood.

Post and his co-authors note, "The feelings of victimization, of being evicted from their family lands, and the sense of despair . . . contributed to the readiness to merge their individual identity with that of the organization in pursuit of their cause."[46] This merging provides, as I discuss elsewhere in this book, a workaround for identity confusion. By joining such a totalistic group, a young man obviates dealing with unfinished and perhaps stalled aspects of his personal development. In group relations theory, this process is thought of as seeking oneness by subverting the individual personality to the group. The group becomes idealized and tyrannical.

Whereas earlier experiences of humiliation and shame may exert potent developmental effects in accentuating alienation, later emotions of rage and contempt become dominant. "You Israelis are Nazis in your souls and in your conduct . . . Given that kind of conduct, there is no choice but to strike at you without mercy in every possible way."[47] This kind of contempt demonizes the other – what is outside and different – and such projection becomes a vehicle for expressing hatred. Within a radically split us-versus-them mentality, total obliteration of the other is viewed as the only desired outcome.

Rage fuels actions of violence. "The extent of the damage and the number of casualties are of primary importance."[48] This rage activates a young man and can remove passivity that may be associated with certain kinds of alienation. A sense of omnipotence coupled with his rage emboldens him, making him feel determined and fearless. Apocalyptic statements and imagery frequently emphasize his destructive intentions. He may not view his self-destruction as contradictory. Rather, he imagines he is part of some greater cause that subsumes his individuality. Martyrdom is often explicit, called *istishhad* in Arabic. Self-sacrifice, in this case, bears a similarity to Tim's delusion that he wanted to save the earth by dying himself. The line between reality and fantasy and delusion is completely blurred because individual willpower counts for little in such a merged group. Tim, however, didn't belong to an outside group negating his individuality, although I could argue that his family formed an analogous group.

The radical group functions to pervert morality and individual conscience. "I don't recall ever being troubled by moral questions."[49] Splitting preserves a strict group boundary between us and them. This totalitarianism, as Erikson notes, does away with questions about identity. Memories of identity crisis are blotted out. An internal split, equally as unyielding as the social one, relegates these problems to the unconscious. This form of dissociation makes for both a lack of depth and intolerance of ambiguity that are characteristic of rigid, paranoid belief systems. Interestingly, representations of destructiveness usually coalesce around apocalyptic themes – the end of world being a kind of goal in itself. Such is the force of rage felt from prior humiliation and shame.

Post and his co-authors assert that there is no one type of terrorist, and they differentiate, for example, between Palestinian suicide bombers and the Al-Qaeda suicide hijackers from September 11, 2001.[50] The latter were "from comfortable middle-class families in Saudi Arabia and Egypt," and almost all of them had lived in the West for years.[51] This differentiation is consistent with more recent research on terrorism that finds many pathways to radicalization and violent action. The September 11th terrorists professed allegiance to Osama bin Laden and his destructive cause against the West. A similarity, however, is in the submission of the terrorists to a radical and tyrannical group. This merging with a group representing the alienated suggests a necessary tipping point for radicalization turning into violence. Individuality is lost. An irony is that the alienation that may have led a young man to joining such a group comes full circle when membership means complete alienation from selfhood. It is as if, in this case, the pale rider claims the terrorist.

Notes

1 W. Shakespeare, *The Tragedy of Hamlet, Prince of Denmark* (1604), World Library Inc., Project Gutenberg, Carnegie Mellon University, 1990–93, Project Gutenberg file #1ws2610.txt. Online, available: <archive.org/stream/1ws2611/1ws2611.txt>.
2 "Millennials: Confident. Connected. Open to change," The Pew Research Center, February 24, 2010. Online, available: <www.pewsocialtrends.org/2010/02/24/millennials-confident-connected-open-to-change/>, p. 1.
3 Ibid., p. 58.
4 W. D. Bales, T. G. Blomberg, and K. Waters, "Inmate tattoos and in-prison and post-prison violent behavior," *International Journal of Criminology and Sociology*, 2013, vol. 2, pp. 20–31. Quote from p. 27.
5 A. Lemma, *Under the Skin: A Psychoanalytic Study of Body Modification*, London, Routledge, 2010, p. 20.
6 "Ink, hole, and scars: The stories our bodies narrative," Panel discussion with A. Lemma, M. Brady, and R. Tyminski, at the Northern California Society for Psychoanalytic Psychology, Annual Conference, Berkeley, CA March 10, 2012.
7 C. G. Jung, "Analytical psychology and Weltanschauung" (1927), *CW* 8, pp. 374–5.
8 KJV, Rev. 6:8.
9 KJV, Rev. 6:8.
10 E. Erikson, *Childhood and Society*, New York, W. W. Norton & Company, p. 269.
11 C. G. Jung, *Memories, Dreams, Reflections*, ed. A. Jaffé, New York, Vintage Books, 1965, p. 356, italics in original.
12 S. Rowland, "Jung and Derrida: The numinous, deconstruction and myth," in A. Casement and D. Tacey (eds.), *The Idea of the Numinous: Contemporary Jungian and Psychoanalytic Perspectives*, pp. 98–116, London, Routledge, 2006, p. 98.
13 W. James, *The Varieties of Religious Experience: A Study in Human Nature* (1902), New York, The Modern Library, 2002, p. 52.
14 Ibid., p. 562.
15 Ibid., p. 195.
16 J. Bowlby, "Grief and mourning in infancy and early childhood," *The Psychoanalytic Study of the Child*, 1960, vol. 15, pp. 9–52. Quote from p. 15.
17 R. Tyminski, *The Psychology of Theft and Loss: Stolen and Fleeced*, London, Routledge, 2014, pp. 121–2.
18 General statistics (2015), Insurance Institute for Highway Safety, Highway Loss Data Institute. Online, available: <www.iihs.org/iihs/topics/t/general-statistics/fatalityfacts/gender> (accessed May 5, 2017).
19 Ibid.
20 "Number of deaths due to firearms per 100,000 population by gender," State Health Facts, Kaiser Family Foundation, 2014. Online, available: <www.kff.org/other/state-indicator/firearms-death-rate-by-gender/> (accessed May 5, 2017). Original source is Centers for Disease Control and Prevention.
21 "Deaths by suicide per 100,00 population in the United States from 1950 to 2015, by gender," The Statistics Portal, 2017. Online, available: <www.statista.com/statistics/187478/death-rate-from-suicide-in-the-us-by-gender-since-1950/> (accessed May 5, 2017).
22 "Drug poisoning mortality in the United States, 1999–2015," Data visualization gallery, National Center for Health Statistics, Centers for Disease Control and Prevention, 2015. Online, available: <www.cdc.gov/nchs/data-visualization/drug-poisoning-mortality/> (accessed June 7, 2017).
23 G. Kolata and S. Cohen, "Drug overdoses propel rise in mortality rates of young whites," *The New York Times*, January 16, 2016. Online, available: <nyti.ms/1OWwo0R>.

24 A. Case and A. Deaton, "Rising morbidity and mortality in midlife among white non-hispanic Americans in the 21st century," *Proceedings of the National Academy of Sciences*, 2015, vol. 112, no. 49, pp. 15078–83.
25 Ibid., p. 15078.
26 A. Case and A. Deaton, "Mortality and morbidity in the 21st century," Brookings Papers of Economic Activity, BPEA Conference Drafts, March 23–24, 2017. This is a working draft of their paper, not a final version.
27 Ibid., p. 3.
28 R. Tyminski, 2016. "Misreading Narcissus," *International Journal of Jungian Studies*, 2016, vol. 8, no. 3, pp. 159–67. doi:10.1080/19409052.2016.1201776.
29 J. Schwartz, "Internet activist, a creator of RSS, is dead at 26, apparently a suicide," *The New York Times*, January 12, 2013. Online, available: <www.nytimes.com/2013/01/13/technology/aaron-swartz-internet-activist-dies-at-26.html?mcubz=0>.
30 L. MacFarquhar, "Requiem for a dream," *The New Yorker*, March 11, 2013. Online, available: <www.newyorker.com/magazine/2013/03/11/requiem-for-a-dream>.
31 Ibid.
32 N. Cohen, "How M.I.T. ensnared a hacker, bucking a freewheeling culture," *The New York Times*, January 20, 2013. Online, available: <www.nytimes.com/2013/01/21/technology/how-mit-ensnared-a-hacker-bucking-a-freewheeling-culture.html?mcubz=0>.
33 Jung, *Memories, Dreams, Reflections*, p. 167.
34 S. Shamdasani (ed.), Introduction to *The Red Book. Liber Novus*, by C. G. Jung, New York, W. W. Norton & Company, 2009, p. 199.
35 Jung, *Memories, Dreams, Reflections*, p. 175.
36 Ibid., p. 176.
37 J. Horgan, 2017. "Psychology of terrorism: Introduction to the special issue," *American Psychologist*, vol. 72, no. 3, pp. 199–204. doi:10.1037/amp0000148.
38 C. McCauley and S. Moskalenko, "Understanding political radicalization: The two-pyramids model," *American Psychologist*, 2017, vol. 72, no. 3, pp. 206–16. doi:10.1037/amp0000062. Quote from p. 208.
39 A. W. Kruglanski, M. Chernikova, M. Dugas, K. Jasko, and D. Webber, "To the fringe and back: Violent extremism and the psychology of deviance," *American Psychologist*, 2017, vol. 72, no. 3, pp. 217–30. doi:10.1037/amp0000091. Quote from p. 224.
40 C. McCauley, "Toward a psychology of humiliation in asymmetric conflict," *American Psychologist*, 2017, vol. 72, no. 3, pp. 255–65. doi:10.1037/amp0000063.
41 Ibid., p. 255.
42 "What happened at the Bataclan," *BBC News*, December 9, 2015. Online, available: <www.bbc.com/news/world-europe-34827497> (accessed July 25, 2017).
43 "The man who attacked Paris: Profile of a terror cell," *The Guardian*, March 18, 2016, Online, available: <www.theguardian.com/world/ng-interactive/2015/nov/16/men-who-attacked-paris-profile-terror-cell> (accessed July 25, 2017).
44 "Unraveling the connections of the Paris attackers," *The New York Times*, March 18, 2016. Online, available: <www.nytimes.com/interactive/2015/11/15/world/europe/manhunt-for-paris-attackers.html> (accessed July 25, 2017).
45 J. M. Post, E. Sprinzak, and L. M. Denny. "The terrorists in their own words: Interviews with 35 incarcerated Middle Eastern terrorists," *Terrorism and Political Violence*, 2003, vol. 15, no. 1, pp. 171–84. doi:10.1080/09546550312331293007.
46 Ibid., p. 175.
47 Ibid., p. 178.
48 Ibid., p. 179.
49 Ibid., p. 181.
50 Ibid., p. 184.
51 Ibid., p. 184.

Chapter 8

What our fathers give us

My father actually believes the earth and the universe are 6,000 years old. And, he just *loves* to argue with me about it.

—thirty-eight-year-old man

My patient who said this felt exasperated by his intelligent father's firm disbelief in evolution. Moreover, his father's long-standing stubbornness in holding various unscientific opinions silently reinforced my patient's doubts about his own intelligence and his ability to stand up for what he believed. Fathers teach their sons many lessons about masculinity, and these often seem to occur magically, without any words or directions but through nonverbal subtleties conveying approval and disapproval. These messages often contradict one another in a confusing array about when to be tough or gentle, when to be independent or part of a team, when to fight for a belief and when not to, and when to be open or stoic. Competition and cooperation can sometimes appear as opposites, especially when strength and dominance are important. Winning an argument may count for more than whether one's point of view has some validity or not. Social, cultural, and family messages frequently coalesce clumsily into what we term "masculine ideologies" about what behaviors, attitudes, and beliefs constitute maleness – what it means to be a boy and later a man.

A father's role in this process is anything but clear, yet he remains a singly important element in the male psyche, including in nontraditional families where we might think instead of a paternal function when no physical father is present. Women can convey this function, as well as ensure that sons have access to other male role models. Certainly, the fact of missing and absent fathers has brought this practical aspect of "What is father's role?" into so many families and necessitated creative alternatives to a physically present father.

Many fathers, however, although present, are not at all available. Searching for the term "father absence," I found over 1.7 *million* results on Google Scholar, and in a scientific database used for psychology articles, just shy of 2,300.[1] The latter includes books, journal articles, and conference papers, with 81% dating after 1980. Although Freud made the father central to his theories, Jung emphasized the relationship with the mother. The mother's role came to dominate much of general psychology as well, with extensive research examining mother-infant attachment and the mother's role in early childhood development. The father was viewed – until somewhat recently – only through a lens of either pulling his children directly away from the maternal sphere or indirectly through his influence on the mother. He was in the background and not conceptualized as primary in his children's early developmental processes.

Michael Lamb began to conduct research on the father's role in the 1970s. He notes, along with others, that fathers engage in a kind of play with their children that is frequently more physical and more stimulating than what mothers usually do. Fathers often hold their infants to play unconventional games that are physically robust and unpredictable. Lamb, in research conducted with others, has found that "gender has a more important influence on parental behavior than does the individual's involvement in caretaking."[2] Thus, even when fathers are in a primary caretaking role, they act differently with their young children than mothers do.

Two views have emerged in the research literature on parent-child interactions. One is that fathers' behaviors vary from mothers' in that fathers are seen to tease more, engage in rough-and-tumble play more, encourage risk taking, socialize gender roles, and prohibit certain activities. The second holds that there are few recognizable stylistic differences between mother-child and father-child interactions. More recent research often stresses similarities in parenting between mothers and fathers rather than their differences.

Catherine Tamis-LeMonda and her coauthors looked at 290 residential fathers in low-income families to assess father-child interactions at twenty-four and thirty-six months and compared them with mother-child interactions. The bulk of previous parent-child research had been conducted on middle-income families. In this study, which used videotaped play records of parents and children, "Fathers were just as sensitive, positive, and cognitively simulating as mothers and did not display more negative or controlling behaviors."[3] The researchers did not find support for significant differences in mother-child and father-child parenting at these ages in how they played with their children. However, they found that fathers' high-quality involvement suggested "beneficial outcomes" for their children's cognitive development.[4]

One area where mother-father differences are frequently noted is rough-and-tumble play (RTP), which is characterized by wrestling, chasing, jumping, grabbing, and play fighting. Joseph Flanders and his coauthors have noted that boys engage in more RTP than girls, although both boys and girls enjoy RTP and fathers are the preferred playmate.[5] This type of father-child play peaks during the late preschool years. Some findings suggest that fathers assist their children through RTP to take risks and learn how to compete, the caveat being adequate discipline and supervision on the father's part.[6] Over-stimulation during pre-school ages can result in a child becoming flooded with emotion if a father cannot restrain himself.

Research on divergences in parenting between mothers and fathers has often focused on children's later behaviors, including those that become problematic. Externalizing behaviors include vandalism, delinquency, cheating, fighting, and stealing. In one study of latency-aged children and their families, researchers examined parental involvement, discipline, supervision, and use of positive parenting to see if there were mother-father variations that correlated with children's problem behaviors.[7] They found evidence of some dissimilarity, specifically related to fathers and sons. Higher levels of involvement from the father were associated with lower levels of externalizing behaviors in their sons.[8] Degree of maternal involvement did not appear to matter, although mothers' positive parenting was related to fewer problems only for their sons (not their daughters).

Since many of these symptomatic behaviors appear in older children, researchers have also looked at the quality of the father-child relationship for adolescents. One study – ironically subtitled "Do Dads Matter?" – looked at more than 6,500 middle and high-school students from the National Longitudinal Study of Adolescent Health and found that adolescents report greater satisfaction in their relationships with their mothers than in those with their fathers.[9] The author of the study, Tami Videon, noted that higher levels of satisfaction with father-adolescent relationship were associated with fewer depressive symptoms in sons and daughters.[10] She reiterated, however, that fathers and mothers are equally important for adolescent psychological adjustment.

Cliff McKinney examined late adolescents' perceptions of their parents' parenting styles (authoritative, authoritarian, permissive, and neglecting), and he noted that having at least one authoritative parent seemed to have a protective effect for late adolescents (ages eighteen to twenty-two).[11] Late adolescence is often viewed as a kind of launch phase into early adulthood, when educational goals, longer-term relationships, life direction, and purposeful activities can all be in states of flux and reorientation. Authoritative parenting, combining higher expectations with warmth and openness, is seen as most helpful for children and adolescents, although an authoritarian parenting style is more likely to occur when parenting sons. McKinney found that late adolescents view mothers and fathers differently in terms of their parenting styles, with mothers more likely to be perceived as authoritative and permissive and fathers as authoritarian.[12] Lower levels of late adolescents' self-reported emotional adjustment are associated with having parents who adopt an authoritarian style of parenting, as well as with a parental couple in which the mother is authoritarian and the father permissive.

The clinical cases discussed later in this chapter typically endorse a view that fathers do act differently from how mothers behave as parents. To elucidate this, I will look at problematic kinds of fathers who show up in clinical practice and discuss how their sons have internalized them psychically, often in hurtful ways. Although these cases come from a clinical sample, they illustrate how some differences in parenting come to affect children and their development.

Peers, culture, and genes

Although fathers may be uniquely important in conveying masculine beliefs, behaviors, and attitudes to their children, other contributing factors include peer influences, the cultural milieu, and genetic background. These are ancillary to the inherent psychological structure of a father-son relationship, however, and they exert varying degrees of impact on it. A father's role is shaped by the interplay of such variables and thus is context dependent. *Father absence* may indicate that these things assume greater significance in how a young man develops his masculine identity and deals with whatever alienation might accompany his fatherlessness. *Father confusion* occurs when fathers are inconsistent figures participating in their children's development, coming and going through what can seem like a revolving door in and out of their children's lives. In addition, *father estrangement* may be a relevant concept when fathers are present but their involvement is only emotionally distant. These fathers usually leave their sons to father themselves, often perpetuating a cycle that they learned from their own fathers.

A peer subgroup can seemingly offer young men an accommodation for father absence, father confusion, and father estrangement. Essentially, these young men are searching for substitute connections to remedy the alienation they experience around facets of their masculinity. Adolescent gangs are one manifestation of this; another comes from social media groups that form echo chambers online around an explicit ideology or affinity grouping, sometimes under the heading of extremism. Such group identity is illusory and based on what group relations theorists would label a *basic assumption group*. Wilfred Bion coined this concept in his book *Experiences in Groups* to describe what happens when groups of people cannot function effectively because of primitive emotional needs being unconsciously transferred into the group field in an attempt to survive collectively.[13] Such basic assumption groups are characterized by unconscious projections of dependency, extreme fear (fight or flight), and messianic hope (pairing). In addition, Pierre Turquet describes another basic assumption group that strives to erase any differentiation among individuals in the group, thereby providing a solution to identity problems. This group, called *Basic Assumption Oneness*, apparently resolves confusion and alienation by offering a person unity with the group in return for surrender of selfhood.[14] "Members seek to join in a powerful union with an omnipotent force . . . to surrender self for passive participation and thereby feel existence."[15] Although this description sounds nearly religious, consider that many young men, searching for meaningful connections to make up for an internal lack of identity fraught with alienating feelings, join groups seeking a kind of initiation. I suggest they are unconsciously looking for a father in the group.

Studying young men aged sixteen to twenty-six, sociologist Michael Kimmel has discovered a configuration that includes young men in such a group – the title of his book reflects their turf, *Guyland*.[16] There are more than 22 million males in this age range in the United States, and many of these young men disavow adult responsibilities while wanting to be men yet not seeming to be men.[17] They are mostly white, middle class, college educated, unmarried, and homophobic.[18] Two characteristics of Guyland are anomie and entitlement.[19] In other words, they are both alienated and troubled by it, but chiefly through a demanding tone of complaint and grievance. These young men rely on their like-minded peers to become adults, although they demonstrate many Peter Pan behaviors, preferring escape, video games, and entertainment.

Kimmel believes these young men are struggling with their masculinity. They are adrift in terms of identity, adopting the stylizations of rage from urban black youth and avoiding any potential "feminizing influence of women."[20] The men of Guyland organize into smaller groups, often like packs or squads, which exhibit some of Turquet's Basic Assumption Oneness characteristics. They rely on the group to provide a fantasized father for them, an illusion of fathering by a collective, to resolve their deep identity crises around masculinity. Why are these young men not prepared for adult life? A generation ago these same young men would have crossed that threshold. Kimmel offers a list of remedies that center on parental involvement, although he finds that mothers may matter more than fathers by encouraging emotional openness and vulnerability.[21] As noted in some of the research cited earlier, parental involvement can make a difference in late adolescence. However, I speculate that most of these young men are attempting to compensate for father-son problems that lead to alienation, fragile masculinity, and identity confusion. Coming together in homogenous groups – by definition seeking "oneness" – is not going to address these issues; it only perpetuates a basic assumption level of psychic functioning that does not lead to continued development.

Whereas Kimmel's research describes the fine grains of an evolving social phenomenon of young men adrift, others have looked at the psychosocial and cultural dimensions affecting fathers, men, and boys. Feminist and queer theorists have tried to understand the social construction of masculinity and fathers' roles in contemporary society. Judith Butler, in an oft-cited paper, writes about the "melancholy" implicit in gender identification from a psychoanalytic perspective.[22] In Freud's classic paper "Mourning and Melancholia," he posits that mourning proceeds by withdrawal of libido from the lost object, whereas melancholia occurs from identification with it – in an attempt to keep it alive internally.[23] Butler wonders what this paradox means for children who come to identify with their same-sex parent. "Is there a way in which gender identifications . . . are produced through melancholic identification?"[24]

Because heterosexuality is usually seen to be a normative outcome in this process, same-sex love must also be disavowed or negated, which is a "mandating of the abandonment of homosexual attachments."[25] Father-son love is, therefore, prohibited if felt as homoerotic and desired, just as mother-daughter love would be. Homosexuality is a threat to gender in this scheme: "in a man, the terror over homosexual desire may well lead to a terror over being construed as feminine, femininized; of no longer being properly a man or of being a 'failed man'."[26] In other words, a boy's soft and gentle feelings for another boy, or even for his father, could be dangerous to his gender identity.

Butler exploits a contradiction in the logic of psychoanalytic theory pertaining to identification, a contradiction that also highlights a certain masculine stance of repudiating anything internal that could appear feminine and/or homosexual. What becomes then of a boy's love for his father in this bleak scenario? It can only be allowed and expressed under strictures of a rigid heterosexuality that implies a distant and feared father whose son can never be sure where he stands because they both have to show an encrusted masculinity. To act otherwise would call into question the presumptive heterosexuality. Butler posits that

> the man who insists on the coherence of his heterosexuality will claim that he never loved another man and thus never lost another man . . . this is an identity based on the refusal to avow an attachment and, hence, the refusal to grieve.[27]

Butler uses what even she calls "hyperbolic" argumentation to unpack a failure to acknowledge why, for such a long time, our society refused to grieve openly for the many gay men who died during the AIDS epidemic.[28] During this period, homosexual loss was disavowed on numerous fronts. Butler uses psychoanalytic theory, perhaps a bit like a trickster, to turn it on its head and illustrate why homosexual attachments are so problematic within psychoanalytic gender conceptualizations. An unwillingness to admit homosexual attachments leads to social ostracization as well as a psychological theory of gender based on unresolved grief, and her social critique places the disgraceful avoidance of AIDS deaths within this context. Later on, Butler argues that one alternative to such an identity problem would be to risk "the incoherence of identity," a position seemingly familiar to Jungians, many of whom, myself included, see our psyches vacillating through identity states under the influences of the collective unconscious, archetypes, culture, and personal history.[29]

Butler's insights into cultural prejudice around homosexuality, explicit favoring of heterosexuality, and fathers' endorsement of it are factors in how fathers – and mothers – interact with their children and convey expectations. Nicholas Solebello and Sinikka Elliott interviewed fathers about how they think and talk to their teenaged sons and daughters about dating, sex, and sexual orientation.[30] Although their results are based on a small sample, and thus are not generalizable, their analysis of the interviews shows that fathers participate little in the sex education of their children. Furthermore, they express a wish that their children be heterosexual, especially their sons.[31] These fathers imply that heterosexuality has to be taught and affirmed, that homosexuality should be actively discouraged, and that their sons' interest in pornography is tolerable as evidence of heterosexuality. The authors suggest that these beliefs stem from a gender binary that sees masculine and feminine as opposite poles. Interestingly, this observation harkens back to earlier research on gender that took a similar point of view until a multidimensional perspective on masculinity and femininity emerged in the 1970s among researchers.

The Jungian analyst Andrew Samuels has written many articles and books that address the topic of fathers in contemporary culture.[32] Samuels has evaluated the father's function in establishing gender identity. He has also reviewed some of the history of why Freud and Jung split so decisively on the apparent grounds of differences in their understanding of libido and incest. Although Jung recognized incest to be a true and reprehensible fact in many tragic situations, he also thought it could be looked at symbolically as a fantasy about growth through love, as reunion with a parent by going back to one's origins and subsequent rebirth. Samuels writes, "The psychological function of incestuous sexuality is to facilitate the closeness of love."[33] This statement is not at all in reference to actual incest, which is sexual abuse.

Samuels believes that the role of father is mainly socially constructed because it arises from a man's intimate relationship with a woman who becomes a mother and his consequent proximity to the mother-infant relationship. He views the father as culturally determined, referring to him as "a created relationship."[34] He maintains this conclusion stems from the fact that a father-child relationship "has to be declared"; only through such a claim does fatherhood achieve validity in psychological and social contexts. I take him to mean that a father can deny his fatherhood or paternity either outright – which, even when false, sets the stage of foregoing any claim to the child – or tacitly by neglecting and distancing himself from his children. This father is not only absent, but also unavailable. Such aversion threatens to leave a family in a complex bind without a parent who claims to be the father, and to that degree, the family can become socially unmoored. I have had many adult men in my practice, speaking about their fathers, say something along the lines of: "He never took me under his wing," "He turned away from me," or "He never saw me." They describe a father who they knew as a fact, but not as a reality. A father without substance. Samuels articulates a view that fathers have to claim their role in a family, with the mother and with their children. This claim underpins the cultural and social meanings within which families develop: "If the patient is describing his or her father, the analyst can scarcely avoid having the cultural parameters in mind."[35]

Children who don't share a reality with their fathers will usually turn to their imaginations for a substitute. I have heard boys assert that their fathers played on champion football or baseball teams, were in famous music bands, and were high-ranking military officers. They were not lying – rather, they were fantasizing about a hero father who they desired in place of a father they only knew as a fact or not at all. In a way, these imaginary fathers came from an archetypal layer of psyche, created to fill a void and inflated to compensate for the ache of abandonment. Samuels notes, "The archetypal father is not in the father at all but in the child's perception of the father."[36] This archetypal father can appear when a boy or man sees someone he wishes had been his actual father and begins to fantasize about this possibility. This process is psyche's way of responding to a cultural and social gap and trying to fill it in.

In discussing the father's role in the family, Samuels emphasizes a containing function around aggression and a feeling function around what he calls "erotic playback."[37] The containing function he envisions is analogous to Bion's concept of *container-contained*, by which the latter means a relationship capable of metabolizing emotions in service of growth when a pair can be open and responsive to one another.[38] Samuels sees a father helping his sons (and daughters) through shaping aggressive play, ambitions, and goals and by emphasizing the process rather than the outcome. In this kind of containment, the father is a flexible partner who does not insist on domination and victory. In other words, he can lose, be a victim, and submit at times in the spirit of assisting his child's evolving mastery. The father's flexibility and ability to reverse roles in play and sport are paramount in this description, because a father who stubbornly dominates is modeling a generational model that is anti-growth – "the young will never learn." One 15-year-old-boy told me that he gave up playing basketball because his father became increasingly rough and aggressive during their practice drills. When his father lost a one-on-one game, he would "throw a fit, getting red in the face." The son couldn't take his father's insistence on victory and gave up, although his giving up also may have unconsciously affirmed his father's view that the son couldn't compete with him.

Although Samuels primarily addresses erotic playback in terms of the father-daughter relationship, he later acknowledges its importance for sons as well.[39] He notes that when fathers hold back their feelings, their children can feel confused and shamed about their own emotional expressiveness. He sees the importance of fathers showing their children that they are desirable and bring pleasure into the father's life. Such erotic playback is implicit in Bion's container-contained as well, since loving and positive feelings are optimally given back and forth between parents and children. One forty-year-old man told me that his father never showed him any physical affection. Although he felt positive toward his father and otherwise described a degree of closeness with him around common interests and books, he cried when he related that his father had never hugged him. "When I left for college, he shook my hand, and I got on the train and started to cry and thought, just this once, why couldn't he have hugged me?" This kind of physical remoteness and inhibition burdens children with ideas of not deserving affection, not being lovable enough, and failing some hidden parental expectation. Samuels's emphasis on a father's erotic playback helps to understand a social stricture that many fathers impose on their sons, who come to suffer from doubts about their self-worth and their own physicality. Boys take cues about their bodies from their relationships with their fathers, and they can form troubling beliefs about appearance, attractiveness, and strength based on a father's distance from and discomfort with affection, showing love, and gentleness. The man whose father had not hugged him was handsome, but he believed himself to be unattractive, "a wallflower" whom women would not find desirable. He had a mother and several aunts who were affectionate toward him as a boy, yet his father's distance in this regard was what continued to weigh on him as an adult. His adult mind kept seeing himself through his father's eyes regarding a boy he wouldn't hug or let close.

Fathers make a genetic contribution to their children, and I will now consider briefly some of the research on understanding masculinity and femininity from this standpoint. This field has been studied for decades yet remains rife with controversy, and perhaps even that is an understatement. A focus of debate is what defines masculinity (M) and what defines femininity (F)? During an initial period of research in the 20th century, the two were seen as bipolar concepts on a single continuum, which implied they were opposites. Around 1970 or so, researchers began to develop a multidimensional perspective that not only looked at these terms M and F separately, but also considered overlapping influences and interactions. They were no longer defined as bipolar traits, but rather as ones consisting of various dimensions and attributes. As a result, the scales and psychometric instruments used for assessing M and F were re-conceptualized.

Twin studies are the primary vehicle for evaluating the variance in genetic and environmental influences for a trait. *Monozygotic*, or identical twins are compared with *dizygotic*, or fraternal ones. Identical twins share 100% of their genetic material, whereas dizygotic twins share about 50% . Twin studies usually compare observable outcomes, including behavioral characteristics, to draw conclusions about genes and the environment, while also trying to account for prenatal factors such as maternal and fetal hormones.[40] Researchers are careful to note disputes and lack of clarity in this area. For example, Karin Verweij et al., using data from over 9,500 Swedish twins, comments, "There is no consensus on whether sex differences in personality arise due to different environmental influences, as social and cultural expectations regarding male and female behavior, or whether they are due to underlying biological differences between the sexes."[41]

With the shift to looking at multidimensional factors in gender M and F, many studies have made use of a common personality test called the *Big Five Inventory*, which has good reliability and validity. It assesses five personality traits: openness, extraversion, conscientiousness, agreeableness, and neuroticism. Many researchers have adapted the responses from the Big Five using statistical modeling to create more complex measures of M and F. Verweij et al. found that "individual differences in the M-F score were moderately heritable; broad-sense heritability estimates were 35% for males and 33% for females."[42] They reported that these figures were in the range of previous estimates, showing anywhere from 30% to 60% heritability for M and F.

Similarly, in an earlier article, Richard Lippa and Scott Hershberger used data from over 800 monozygotic and dizygotic twins collected during a prior study from the 1970s.[43] They selected items from personality inventories those subjects completed to create their own measures for femininity and masculinity; however, their scales were based on conceptual parameters that we might no longer hold to. Although the authors noted that M and F were not static, either over time or place and culture, they defined masculinity in terms of "instrumental personality traits (aggressive, dominant, independent)" and femininity in terms of "expressive personality traits (warm, sensitive, nurturant)."[44] They admitted this choice was a limitation; we can argue that what such scales measure are not M and F, but rather instrumentality and expressiveness. To address this constraint, the authors devised a way to measure *gender diagnosticity (GD)*. This term refers to "the probability that an individual is predicted to be male or female based on some set of gender-related indicators . . . a masculine person is an individual who shows 'malelike' behaviors in comparison to a contemporaneous reference group."[45] The authors believed that the concept of gender diagnosticity illustrated more accurately gender-related differences within the sexes. Examples included non-verbal behaviors, areas chosen for college studies, attitudes toward gay people, and authoritarianism.

Lippa and Hershberger reported that their analyses confirmed that there were "significant genetic effects" for masculine instrumentality, feminine expressiveness, and gender diagnosticity, and that estimated heritability of within-sex gender diagnosticity (.53) far exceeded that of either M (.36) or F (.38).[46] They found that shared environmental effects for personality traits were small. Gender diagnosticity seems to measure a tendency for men and women to prefer things, interests, and behaviors, and thus, it may provide descriptive clusters of what constitutes maleness and femaleness. However, given the lack of clarity about the concept and its measurement, it seems reasonable to question if the reported heritability was as meaningful as these authors suggested.

Ariel Knafo, Alessandra Iervolino, and Robert Plomin pose the question, "What causes some boys to become different than most boys and behave more like girls?"[47] By the age of two, most children are aware of their gender, and by ages three to four, they show awareness of their expected sex role. For example, more boys at this age are observed to pursue risk-taking activities, and their pretend play is often more violent in content and oriented toward heroic fantasies. Much of this comes about through gender role socialization, and fathers are often more directive and prohibitive in this area than mothers. In my practice, I regularly observe four- and five-year-old boys staging violent combat scenes with the sand-play figures, and sometimes, the dismemberments and decapitations that they describe startle me because of the passion with which they are enacted. This kind of play is often in service of the boy's attempting to gain mastery over aggressive urges and intensely angry and rageful feelings.

Researchers often note that parents, teachers, and peers look down on gender-atypical behavior in boys and reward gender-typical displays more consistently. The area of genetics and environment in gender-atypical behaviors has been relatively under-regarded for research. Knafo, Ievolino, and Plomin mentioned one prior study finding that the environment was associated with 67% of the variance in boys' femininity.[48] In their study, they looked at more than 5,000 families in the UK with twins and had parents assess gender role behaviors at ages three and four. They found that gender-atypical children fell well within the range of all children, but that their behaviors often differed from most of their same-sex peers. Interestingly, they concluded that the environment exerted a greater influence on gender-atypical children, and they stated that for gender-atypical boys there was "a modest heritability effect and a large shared environment effect account[ing] for about 80% of the variance in femininity."[49] As they used parent-rating scales, the authors speculated this result may stem from parents' greater tendency to socialize their sons for normative masculine behaviors, thus perhaps indicating parental overcompensation when parents see feminine behaviors in their sons. Another possibility could be that genetic influences emerge over time and become greater as boys mature and different genes are activated.

I include this research about genetic factors and the environment to illustrate how far we still are from more fully understanding their relative contributions to a boy's masculinity or a girl's femininity. Heredity seems to play a somewhat significant role in how a boy's masculinity is initially expressed within the family. Yet the environment probably plays at least as significant a role, and perhaps a greater one, in shaping masculine behaviors as development progresses and a boy matures. Much of this environmental effect will be determined by what a boy internalizes about masculinity from his parents, a process that also occurs over time and is subject to wide variability, particularly as parents' perceptions of their sons change with their growth.

Psychoanalytic considerations

Many analysts and psychotherapists emphasize environmental effects for developing masculinity and see much evidence for its social construction. Bruce Reis articulates a view that masculinity cannot be viewed simply as built up based on a rejection of femininity and homosexuality.[50] He describes the latter as a version of psychoanalytic theory about gender that has become antiquated. He writes, "Such monolithic descriptions fail to recognize that men can be hard and soft, and that these qualities together form an essential contradiction of masculine gender."[51] He disputes a cultural trope of putting heterosexual men into straitjackets of traditional masculinity, often depicted as mindless or dopey.

He envisions that an opening to recasting masculinity is through eroticizing the father's role, including the father's body, and suggests that this possibility would "mean imagining a role not dominated by prohibition, but rather open to delight and pleasure . . . of visceral excitement and indulgence."[52] This is a passionate father, capable of evoking erotic playback, as Samuels suggests, without becoming dangerous and boundary breaking. In a way, he is arguing for variety in the kinds of fathers we acknowledge and perceive. This position, however, is almost Jungian because it implies that there are numerous father archetypes. Jung's collective unconscious conceives of infinite possibilities.

Michael Diamond provides earlier psychoanalytic background for a long-held hypothesis about masculinity, which is exactly what Reis, too, describes and takes issue with. Diamond reviews the Greenson-Stoller theory of masculine identity that is based on two cumbersome developmental tasks, namely a boy's disidentification with his mother and his subsequent counteridentification with his father.[53] Briefly, this theory proposes that in order to become fully a boy, since a boy is usually first attached primarily to his mother, he must separate from her and repudiate the female in mother, while turning to his father as a replacement figure and identifying with what is male in father. This convoluted do-si-do is an analog to the older bipolar M-F scales mentioned previously, in which masculinity and femininity are seen as opposites. Diamond, however, rejects this theory because he understands it to describe a defensive masculinity, not a genuine one. This defensive masculinity is organized around being phallic and narcissistic. This kind of masculinity is a closed system, inflexible and based on a need to dominate or always be the hero (or anti-hero). The Greenson-Stoller theory is not supported by clinical or observational data, and its suppositions run counter to attachment theory, social learning theory, and modern developmental theory.

Diamond notes that a mother's role in her son's masculinity can be pivotal, especially as a boy grows from being a sweet baby and toddler into a sexually curious preschooler. A boy's internal sense of mother usually undergoes a change during this period, when she is not only someone who soothes and comforts, but also someone who is evocative, stimulating, and even arousing. Diamond believes a father helps his son through this process by supporting mother and by tolerating that his son may resent awareness of sexual connection between mother and father.[54] Diamond does not resort primarily to the theory of the Oedipus complex to explain this, but suggests that father stands for a different kind of growth coming from the external world that encroaches on the child in a positive way. The father at this stage represents a developmental shift to triadic reality, more complicated than the dyadic one of infancy and early childhood.

Diamond's insight into a shifting mother-son relationship at the ages of 3 to 4 can be informative. Mothers, too, may struggle with no longer being just a soothing figure as they deal with sons' vigorous and passionate demands for attention of a different sort. A mother's validation of her son's developing maleness can be key to whether he resorts to more defensive kinds of masculine behavior. One mother told me that as her son became a preschooler, he "lost his sweetness." She didn't like his fiery side, his curiosity about her body, and his harder edges in play. She withdrew from him emotionally and even believed he needed less open affection from her to get through this phase. As a result, he became more insistent on dominating the family like a mini-Napoleon. His outbursts were a masculine opera of posturing and projecting bigness.

When I heard that she no longer showed any physical affection for him, I asked why. She related that she grew up with sisters and said she didn't "get boys." Over a period of time, I worked with her and her husband to address their anxieties about their son and to suggest that physical affection at this age was crucial; otherwise, he would probably end up feeling rejected and trying more outrageous displays to convince her of his worth. I involved her husband in encouraging and praising her for reaching out more to their son. They worked hard at being more open and expressive within their family, and eventually, the boy calmed down considerably. She proudly told me one day that while he was practicing the piano, she sat next to him on the bench, hugged him, and suggested they try a duet. She reported, "His eyes lit up with excitement," and after this encounter, he regularly asked that they play "their song" together.

Reading psychoanalytic writers such as Reis and Diamond, I get the sense they are trying to catch up with the pace of sociocultural changes that disprove or discredit many of psychoanalysis's older theoretical assumptions about men, women, masculinity, femininity, and gender development. Coming at the topic differently, Luigi Zoja, a Jungian analyst, authored a book about various perspectives on fathers and fathering.[55] He squarely sees the role of father as a social construct and notes that this implies a paradox because the father operates in two realms that are not congruent, namely within the family and within society.

Zoja posits, "The father is in fact more frequently pathological, both disturbed and disturbing, than the mother, just as is generally true of men with respect to women. The phenomenon of the anti-paternal father arises much more easily than that of the anti-maternal mother."[56] He discusses the character of Hector from the *Iliad* as representing an appealing father because he lifts up his son above him and prays for him to be stronger than his father.[57] This gesture and the prayer express some of the best in a father: generosity, future perspective, direction into the world, and spirit. Although Zoja notes that Hector dies and thus the *Iliad* leaves us "with a problematic nexus of symbols," he sees in Hector a good-enough father to contrast with what is missing in much contemporary fathering and discussions about it.[58] In particular, the father can represent a hopeful link between generations that does not insist on keeping power out of envy and jealousy. Zoja also notes that this good-enough father promotes differentiation as an aspect of growth, unleashing potential and encouraging his children to strive by undertaking challenges.

Zoja is concerned by all the contemporary problems engulfing fathers. He reminds us that a son will always seek his father. "He wants to know him from the inside, just as once he knew him from the outside."[59] This search takes the son inside himself to find what of his father lives there. What he discovers may not be at all like an Oedipal father, because there are numerous archetypal configurations of father. The form and condition of the internal father will be vital for understanding masculine development and when it gets stuck because of alienation. More frequently than perhaps we know, it is on the fate of this relationship that boys and young men suffer.

Next, I want to discuss why and how certain kinds of fathers contribute to their sons' states of alienation, often centered on flawed ideals of masculinity. These fathers, the ones I have chosen here, do not comprise the full scope of problematic fathers. Rather, they are types of fathers that I have heard about many times in my practice, teaching, supervision, and consultation with colleagues. Three, in particular, will be addressed: a thieving and corrupt father; an overly demanding, highly principled father; and an abandoning and emotionally abusive father. Additionally, I will discuss what happens when a father dies during boyhood and what "good-enough" fathering, to borrow Winnicott's useful term about reasonably expected mothering, looks like. Because my examples are drawn from clinical practice, they reflect boys and men already struggling with a state of alienation interfering with their emotional adjustment and causing them emotional distress.

Thieving fathers

In a previous book, I discussed the myth of the Golden Fleece and its meanings in regard to stealing.[60] The myth is complicated and has been told in many different ways by writers from the 5th century BCE on. The main characters are Jason and Medea, both known to us today, but in a polarized manner, with Jason often viewed as the gleaming hero and Medea the scheming witch. Neither is true in the original texts, although there are elements of heroism and witchery throughout the myth. When I reviewed many of the interpretations of this story, what emerged was a different emphasis on the characters. Medea is sometimes the victim, sometimes the wicked wife, and frequently the hero. She comes closer to upholding the classic Greek heroic code than Jason does, and many classics scholars have discussed the implications of this reversal. A fuller account can be found in my book.

Jason, on the other hand, is often a sneak, at best a compromised hero, and at worst a scoundrel. He orchestrates the stealing of the Golden Fleece, which he only gets through Medea's help. He is a thief, and his corrupt actions lead to disaster once he and Medea return to the Greek mainland from their adventure on the far side of the Black Sea, which was her homeland. We know of their mutual tragedy mostly through Euripides's drama *The Medea*. In that work, Jason betrays Medea by planning to marry the local king's daughter. Faced with possibilities of exile and losing her two sons, she instead kills Jason's bride and her own two children. Although this infanticide is horrific, within the context of classic Greek tragedy, she acts somewhat heroically to avenge Jason's treachery by sacrificing her beloved children. Infanticide has occurred throughout much of early human history, and the tale of Abraham and Isaac, a near infanticide between father and son, is another example that I will look at in the next section.

My study of that myth led me to an idea that the universality of stealing among us implies that we each have a version of an inner thief. What might happen when this thieving figure is activated within a family, especially by a parent? I discussed my patient Nicolas in Chapter 5 and return to him now. I mentioned Nicolas's issues with lying and his uncertainty about truth and pursuing it. During the middle phase of our work together, Nicolas became curious about what was behind the scandals his father had been involved in. He found himself also being quite hard on himself, working long hours and cleaning at home beyond what was necessary. His compulsiveness puzzled him and made him anxious that he was losing control. Around this time, Nicolas had written to his father after a long period of not communicating with him. I asked Nicolas if he had heard anything from his father, and he said no. In the session when we discussed this, he seemed to calm down right after I had brought up his father. I commented on this change in his mood, and he agreed. I wondered if he had other feelings about his father that might be troubling him?

Nicolas responded by telling me he was very angry with his father. He wished that he could tell him this himself, but he felt constrained by an idea that to do so would be a "violent revenge" because they didn't share such feelings in the family. Nicolas felt he'd be breaking a taboo. I inquired what made him so angry, and he said, "I have all these questions!" Nicolas imagined interrogating his father, and I asked what evidence was he seeking? Nicolas then replied that he wanted to know why his father left when he had, why did he involve other family members in his corrupt schemes, and "did he ever try to change from being a scoundrel?" I remarked that Nicolas wanted to know some truth about his father and that bottling up his questions may have put him under a lot of pressure that he felt he could only rid himself of by working more and cleaning. Nicolas smiled. He was both glad and upset that I'd made this connection: glad because he felt relieved and upset because I had seen something inside him and that made him uncomfortable.

Nicolas continued to explore his anger at his father, who took months to answer the letter. He wondered, for example, if his own provocative behaviors had something to do with his feelings about his father. He professed to enjoy pranking others because it gave him a feeling of dominance. I mentioned that he might occasionally be misunderstood by others when he did this, and he agreed, telling me how surprised he was when someone got irritated with him. I asked where he thought he had learned this behavior. He told me his parents had split up when he was 4, and his mother had told him if they hadn't separated, then the family would have ended up "on the street." No other explanations were given to him. He remembered that after this event, he developed an interest in magic, tricks, and practical jokes. As we talked about his prankster nature, I commented that a child hearing his family could end up on the street might think a real bad trick was being played on him and would probably feel frightened. Nicolas responded that not knowing any details about what was behind this statement felt mysterious and contributed to his hating his father.

His father's exit from his daily life at such an early age probably felt to Nicolas like a rip off; he was losing someone important. This loss represents a stealing father, who takes from his son an ongoing developmental presence that would have held love, useful conflict, and aspects of identity. Nicolas would overhear random comments from his mother and other relatives that his father was a schemer, yet even as he matured into adolescence, he never felt entitled to ask why they claimed this. Nicolas at last heard from his father, who admitted he felt like "a stranger" to his son.

They began a correspondence in which Nicolas asked his father many questions, including why he had left. His father responded by saying that he had been involved in something illegal and the strain on the marriage became too much. Although Nicolas continued to voice much anger and disappointment in his father, and at one point called him "a thief," he experienced their renewed communication as an opportunity to ask many questions about family secrets. His father surprised him by not being judgmental, vindictive, or bullying in response to

Nicolas's many inquiries. Nicolas felt this was a hopeful sign that the rift between them could be somewhat bridged.

Nicolas came to understand that his deeply conflicted relationship with his father had been nearly frozen in time. Shrouded in family secrets, he consciously avoided thinking about what had happened between his mother and father. However, this thieving internal father was unconsciously nagging at his wellbeing. Nicolas's anger and sadness had to be meaningfully reconnected with his father in order to be emotionally processed, and his following through on his desire to resume a relationship with his father eventually led to an easing of his depressive and compulsive symptoms.

Principled, overly demanding fathers

Some fathers make a point in their families of demanding adherence to high principles, which can derive from various sources such as educational, military, professional, social, ideological, or religious ones. This stern father figure appears biblically in the archetypal relationship of Abraham to Isaac. Presented as a temptation, God orders Abraham to take his son Isaac to the land of Moriah and offer him there for a burnt offering.[61] Abraham obeys. As they make their way, Isaac asks, "Where is the lamb for a burnt offering?"[62] Abraham lies, leading his son onward and building an altar. He then binds his son. "And Abraham stretched forth his hand, and took the knife to slay his son."[63]

An angel intervenes, and a ram is discovered to be sacrificed instead of Isaac. Because of Abraham's devotion, he is then promised that his seed will multiply and "in thy seed shall all the nations of the earth be blessed; because thou hast obeyed my voice."[64] Theodor Reik notes that "Isaac was about thirteen years old and bound against his will on the altar."[65] He cites research pointing to an interpretation that this biblical story was intended to counter the practice of child sacrifice during the early Iron Age.[66] It was also, he suggests, a replacement for a more ancient puberty rite.[67]

Abraham is a patriarch of three worldwide religions originating in the Middle East: Judaism, Christianity, and Islam. God's earlier covenant (*berith* or בְּרִית in Hebrew) with Abraham occurs in the book of Genesis when God requires that Abraham's male descendants be circumcised.[68] The command to sacrifice Isaac comes after this. What might this mean psychologically about his relationship with Isaac? Reik comments, "Isaac was not sacrificed, nor did he offer himself as a sacrifice, as Christ did. He was condemned to have a shadow existence, compared with the life of his father Abraham and of his son Jacob."[69] Reik suggests that the figure of Isaac disappears strangely from biblical narrative as if this sacrificial moment, indeed, crushed his presence. Abraham's principled obedience apparently was ready to extinguish his son's life without giving his son any reason for this act.

Larry Powell and William Self comment, "Indeed, the details of Isaac's life are withheld from most of the remainder of the story," and they cite others who describe Isaac as diminished and even "shattered."[70] In trying to explain Abraham's near sacrifice of Isaac, they note, "In the case of human sacrifice, something is given that does not belong to the giver."[71] This radical offering is frequently based on obedience to highly inflated ideals.[72] Such a father does not see his son. The Renaissance sculptor Donatello captures this lack of relatedness in his masterpiece *The Sacrifice of Isaac* (ca. 1418), in which Abraham looks askance upward while the bound Isaac exposes his neck and looks downward. This division in where their line of sight is directed captures the rupture inherent in the father's brutal gesture.

I discussed my patient John in Chapter 3, where I wrote about his demanding father who insisted on a push-along lawnmower to teach his son a lesson about hard work. I heard many such stories from John, who described his father as unrelenting in "mouthing grand principles." The whole family suffered, and John told me there was no escape. "I was a dutiful son. He always had the last word." John neither felt seen nor loved by his father, who insisted on unquestioned obedience. As an adult man, John described feeling depleted and alienated from himself, afraid of what might be inside. Discovering his ruthlessly principled father as an inner figure who continued to punish him was a harrowing but necessary therapeutic task for John in his individuation.

John referred many times to one particular story about his father. When John was about ten years old, the family went on a vacation along the northeastern coast of the United States. His father rented a boat for a day to take them on a ride in the ocean. It suddenly became stormy, and the captain recommended they turn back to the harbor. John's father said no, insisting they push through the storm. Rain and waves battered the boat, and John, his mother, and siblings all became seasick. His father simply stood on the deck in the wind and rain not looking at his family's distress. Like Abraham in Donatello's sculpture. Later, when they returned safely to the harbor, John's father said, "Now wasn't that splendid!"

John's father, although behaving narcissistically, did embody and represent characteristics of a father willing to sacrifice his family in the name of a principle – of man not bowing to forces of nature. His father's persecutory idealism was similar to what we find from a psychological perspective in the sacrifice of Isaac. In a parallel way, Isaac's disappearance from the narrative afterward corresponds to what John described about feeling depleted and empty inside himself. John felt he was not even the main character in his own life story.

John's personal narrative seemed hijacked by his inner father's continued demands on him. John often criticized himself for not being masculine enough and not competing as hard as his father would have done. Instead he thought himself "too soft." Such a relentlessly demanding father is not easy to come to terms with. A son of such a father continually runs the risk of never measuring up and of being discarded from the father's view. This is a son who, when he tries to see himself through his father's eyes, might see a sacrifice, someone the father was willing to crush.

Abandoning and emotionally abusive fathers

The Oedipus complex is no longer presumed to be universal or normative. Richard Friedman and Jennifer Downey propose that the erotic component of the Oedipus complex is "not a normatively occurring . . . event."[73] Frank Lachmann, after reviewing new evidence about Freud's Little Hans case history, goes even further, "the concept of the universal unconscious fantasy of the Oedipus complex is not substantiated."[74] Mikkel Borch-Jacobsen attributes Freud's investment in this idea of the Oedipus complex to "arbitrary constructions designed to explain away his patients' stories of incest and perversion while . . . excusing the method that provoked them."[75] Still, there is something about Oedipus's story in myth that tells about a kind of father who abandons and abuses his child. While not assuming this is true of all such fathers, the myth offers some elaboration of what happens when a father-child relationship turns lethal. I discuss maternal aspects of this pattern in an article about Medea and mothers who act destructively toward their children.[76]

John Munder Ross describes the cruelty of Oedipus's father Laius, king of Thebes, and calls him "the paradigm of the 'bad father.'"[77] Although Munder Ross interprets that the curse on Laius that he would be killed by his own son follows from Laius's abduction and rape of another king's son, Timothy Gantz notes there are alternate versions of Laius's story and background, and he offers the opinion that the abduction does not directly link to the Oedipus drama.[78] Nonetheless, Laius behaves cruelly toward Oedipus out of fear for his own fate and has his son sent away with feet pinned together (*Oedipus* means "swollen foot") to be left exposed to the elements on a mountain. He is saved by a shepherd, who gives him to the king and queen of Corinth to adopt.

Munder Ross summarizes what he calls the *Laius complex* as the family dynamics when an unfathered father dominates his wife and children, demands their loyalty, and constantly threatens the mother-child relationship. "Such men may parade their power to hide their infantile fears and fixations, give vent to their unalloyed hostility, and murder, abuse, ridicule, or otherwise injure their own offspring."[79] This kind of father tyrannizes a family, although this tyranny can assume different forms. There are, for example, outright abusive fathers who are violent and inflict physical as well as emotional injury. But there are also fathers who monopolize power within a family, never cede a central position, and fragment all other family relations; these men, too, act cruelly by dominating and absorbing any positive energies into themselves. They are emotionally abusive.

I discussed my patient Luke in Chapters 1 and 6 and return to him briefly in this context of his relationship with his father. Luke described his father as quite successful in his career, holding a top post in the nonprofit sector. He told me his father was handsome and full of confidence, someone who people noticed when he entered a room. His father enjoyed being fawned over. He traveled frequently, but when he was home, he demanded that the family revolve around him. He asserted his needs without much concern for what his wife or children wanted. I asked what he and his father did together when Luke was a child, and he smirked, saying that his father called the shots. He rarely showed any interest in his son's activities, school, or hobbies.

The family relocated several times during Luke's childhood and adolescence because of his father's career, and each time, Luke recalled his father telling them, "You'll adjust; you'll make new friends," although Luke said it was never that easy. Luke grew into an isolated adolescent who felt he shouldn't ask his father for time or attention. Luke reported that his father also ignored his mother, who became increasingly depressed, and that he paid no attention to his older brother when this brother began smoking marijuana daily during his mid-adolescence. I asked Luke how he made sense of his father's emotional disengagement within the family, and he replied that his father operated "on a different planet" and rarely involved himself with the family. Luke speculated that his father continued to live out permissive attitudes from the 1960s and his personality did not seem suited to family life.

Luke's father received many awards for his work, and these seemed to matter most to him. Luke recalled a few occasions when the family entertained, and these parties were inevitably organized around his father's professional life. Luke struggled with his masculine identity because he felt the father he held inside himself was "crumbly like brittle shale." This inner father felt not only fragile to Luke but also depleted his initiative and curiosity. Luke felt that whenever he started to make a change, he felt something inside telling him "why bother?" as if it would be futile. He associated this obsessive inner voice with his father, and Luke came to express that he often felt that his father viewed him as useless.

Luke sought out being affiliated with more powerful men, and he usually assumed a somewhat submissive role. He often described his bosses as domineering. He spoke about craving a kind of male attention that he felt he rarely had gotten earlier in his life. Luke often wondered if what he was looking for from these men was something that would make up for what he felt he'd never received from his father. He frequently commented, "It's like I never got initiated into the guy tribe because he [father] was never that interested in me." When he could let himself feel this sadness, Luke's eyes would well with tears, but he fought them because he believed, "If I start [to cry], I might not stop."

Luke's father enacted an emotional abandonment that many psychotherapists and analysts often hear about. A family might outwardly look good – but those appearances deceive because they are often dependent on orchestrated images, a kind of family persona, with not much substance beneath them. Luke had to deal with profound paternal neglect that hampered his development and created such deep alienation that substance abuse appeared to offer him relief from his painful emotions. His father was seemingly oblivious to the psychological harm that he inflicted on his wife and children. This is a disturbing portrait of a family, in which a father neither acts like a father to his children, nor as a husband to his wife. In that way, Luke's father resembles the kind of father that Laius represents – a selfish man who does not seem to want the responsibilities of family life.

Luke eventually got in touch with his anger and rage at his father. He wondered over a long period of our work what it might feel like to express these feelings to his father. On the one hand, he imagined that his father might be hurt and fall apart, perhaps coming from an inflated fantasy of a child's having responsibility for a parent's emotional wellbeing. On the other hand, Luke feared that he'd simply get no response. "He'd look at me blank and turn away." That second idea conveyed the alienation between them that seemed unbridgeable and beyond repair. I suggested that with time Luke might have further ideas about his father's reactions to his anger, that he might not always feel like a boy suffering the consequences of his father's neglect. He nodded, "I'd like to get there."

What are the effects of having such problematic fathers as internal figures? Coming to terms with them can burden a boy's and man's developmental course. These types of fathers evoke feelings of rejection, depletion, disappointment, and hopelessness. A son's negative self-image, which is at the mercy of these inner fathers, typically contributes to severe alienation and a fear of exploring the inner world. The unconscious may, in turn, be activated to pursue destructive, morbid imagery as a way of representing inner turmoil. Apocalyptic content often appears in the dreams and fantasies of these males. For example, Nicolas, who I discussed earlier in the chapter, was preoccupied with reading war histories about grueling and vicious battles. He believed this interest stemmed, in part, from his father's shameful involvement with the military in his country of origin. John reported bleak, violent images suddenly breaking through into consciousness and upsetting him. He would feel depressed after such incidents because he believed they demonstrated "rottenness inside" him. Luke also had such grim images break through unexpectedly; for instance, when he saw himself in a mirror, he might see himself as a zombie or corpse. For these men, a kind of tormenting apocalypse existed within their psyches.

Developmentally, these problematic fathers can be viewed as anti-growth. In each myth or story, the father exposes his sons to danger that prevents them from growing. Jason's thievery brought on Medea's revenge, and his sons paid a price. Abraham's binding of Isaac brought his son to near death. Laius's pinning of the baby's feet is a dramatic representation of cruelly stopping any ability to grow and move. Each of these fathers acted in ways that exposed their sons to terror and trauma, thus thwarting their sons' normal development. These anti-growth fathers within a male psyche leave a boy stuck *and* alienated, a double problem in psychological terms. Growth is derailed, and attempts at healing are potentially frightening because they require looking inside oneself.

A dead father

Conor was seven years old when we met. His father had died of a quick and fatal illness six months before. Conor had one older sister. His mother was concerned with Conor's adjustment because he refused to talk about his feelings around what had happened to their family. When we first met, I asked Conor to draw a picture of himself, and he drew a picture of a boy with one eye open and one eye shut.

I wondered to Conor what it might mean, and he said it "looks creepy." I replied that maybe this boy was just half-awake, and he smiled, nodding yes.

During the eighteen months that I worked with Conor, he went through a process of waking up. After our first few sessions, I noticed a peculiar tic. He would move his head rigidly and slowly from side to side as if slowly scanning the room. Sometimes, this movement could take a full minute. Whenever I asked about it, Conor told me he felt fine, had no pain, and was "just looking." I asked his mother if she had noticed it, and she said yes. I suggested she see a pediatric neurologist to make sure there was nothing organic occurring. The neurologist confirmed that the tic was behavioral.

In Chapter 5, I wrote about ten-year-old Carlos who had an embodied identification with his lost father. I wondered if something similar was true for Conor. I met with his mother, and I explained that it could be helpful to me and to Conor if she could tell me about her husband's illness. She said he had deteriorated quickly, and when it became apparent that he would not survive, they moved his bed into the living room. Mother, Conor, and his older sister would spend time sitting around the father's bed reading to him, talking, watching movies, and telling one another stories. It sounded like a moving and compassionate farewell time for the whole family. I asked Conor's mother if her husband had developed any unusual movements because of his illness. She recalled that he lost a lot of muscles from staying in bed and that toward the end he could only move with great effort. I wondered if Conor's tic might be a way for him to express an unconscious memory of this time. She thought this was possible. She added that Conor had always been "a physical kid" until the last several months.

Over the next couple of months, I looked for ways to ask him about his father. What was his favorite memory of a time they shared? What did his Dad look like? What was something funny they did together? What did Conor miss most about him? Could he show me a photo of his Dad? These questions and others were not raised all at once. I had to select carefully and make sure my timing was good; otherwise, Conor would say, "I don't want to talk about that." But if I found the right moment, he would answer, look sad, and eventually say, "I miss him."

Conor's tic disappeared shortly after the period of therapy that I describe here. I want to mention a parallel aspect of his play during and after this time. I have a sand tray in my office, and anyone is welcome to put various small figures from a collection into it to create a scene. Boys like Conor frequently love this option. It is nonverbal and expressive as well as symbolic and cathartic. Conor made a series of scenes over many months in which the characters varied and the themes shifted, but there was one figure that remained constant. This was an old man whom I called grandpa. He had white hair, was wearing a tie and cardigan sweater, and was reading a book.

Conor placed grandpa in virtually every sand-tray scene that he made and, usually, in the most violent positions. Grandpa would have an ax to his head, a gun to his back, a knife to his throat. A knight aimed an arrow at his belly. A dinosaur or three-headed dog would try to bite him. Grandpa was a target of repeated vicious attacks. I occasionally asked Conor about grandpa, and he would typically laugh and say, "I don't know; it's funny." Conor's mother told me that he got along well with both his grandfathers, who had been helpful male figures around her husband's death. She was unaware of any friction between Conor and them. Conor also liked his male coaches and teachers, and he seemed to be at ease around them. I considered too whether grandpa had anything to do with me, yet I could not find a meaningful connection between this figure and me.

I never really found a satisfying answer to the mystery of grandpa's tortures. It seemed that Conor was showing anger at an older man, who stood for generational change and, possibly, the future. I wondered, at times, if his hostility might have been unconsciously aimed at his father who would not grow old and become a grandpa. The loss of a parent at this age is devastating, and expressing anger can upset whatever tenuous emotional equilibrium there is. Conor did the best he could in representing this dilemma. Importantly, later in his therapy, he did get visibly angry with me around my vacations. I told him that I was proud of him for telling me and it made sense that he'd be angry at me leaving because I was someone who he depended on. After one of these exchanges, Conor said, "Yeah, I was mad. I really needed to talk to you."

Conor's situation illustrates how difficult loss is for children and also how a boy may struggle to hold on to his father when the latter dies. The embodied identification of Conor's tic was an attempt to show that his father was very much on his mind. His symbolic play with grandpa may have revealed Conor's alienation related to his father's death. He lost a future with his father, and for many children, that loss transports them into psychic alienation because their feelings are jumbled and turbulent.

A "good-enough" father

Winnicott realized with admirable compassion that the demands and expectations on parents are many and unending. He saw that there was no ideal parent, only a parent who functioned good enough, and that this was actually what infants and children needed to grow up reasonably well. He coined the terms "good-enough mother" and "good-enough mothering" to describe that parents let go of managing so tightly most of their infants' needs and later allow for increasing amounts of frustration to enter into the child's repertoire of experiences.[80] The child thus internalizes a "good-enough" caretaking object that is not persecutory because he has learned over time to cope without being flooded.

In this chapter, I have discussed many examples of fathers who are problematic because their behaviors lead to internalization of inner fathers that contribute to their sons' alienation. In addition, these inner fathers attack and undermine their sons' masculinity. I want to conclude this chapter, however, with an example of what good-enough fathering might resemble and why it matters to a son's adaptability and mental health.

I met Andy when he was in his late twenties and experiencing a choppy ending to his marriage. It would take another year until they divorced. He described what it was like when his wife was angry as "trying to touch a dragon." Andy was intelligent and had a knack for metaphor that helped him to articulate the emotional pain he was going through. For example, he often remarked that his life was "a book with sad chapters and pitiful parts, which would shock a reader for how off track" he'd gone. Andy was depressed and obsessed about his relationship with his wife. He frequently faulted himself for not standing up to his wife's hot temper.

Andy's self-criticism seemed to originate more from his childhood experiences of his mother's distance and emotional constriction than from his relationship with his father. He said his mother's reserve was confusing to him as a boy, and he often believed she was thinking the worst of him. He spoke affectionately about his father, although he wished that his father had been more open with him. His father's business went downhill during Andy's adolescence, and they lost their house, but no one discussed what was happening. Andy believed his father was too embarrassed to tell them. Yet he continued to show up for Andy's athletic activities and school events. He encouraged Andy in subtle ways to aim high and to get the most out of trying his hardest. When things didn't work out in a game, he'd remind his son that there'd be another day, another game. When I asked Andy to describe his father, he replied that, although his father was "stern, he was kind and fair minded." When one of Andy's friends committed suicide during high school, Andy's father went with him to his friend's funeral. Afterward, he asked Andy what he'd remember most about his friend, a meaningful gesture since Andy could not believe what his friend had done.

Andy's father was by no means a super dad, but he sounded good enough. He had his difficulties in life, but seemed to have taught his son important lessons about persistence and finding a purpose. Once, when Andy was especially down on himself and said he was "pathetic," I commented that sounded too harsh, and I hoped he'd find a way to be gentler with himself. Andy's eyes welled with tears, and he said that I reminded him of his father after his high-school team had lost a state championship. Andy seemed to be indicating that just as I could see into his emotional life, his father, too, had done this. This inner father opens up a psyche rather than threatening and closing it down.

Andy looked forward to our sessions, and I also had a feeling of pleasant anticipation about seeing him. When I mentioned that he might consider coming twice weekly, he thought about it and responded, "Sounds great." To me, this affirmation was a sign of a good-enough father in Andy's relationship to me, what we'd call his transference to me. It also implied he was eager for more of this experience. Shortly after this, Andy told me he had started to volunteer in a mentoring program with a teenaged boy whom he met twice a week, once for homework and once for fun. He told me he liked the opportunity to give back something, and that he learned a lot from the boy he was mentoring, especially from the boy's "wise cracks."

The references to meeting twice a week and "wise cracks" struck me as not coincidental, but also not entirely conscious. I thought that Andy was replicating something helpful from his relationship with me, by taking on a parallel role with someone younger needing help and guidance. He seemed to feel the liveliness and attention of a good-enough father and wanted to experience it from both sides, receiving and giving. This kind of therapeutic identification, building on what Andy had already internalized from his father, nurtures a psyche by providing it with inner resources and aspirations. I was careful not to make an explicit interpretation, because I believed Andy might feel I was infantilizing him. Instead, I said that I thought it was interesting his student challenged him with wise cracks because we all have to learn that authority shouldn't get too comfortable. Andy smiled, mimicked a high-five toward me, and said, "Right on!"

Notes

1 Google Scholar (available: <https://scholar.google.com>) and PsycINFO (available: <www.apa.org/pubs/databases/psycinfo/index.aspx>), accessed August 9, 2017.
2 M. E. Lamb, A. M. Frodi, C. Hwang, M. Frodi, and J. Steinberg, "Mother- and father-infant interaction involving play and holding in traditional and nontraditional Swedish families," *Development Psychology*, 1982, vol. 18, pp. 215–21. doi:10.1037/0012-1649.18.2.215.
3 C. S. Tamis-LeMonda, J. D. Shannon, N. J. Cabrera, and M. E. Lamb, "Father and mothers at play with their 2- and 3-year-olds: Contributions to language and cognitive development," *Child Development*, 2004, vol. 75, no. 6, pp. 1806–20. doi:10.1111/j.1467-8624.2004.00818.x.
4 Ibid., p. 1817.
5 J. L. Flanders, V. Leo, D. Paquette, R. O. Pihl, and J. R. Seguin, "Rough-and-tumble play and the regulation of aggression: An observational study of father – child play dyads," *Aggressive Behavior*, 2009, vol. 35, no. 4, pp. 285–95. doi:10.1002/ab.20309.
6 D. Paquette and C. Dumont, "Is father – child rough-and-tumble play associated with attachment or activation relationships?" *Early Child Development and Care*, 2013, vol. 183, no. 6, pp. 760–73.
7 M. R. Gryczkowski, S. S. Jordan, and S. H. Mercer, "Differential relations between mothers' and fathers' parenting practices and child externalizing behavior," *Journal of Child and Family Studies*, 2010, vol. 19, no. 5, pp. 539–46.
8 Ibid., p. 543.
9 T. M. Videon, "Parent-child relations and children's psychological well-being: Do dads matter?" *Journal of Family Issues*, 2005, vol. 26, no. 1, pp. 55–78. doi:10.1177/0192513X04270262.
10 Ibid., p. 69.
11 C. McKinney, "Differential parenting between mother and fathers: Implications for late adolescents," *Journal of Family Issues*, 2008, vol. 29, pp. 806–27.
12 Ibid., p. 817.
13 W. R. Bion, *Experiences in Groups*, London, Tavistock Publications, 1961.
14 P. M. Turquet, "Leadership: The individual and the group," in G. S. Gibbard, J. J. Hartman, and R. D. Mann (eds.), *Analysis of Groups: Contributions to Theory, Research, and Practice*, pp. 349–71, San Francisco, CA, Jossey-Bass, 1974.
15 Ibid., p. 357.
16 M. Kimmel, *Guyland: The Perilous World Where Boys Become Men*, New York, HarperCollins, 2008.
17 Ibid., pp. 4–5.
18 Ibid., pp. 8–9.

19 Ibid., p. 42.
20 Ibid., p. 167.
21 Ibid., p. 275.
22 J. Butler, "Melancholy gender – refused identification," *Psychoanalytic Dialogues*, 1995, vol. 5, no. 2, pp. 165–80.
23 S. Freud, "Mourning and melancholia," *SE* 14, 1917, pp. 243–58.
24 Butler, "Melancholy gender," pp. 167–8.
25 Ibid., p. 168.
26 Ibid.
27 Ibid., p. 172.
28 Ibid., p. 169.
29 Ibid., p. 179.
30 N. Solebello and S. Elliott, "We want them to be as heterosexual as possible," *Gender & Society*, 2011, vol. 25, no, 3, pp. 293–315. doi:10.1177/0891243211403926.
31 Ibid., p. 297.
32 A. Samuels, "A relation called father, part 1: The father in depth psychology," *British Journal of Psychotherapy*, 1988, vol. 4, no. 4, pp. 416–26; "A relation called father, part 2: The father and his children," *British Journal of Psychotherapy*, 1988, vol. 5, no. 1, pp. 66–76; *The Plural Psyche: Personality, Morality and the Father*, London, Routledge, 2016 (first published in 1989).
33 Samuels, "A relation called father, part 1," p. 417.
34 Ibid., p. 419.
35 Samuels, *The Plural Psyche*, p. 27.
36 Samuels, "A relation called father, part 1," p. 420.
37 Samuels, "A relation called father, part 2," p. 75.
38 W. R. Bion, *Learning from Experience*, Lanham, MD, Rowman & Littlefield, 1962, p. 90.
39 Samuels, "A relation called father, part 2," p. 75.
40 J. C. Loehlin and N. G. Martin, "Dimensions of psychological masculinity – femininity in adult twins from opposite-sex and same-sex pairs," *Behavior Genetics*, 2000, vol. 30, no. 1, pp. 19–28; K. J. H. Verweij, M. A. Mosing, F. Ullén, and G. Madison, "Individual differences in personality masculinity – femininity: Examining the effects of genes, environment, and prenatal hormone transfer," *Twin Research and Human Genetics*, 2016, vol. 19, no, 2, pp. 87–96; R. Lippa and S. Hershberger, "Genetic and environmental influences on individual differences in masculinity, femininity, and gender diagnosticity: Analyzing data from a classic twin study," *Journal of Personality*, 1999, vol. 67, no. 1, pp. 127–55; A. Knafo, A. C. Iervolino, and R. Plomin, "Masculine girls and feminine boys: Genetic and environmental contributions to atypical gender development in early childhood," *Journal of Personality and Social Psychology*, 2005, vol. 88, no. 2, 400–12; J. E. Mitchell, L. A. Baker, and C. N. Jacklin, 1989, "Masculinity and femininity in twin children: Genetic and environmental factors," *Child Development*, 1989, vol. 60, no. 6, pp. 1475–85.
41 Verweij et al., "Individual differences in personality masculinity," p. 87.
42 Ibid., p. 97.
43 Lippa and Hershberger, "Genetic and environmental influences on individual differences in masculinity, femininity, and gender diagnosticity," p. 130.
44 Ibid., p. 133.
45 Ibid., p. 135.
46 Ibid., pp. 145–6.
47 Knafo, Iervolino, and Plomin, "Masculine girls and feminine boys," p. 400.
48 Ibid., p. 401.
49 Ibid., p. 407.

50 B. Reis, "Names of the father," in B. Reis and R. Grossmark (eds.), in *Heterosexual Masculinities: Contemporary Perspectives from Psychoanalytic Gender Theory*, pp. 55–72, Hove, Routledge, 2009.
51 Ibid., p. 65.
52 Ibid., pp. 66–7.
53 M. J. Diamond, "Masculinity unraveled: The roots of male gender identity and the shifting of male ego ideals throughout life," *Journal of the American Psychoanalytic Association*, 2006, vol. 54, no. 4, pp. 1099–130; and "The shaping of masculinity: Revisioning boys turning away from their mothers to construct male gender identity," *International Journal of Psychoanalysis*, 2004, vol. 85, no. 2, 359–80.
54 Diamond, "Masculinity unraveled," pp. 1116–7.
55 L. Zoja, *The Father: Historical, Psychological and Cultural Perspectives*, Hove and New York, Brunner-Routledge, 2001.
56 Ibid., p. 15.
57 Ibid., p. 87.
58 Ibid., p. 96.
59 Ibid., p. 280.
60 R. Tyminski, *The Psychology of Theft and Loss: Stolen and Fleeced*, Hove, Routledge, 2014.
61 KJB, 22:2.
62 Ibid., 22:7.
63 Ibid., 22:10.
64 Ibid., 22:18.
65 T. Reik, *The Temptation*, New York, George Braziller, 1961, p. 28.
66 Ibid., p. 40.
67 Ibid., p. 171.
68 KJB, 17:9–14.
69 Reik, *The Temptation*, p. 233.
70 L. Powell and W. R. Self, *Holy Murder: Abraham, Isaac, and the Rhetoric of Sacrifice*, Lanham, MD, University Press of America, 2007, p. 160.
71 Ibid., p. 163.
72 I am not interpreting the religious meanings of Abraham and Isaac's story. Rather, I use it here to explore certain psychological dynamics in a father-son relationship.
73 R. C. Friedman and J. I. Downey, *Sexual Orientation and Psychoanalysis: Sexual Science and Clinical Practice*, New York, Columbia University Press, 2002, p. 113.
74 F. Lachmann, "Addendum: Afterthoughts on Little Hans and the universality of the Oedipus complex," *Psychoanalytic Inquiry*, 2010, vol. 30, no. 6, pp. 557–62. Quote from p. 561.
75 M. Borch-Jacobsen, "Self-seduced," in F. Crews (ed.), *Unauthorized Freud: Doubters Confront a Legend*, pp. 43–53, New York, Penguin, 1998, p. 52.
76 R. Tyminski, "The Medea complex: Myth and modern manifestation," *Jung Journal: Culture & Psyche*, 2014, vol. 8, no. 1, pp. 28–40.
77 J. Munder Ross, "Oedipus revisited: Laius and the Laius complex," *The Psychoanalytic Study of the Child*, 1982, vol. 37, no. 1, pp. 169–200. Quote from p. 171.
78 T. Gantz, *Early Greek Myth: A Guide to Literary and Artistic Sources*, Volume 2, Baltimore, Johns Hopkins University Press, 1993, pp. 488–91.
79 Munder Ross, "Oedipus revisited," p. 185.
80 D. W. Winnicott, *Playing and Reality*, New York, Routledge, 1982.

Chapter 9

I'm broken

Love with his gilded bow and crystal arrows
Has slain us all,
Has pierced the English sparrows
Who languish for each other in the dust,
While from their bosoms, puffed with hopeless lust,
The red drops fall.[1]

Elizabeth Bishop, "Three Valentines"[2]

"I'm broken." I have heard this statement repeatedly in my work with adolescent boys and men of all ages. It seems both curious and sad. Broken implies a unity that has been lost, and it refers to a past time that apparently was perceived as better, more whole and not so jagged. It is a lament that expresses disappointment with a self-image that seems tattered and torn and unable to mend. Broken can mean defeated, weakened, unable to rally, and hopeless of a future that may not be coming.

Ted was seventeen years old when he told me that he was broken. He was an avid videogamer, obsessed with playing the point-and-shoot game *League of Legends*. *League* is team-oriented, a multiplayer, online, battle arena, or "MOBA" game. It takes place in a fictional land named "Runeterra." Players are ranked according to the number of levels each of their characters achieves. The characters, called champions, are a marksman, a mage, and a slayer, among others.

To participate in tournaments, players seek out similarly ranked players. Tournaments award special weapons, armor, powers, and treasure that are usually not won during play of the regular game. Highly skilled players have *YouTube* and *Twitch* channels, so others can watch them play live or see videos of how they won difficult quests. It is estimated, as of 2014, that *League of Legends* has 67 million monthly players worldwide, and the game is now thought overall to have 100 million players.[3] In addition, Riot Games, the company that created *League of Legends*, organizes official world championships, televised online as e-sports, and the winners are awarded substantial cash prizes.[4] Videogaming now generates more revenue than the music industry.[5]

Ted frequently played *League* for forty or more hours a week. He sometimes skipped school to play, and because he often played through the night, he often slept through his classes when he attended. His grades suffered, and his friendships were sparse and fleeting. His parents worried about him, yet he reacted explosively when they verbalized their concerns. He was the youngest of four children by ten years, and his parents were older and described themselves as less involved in his life than they had been with their three older children. His father said, "We're tired. We never expected Ted would be this difficult as a teenager, and we're running on fumes right now trying to cope with him."

The last thing that many young men like Ted want is therapy. How did he make it into my office to tell me he was broken? Ted was caught at school searching the dark web for guns to buy, although he later insisted he would not have purchased them. His school suspended him and informed the family that Ted could only return on the condition that he was in therapy. Ted protested and initially refused to get any help. His father, frustrated and feeling out of options, canceled the family's Internet subscription, confiscated Ted's cellphone, and told Ted that if he wanted to have Internet access, then he would have to get a job to pay for it himself. Within two weeks, Ted began sleeping twelve or more hours a day and lost several pounds. Deprived of his addictive outlet, he became depressed and finally agreed to see a therapist.

Ted's addiction to videogaming is an example of an increasingly common situation that many adolescents and young adults bring nowadays to psychotherapy and analysis. How do we engage with cyber-related problems that suggest a lack of psychological containment? How will these patients make use of a therapeutic relationship?

As I mentioned in Chapter 6, the American Psychological Association recently convened a taskforce of experts to look at the effects of violent videogaming. They reported that exposure to violent video games was associated with increased aggression in the mind (in what a person thinks and imagines) and in the world (in how a person behaves). They documented physiological effects (increased heart rate and higher blood pressure) as well as behaviors like overt hostility, hitting, pushing, and fighting. Playing these violent video games was also associated with desensitization to aggressive actions, decreased empathy, and heightened physiological arousal.[6] These are relational problems, which require containment from a psychotherapist willing to provide a therapeutic experience to repair a rupture in the patient's internal sense of himself and others. It bears repeating that their report found *no evidence* for positive outcomes after exposure to violent video games.[7]

Ted was, at first, a reluctant participant in therapy; however, he eventually began to make use of me and our sessions to describe how alienated he had felt at home and at school. Speaking about being the youngest by many years, he reported, "I was the surprise guest they [family] weren't ever expecting to show. They never said anything about it, but I thought I was the odd guy out." He believed the age difference between him and his siblings made them seem remote and that they were more like cousins. Ted had done well until high school when he said, "I got off track. The place was huge. I didn't seem to find my crowd." Ted began to notice that he had felt broken for a long time, associating this feeling with not being able to connect meaningfully to others and with seeing himself as a misfit.

In this chapter, I discuss the therapy setting and many of the challenges that boys and men present when they are alienated, adrift, and acting out their troubles in the outside world. Many feel they are brought to therapy by the complaints of others – parents, teachers, marital partners, siblings, managers, and coworkers. This belief that they are doing therapy because of someone else means that many of these boys and men are already alienated from what a therapist may have to offer them. Their alienation toward us can appear as guardedness, suspicion, skepticism, stubbornness, and veiled or outright hostility. As my father would have put it, starting off in this way can be like trying to drag a dry horse to water.

How broken?

Of the $2.4 trillion that we spent in the U.S. on healthcare in 2013, nearly $188 billion went for mental health and substance abuse treatments, which ranked fourth behind cardiovascular diseases, diabetes, and other noncommunicable diseases.[8] Depressive disorders were the sixth most costly health condition. Mental health treatments are part of our society's overall health picture, as these numbers show, and access to psychotherapy has been improving, although it can vary by specialty need, by geographic location, and by training of mental health clinicians. A 2016 survey in the UK found that more than a quarter of men had not gotten help for a mental health problem, a higher figure than for women.[9] In the U.S., changing economic times have upended men's traditional roles in the workforce; for example, now more than 11% of men aged twenty-five to fifty-four are unemployed and not seeking work, a figure trending upward during the past decade.[10] Many men feel threatened by these societal shifts because the fastest-growing job markets are in "fields traditionally embraced by women, such as child care, health care, education, and food preparation."[11]

Y. Joel Wong and others studied conformity to masculine norms in meta-analyses of seventy-eight samples, from published work between 2003–2013 with over 19,400 subjects, to look at mental health-related outcomes.[12] He and his co-authors used a scale, Conformity to Masculine Norms Inventory – 94, that consisted of dimensions like winning, emotional control, risk-taking, violence, dominance, playboy behavior, self-reliance, primacy of work, power over women, disdain for homosexuals, and pursuit of status.[13] Wong et al. found that "conformity to masculine norms was positively associated with negative mental health as well as inversely related to positive mental health and psychological help seeking."[14] In other words, men who tried to fit in with masculine norms tended to have worse mental health and to seek help less often for their psychological problems. The authors speculated that these findings showed that the significant relationships of men who struggled with "negative interpersonal consequences" from conformity to masculine norms suffered accordingly.[15]

Three dimensions of masculine beliefs and norms were noteworthy for contributing heavily to these results, namely, self-reliance, playboy behavior, and power over women. One dimension, risk-taking, had both positive and negative associations with mental health, perhaps showing the Goldilocks problem of locating the "just right" place of risk-taking that was neither too much nor too little. Risk-taking makes our lives challenging, but when out of bounds, it can become dangerous. The authors noted that their data were based on correlations and thus could not show causality, only associations. Still, we are left with a grim picture of men trying to conform to unhelpful versions of themselves, versions that alienate them and put them at disadvantage for their mental health and for satisfaction in their relationships. Further, this picture shows men isolating rather than connecting with others and trying to improve their situations. Their refusal of help seems obviously self-defeating, yet it is persistent, and it likely leads to avoidant behaviors within other relationships and social settings.

David Deming, in a paper for the National Bureau of Economic Research, proposes that the labor market is evolving to place a premium on social skills. He cites research that "the labor market return to cognitive skill was substantially lower in the 2000s than in the 1980s."[16] Interestingly, he mentions *theory-of-mind capacities*, which most psychologists would recognize, as relevant for social skills that require empathy and imagining the responses of others. Theory-of-mind (ToM), also called *mentalization*, emerged from autism research in the 1990s. It refers to a normatively developing capacity in children around age four to comprehend that we all have minds that can lie, deceive, play tricks, pretend, and imagine alternate outcomes to situations. "The 'theory of mind' explanation of autism suggests that autistic people lack this ability to think about thoughts, and so are specifically impaired in certain (but not all) social, communicative and imaginative skills."[17]

Theory-of-mind is believed critical for predicting and explaining observed behaviors in oneself and others. Deming implies that impairments in this area of ToM would influence the effectiveness of social skills and presumably make for problems in jobs requiring them. He notes that current labor market demand for higher wage jobs is driven by both cognitive and social skill abilities. The latter would include teamwork, being able to communicate articulately and sensitively, and cooperation. Many of these abilities, in his view of his research, favor women over men in terms of what employers seek: "The pattern is clear – occupations with higher social skill requirements employ relatively more women in 2012 than they did in 1980."[18] There is evidence that ToM can be taught; however, this is not entirely what a therapist would characterize as a smooth or straightforward process. Many boys and men struggle with empathy, in particular, when it seems feminizing to them and threatens their beliefs about masculinity. One adolescent boy, after arguing with his girlfriend, responded to my question about whether he could see her point of view with, "Why would I want to do that, dude? Get in her mind, is that what you're saying?" He was somewhat outraged I would suggest something that might open him to her because this seemed too feminine to him. In other words, he was telling me that ToM was girlish and conflicted with his masculine ideas of himself.

Often, when boys and men say that they are broken, they mean they have a problem communicating what is inside them to others. They essentially substitute the word *broken* for *alienated*. Thus, "I'm broken" could be a statement indicating one of these categories of problems:

(1) A problem of even identifying a feeling and realizing it is there. "I'm broken" may indicate little awareness of an internal world. Ted's presenting situation belonged to this category, as did Zack's from Chapter 2. Many Internet-related and other addictions fit this category.

(2) A problem with naming the feeling in order to communicate it. This individual lacks a useful emotional vocabulary to label an internal state. The cases of Anthony and Tom from Chapter 4 are suggestive of this category. Substantive language for emotions is inaccessible.

(3) A problem with recognizing the causes and effects of a feeling, for example, on a person's body as with blushing, sweating, racing heartbeat, and jumpiness. Feelings are commonly expressed through the body. My close colleague Mary Brady writes about when difficult feelings turn into body-based symptoms in adolescence; in such situations, the clinical presentation often shows "little internal thinking space" and "require[s] a greater need to work with projective identifications and concepts of container/contained."[19] She describes a variety of these bodily symptoms, which can be attempts to express the pain of acute isolation. The cases of Edward in Chapter 4, Carlos in Chapter 5, and Conor in Chapter 8 are illustrative of this category.

(4) A problem with admitting a feeling because it conflicts with one's self-image. The feeling is seen and known, but devalued and unwanted – defended against. The cases of John and Charlie from Chapter 3 and Nicolas from Chapter 5 correspond to this category. Many of the other cases in this book also fit this last category, which arises when beliefs about masculinity, self-image, and relationships collide in ways that hurt. But someone struggling with category 4 is much different from someone in category 1, who may insist that there's nothing inside to examine or understand.

Categories 1–4 are helpful indicators for deconstructing the statement "I'm broken" and then applying it therapeutically. These categories move progressively toward greater internal organization and more emotional availability. Category 1 indicates low access to inner life and highly restricted availability of emotional responses, whereas category 4 implies conflicted awareness of an inner world and ambivalence about emotions. In my earlier house metaphor, category 1 is a closed and sealed structure with no entry; category 4 is a place with doors and windows that are locked and in need of a set of keys. Categories 2 and 3 are intermediate conditions, in which category 2 requires remodeling to get at what's inside, and 3 shows some problems with the passages between interior and exterior.

Patients often need help in figuring out what they mean when they tell us something is wrong and painful. Recall that alexithymia, which I discussed in Chapter 4, means an inability to read emotional states and thus articulate them to others. Graeme Taylor and R. Michael Bagby argue that alexithymia overlaps with low emotional intelligence and that these two problems stem from "failures in early caregiver-child relationships."[20] They note that the concept of alexithymia is associated with externalization and difficulties in symbolization. In my first clinical paper, I discussed patients who appeared to symbolize poorly and who pulled for enactments in the therapeutic field.[21] I was struck then by an intelligent male patient's inability to verbalize his emotional states and how he pulled me into situations where I felt compelled to do this for him. Taylor and Bagby note the important connection between emotional intelligence and ToM because the former relies on the latter to read the emotions and intentions of others.

Citing their research, they write that their findings

> are consistent with clinical observations and some empirical evidence that alexithymic individuals not only lack emotional self-awareness and empathy, but also have difficulty establishing warm, intimate relationships, manifest a propensity to dysphoric states, and are unable to think about and use emotions to cope with stressful situations.[22]

This limitation would predispose those affected to many significant difficulties in maintaining relationships, and the authors believe that arises from early developmental precursors that reinforce insecure attachment styles. Their view of alexithymia being associated with low emotional intelligence emphasizes some of the distinct therapeutic challenges in working with boys and men who may present this way, claiming they are broken.

Allan Schore argues there may be important physiological differences in brain structures that account for some of these problems that boys and men have. He suggests the "right hemisphere, which is dominant for the processing, expression, communication, and regulation of emotion, develops more slowly in male than in female infants."[23] He finds this comparative lag creates a specific vulnerability for male infants to chemical disruptors found in herbicides, fungicides, insecticides, and plasticizers. Exposure to such toxins at vulnerable periods of development might result later in diagnoses that are predominantly given to boys such as attention deficit hyperactivity disorder, autism spectrum disorders, and oppositional defiant disorder.[24]

Schore proposes that the boy brain continues to develop at a slower pace than the girl brain into early adolescence and that males only catch up in early adulthood. At that point, he remarks on numerous observations that men process their emotions differently from women: "men's subjective affective experience is relatively more rooted in sensations from the world whereas women's affective experience is more rooted in sensations from within the body."[25] Schore comments that men tend to use cognitive empathy whereas women rely on "bodily based affective empathy."[26] Louann Brizendine, in her book on the male brain, refers to this same difference in two kinds of empathy, one characteristic of women, the other of men.[27] Thus, there are social, economic, psychological, and neurophysiological explanations for why some boys and men might claim they are broken.

Showing up in the office

Given this outline of manifold vulnerabilities, what happens when boys and men make it into our offices? What makes for an effective psychotherapy? How do we as therapists and analysts build rapport when alienation may define the initial contact point?

There are not many contemporary psychology books dedicated to the topic of treating men and boys. One quite good book, *Therapy with Young Men*, is by Dave Verhaagen.[28] He notes that young men can be resistant to psychotherapy, yet their externalizing behaviors put them at risk for a multitude of behavioral problems. He views sixteen- to twenty-four-year olds as "pre-adults," a somewhat new term for this age range, implying that young men of these ages are still in training for adulthood.[29] It is interesting to consider whether this same term would apply to young women these ages. In my clinical experience, I have seen many young women fully up for the challenges of early adulthood and not "pre-adult" in the sense Verhaagen means, although his idea certainly is consistent with Michael Kimmel's formulations in his book *Guyland*, which I discuss in the previous chapter.[30]

Verhaagen uses a cognitive-behavioral therapy (CBT) approach with his young patients and blends in aspects of positive psychology and motivational interviewing. He finds four "protective factors" are more likely associated with good therapeutic outcomes: ability to talk about feelings, empathy, setting realistic goals, and confidence in one's choices.[31] From a depth psychology perspective, I suggest that Verhaagen emphasizes the importance of developing an attitude toward inner life that includes openness to feeling and of having sufficient ego strength to modify grandiose ideas and projections.

Verhaagen illustrates his ideas through clinical examples that demonstrate sensitivity and tact in working around defenses that keep others at a distance. He describes, as I have throughout this book, that many boys and men resist the notion of admitting their feelings because they are viewed as feminine and feminizing. "They take pride in how they are non-emotional. . . . Even among the more emotionally expressive guys, there is often an underlying belief that emotions belong to the feminine and not the masculine."[32]

The losses accompanying such beliefs are immense. Those reading this book probably already hold their inner life in some esteem, but that belief is not as widespread an attitude as we might assume. Many boys and men readily adopt a stance fitting category 1, described in the previous section. Robert Waldinger and Marc

Schulz conducted a study on eighty-one men who provided data from adolescence into their eighth and ninth decades of life.[33] Their research data included observations, ratings, and interviews spanning more than seventy years. They investigated the role of attachment and family relations in mediating a man's capacity to regulate his emotions and to form secure adult relationships. For example, the mean length of these men's marriages was 40.8 years.[34]

The authors noted,

> Our findings suggest that individuals raised in nurturing environments and those who have more adaptive emotion-regulatory styles are better able to meet two developmental challenges of aging: accepting the vulnerability associated with depending on a partner for one's needs and the responsibility of being depended on by that partner.[35]

In their model, a nurturing family environment in early childhood contributed to both adaptive regulation of emotions as an adult and to secure attachments in later life, although they explained that they based this model on correlations and, therefore, no causality could be determined. They emphasized that adult men dealing with nonnurturing childhood histories might need therapeutic intervention to help them with emotional regulation. They found evidence for "the long reach of warm parent-child relationships," an idea that most analytic psychotherapists know from clinical experience.[36] Their conceptualization helps to define a theoretical background for the statement "I'm broken": emotional dysregulation that leads to avoidance of interpersonal contacts. Categories 1, 2, and 3 imply degrees of this condition, with category 1 being the most problematic.

A common source of referral for psychotherapy is poor impulse control, which is especially true for boys and men, as many of the cases in this book have shown with examples of addiction, aggressive behaviors, and extreme risk-taking. Many behavioral approaches can mitigate these problems. The non-public school where I worked for many years used behavioral plans for all the students.[37] However, we also provided each of them with dynamically focused individual therapy because these children, primarily boys, needed a place to process their emotional suffering and develop trust. Learning to control ourselves is not a linear project, nor is it one amenable solely to rationality. Walter Mischel's work on delayed gratification has shown the importance of impulse control for a variety of measurable life outcomes. He began by looking at how young children reacted to a visible temptation – marshmallows – when instructed to wait so they might get more of them. This situation is a bit like the fable of the ant and the grasshopper, in which the industrious ant saves food for winter whereas the grasshopper sings the summer away.

Mischel's early work found that the visual presence of the marshmallows appeared to increase temptation and desire rather than help to delay them. Children begin to develop more delaying strategies and an ability to inhibit impulses – to wait – between the ages of three and four, although this should be regarded as something of an ongoing maturational project. Faced with waiting to get more of a reward that they could see, when the experimenter left the room, many children could not stop themselves from eating the marshmallows. Mischel wrote that seeing the reward – whether marshmallows, pretzels, or cookies – often became too much for children, who "devised elaborate self-distraction techniques . . . they talked to themselves, sang, invented games with their hands and feet, and even tried to fall asleep."[38] He concluded that learning "not to think" about the reward may be more important than imagining eventually having it.

Why might this matter for a three- or four-year-old boy or for a teenager or young adult? Mischel continued to study his subjects as they got older, and he found that those preschoolers who could wait longer did better later on in life academically and socially. "The seconds of time preschool children were willing to delay for a preferred outcome predicted their cognitive and social competence and coping as adolescents, as rated by their parents a decade later."[39] Mischel's research has stood the test of time regarding what has become known as "the marshmallow test." In a review article, the authors noted, "In numerous follow-up studies over 40 years, this 'test' proved to have surprisingly predictive validity for consequential social, cognitive and mental health outcomes over the life course."[40] Being able to delay gratification at a young age has also been associated with less externalizing behaviors, less physical and verbal aggression, less bullying and higher self-esteem.[41] These authors speculated that this ability helped construct a foundation for willpower and enabled a person to block unwanted temptations and distractions.

Like with the ant from Aesop's fable, planning, working, and persisting are worthy aspects of a psyche that has three-dimensionality and is not phobic toward inner space. Self-control presupposes a self to have a relationship with, an internal working of a psyche that wants, desires, and needs, but can't always have or get. The grasshopper in the fable is lazy, and he also does not limit his summer singing to redirect himself toward other productive activities. "I'm lazy" is a different self-concept than "I'm broken," but also one that therapists hear from adolescent boys and young men to account for their troubles. Such a complaint may indicate, as in categories 2 and 3, that the house/self needs work and repair, but a motivational issue stands in the way. Resistance to therapy can appear as a defensive move to excuse bearing pain and trying to change. Refusing help, however, is relational avoidance, more entrenched, and more difficult to address because this person's alienation obstructs his interacting with others.

The analyst's mind

Having been trained as a Jungian analyst, I work with particular attention to the intersubjective and largely unconscious field created between me and my patient. This kind of analysis and psychotherapy requires a high degree of freely meandering attention, capacity for reverie, and introspection. My colleagues and I frequently discuss the psychological intensity this takes, although it is deeply rewarding at the same time. Jung pioneered an understanding of the analytic field in his work from the 1940s titled *The Psychology of the Transference*.[42]

There, he makes many intriguing and beguiling statements about analytic process. "Doctor and patient thus find themselves in a relationship founded on mutual unconsciousness."[43] Jung was ahead of his time in understanding that analysis is fundamentally intersubjective and that the patient and doctor influence one another unconsciously. His remark here underscores the importance of those unconscious projections that are activated from the very first contact, whether by phone, or nowadays, by an email communication. I may believe I already know something about the person I am going to meet, and I may even have a feeling corresponding to this impression. But I rarely know anything predictive or specific beyond some facts of personal distress, upheaval, and emotional pain. I am usually surprised by what happens in the first session when we meet in person.

In our first parent meeting, Mrs. C complained to me about her twelve-year-old son Pat because she found him disruptive to family life. She listed ways in which she believed he was uncooperative and demanding. He recently had fainted several times at school, and his school counselor recommended therapy as there were no medical reasons for Pat's fainting spells. Mrs. C led me to believe that I'd meet a rebellious and surly boy, and Mr. C affirmed his wife's view of their son, although I had a feeling that his agreement was tentative. When I first met Pat, however, he was polite, even sweet, and told me that when he got angry, he sometimes "talked louder than I should." This session seemed unremarkable as he and I got acquainted, until the end when I stood up from my chair and, for only a few seconds, felt dizzy. This sensation passed so quickly that I might not have registered it, as Pat said goodbye and went out the door.

I realized in writing my notes of this session that I couldn't account for any physical reason that I'd have been dizzy. Nor was there any clear evidence during the session from any of Pat's behaviors that he had done anything to disturb me. He hadn't pressured me or demanded anything from me. He wasn't an overly active boy, fidgeting throughout the hour. He didn't test any of the usual limits. On the contrary, I was struck by how different he seemed on first meeting him from what I had expected based on what his parents, particularly his mother, had told me in their meeting with me. Why had I become momentarily dizzy on meeting a boy who was seeing me after a series of fainting spells? I came to understand that this sensory reaction was unconscious information about Pat and his family that arose from an initial link formed between his parents, me, and him. Later in our work, I would learn that he felt under tremendous pressure from his parents to achieve academically and athletically – dizzying expectations that even they were not entirely aware of.

Jung writes that an analyst should realize that "psychic infections, however superfluous they seem to him, are in fact the predestined concomitants of his work."[44] These "infections," usually the result of projective identifications, are helpful in thinking about a patient's needs and conflicts. I began to wonder, for example, why a twelve-year-old boy might faint – was a loss of consciousness a release from something troubling in his waking reality? The apparent normality of Pat's family life was rather misleading. I came to wonder how crushed he might feel by what his parents expected from him, and in that sense, fainting would communicate a sense of being flattened. Perhaps, I had to have a taste of it in order to understand how insidious this process was, how hidden it was, and how disorienting its effects were.

Jung did not believe that hero identifications in analysts were useful. He adhered more to a wounded-healer idea, in which an analyst's own wounds help him or her to continue to learn about psychic life, even as these get reactivated time and again: "Psychological induction inevitably causes the two parties to get involved in the transformation of the third and to be themselves transformed in the process."[45] This is Jung's articulation of the field between two people as a third thing in its own right, or as Joseph Cambray explains, "His exploration of the deep background to transference phenomena brings him to postulate a bipersonal interactive field model for the analytic relationship."[46]

This field is organic and unique, along the lines of Gestalt psychology, postulating the whole as more than the sum of its parts. Jung believed that analyst and patient participate in this field, which changes them both. He viewed the analyst as having the greater role in initiating this process: "The doctor must go to the limits of his subjective possibilities, otherwise the patient will be unable to follow suit."[47] His counsel means that analysis is quite different from other forms of therapy because the analyst gets so involved at an intimate level of interaction by using the field as a vehicle for transformation. This method is not without risks. "Unless both doctor and patient become a problem to each other, no solution is found."[48]

When I conveyed to Pat's parents that I believed they might be imposing too much on him with their expectations, they were not pleased, to say the least. I began to feel their expectations of me and not in a pleasant way. But, through this discussion, we became problems for each other; I served as an advocate for their son's mental health, and they wanted results and valued outcomes. Our discussions were occasionally heated, yet they helped us to understand why achievement and high standards meant so much in their family, which was a loving one. They came to see that Pat's fainting did not imply giving up or weakness, but rather was a communication that his parents' demands felt too heavy to him.

Other analytic traditions endorse a view of an interactive field as the way that patients and analysts engage so that transformation might occur. Wilfred Bion's concept of container/contained offers another model for such a field into which emotions are projected and worked on.[49] Bion's theories are increasingly referred to by contemporary psychoanalysts of Freudian and Kleinian traditions, as well as by many Jungians. Bion attended Jung's 1935 lectures in London at the Tavistock Clinic and participated in discussions then.[50] A German Jungian analyst, Christian Maier, suggests that Bion likely heard Jung's idea of analysis as a living container and later expanded it, adding his own theoretical concepts to it.[51] Maier sees considerable overlap in Jung's and Bion's models for psychic growth. Antonino Ferro has further elucidated Bion's theories and shown their application with children in what he also calls a bi-personal field.[52]

An analyst's reactions have typically been termed *countertransference*, which can be of a general kind, a feeling or fantasy in response to a patient, or more specifically, of an activating kind that stirs something conflictual in the analyst's own history. Like most analysts, I rely on my countertransference to inform me about what is happening in the field. Harold Searles wrote a moving article in the late 1950s about countertransference that is, to me, a hallmark for advocating openness to an analyst's feeling responses.[53] Early in this piece, he admits he has experienced "romantic and erotic desires to marry, and fantasies of being married to, the patient."[54] For that time in the history of psychoanalysis, this was a radical admission; nowadays, thankfully not so much.

Searles makes the point that in "normal" development parents will reciprocate their children's love, even when the child insists on something impossible or unattainable. Parents, one hopes, would not turn away and distance from their children around these desires, although they do set boundaries so children can learn about them. Searles argues that when an analyst inhibits or forbids himself or herself an experience of loving the patient, it is the patient who loses out. For Searles, a more open stance about countertransference encourages analysts to not be afraid of recognizing their positive feelings for their patients. When these feelings can enter consciousness, there is an opportunity to think about their meanings for the patient's growth within the analytic relationship.

Searles writes, "I came to the conviction, some time ago, that such moments of relatedness could only be nourishing for her [the patient's] developing personality as well as delightful for me."[55] He believes that these emotionally intimate connections help a person's ego to develop by reinforcing a sense that he or she is loveable. Part of this process then permits the patient to identify more meaningfully with the analyst. Searles warns that, in many instances, if an analyst defends against such tender feelings in him- or herself, then the patient may end up feeling defeated and worthless.[56] I read Searles, like Jung, to mean that intimacy and relatedness involve an array of human emotions, including love and desire, and hiding from these affectionate and erotic feelings can restrict the meanings and importance that patients derive from their therapy. Participating in the uncertainties of an analytic field implies that we will show up for whatever awaits us.

The dog bite

Often, in my work with men, there comes a moment when a boy shows up, and it is not the boy the patient wants to remember. Frequently, this psychic distance is associated with self-alienation, which may come from having disowned and abandoned this boy because the now-grown man does not like what he represents. The result is a bit like a book with chapters torn out, and their loss means the story is not understandable.

My patient Luke, discussed in Chapters 1, 6, and 8, struggled with his self-image, believing he was not assertive and masculine enough. During the course of our later work together, Luke was bitten by a dog on the street. He berated himself for being "feeble," a "sissy," because he hadn't confronted the dog's owner. These nasty self-criticisms were often hard to hear, and I remarked how Luke beat himself up in front of me, and he must have wondered why I did not stop him. I often wanted to, but considered that if I had, then I might be indicating I could not bear what he was doing, or that I had to show him how "real men" behaved. To me, this problem stemmed from a bullying figure in Luke's unconscious that I could not excise even if I wanted to. This was a part of his psyche.

After this incident, Luke dreamed that *he was a boy walking toward a hut. He realized there was a wild animal inside, a weasel. He worried he would not be able to keep it inside. He thought he saw a man approaching.* Luke clarified that he believed the approaching man was someone like me who would protect him. He also said this dream seemed related to the dog bite, and that the boy could not even handle a weasel. He then disparaged himself again for being "pathetic" because he had not taken the dog owner's name and phone number.

When I heard Luke's dream, I wondered about the weasel, and I asked if he could describe why it had to be kept inside the hut. Luke replied that it was vicious. His comment made me think of Luke's unresolved anger at himself over the dog bite. In the dream, he appeared to hope that I might rescue him from this animal inside, but in listening to his dream, I chose not to comment on this aspect. Instead, I asked whether the vicious animal might have something to do with him and how he felt about what had happened with the dog.

Luke paused before replying. "Inside me, there's this defiant, pissed off, hurt kid. He's pouting and inconsolable. People won't care about him." Luke hadn't described himself in this way before. I asked who those people might be, and Luke recalled telling his father "I hate you," and next running out of the house when he was a boy of about ten. His father didn't follow; now Luke said he "wasn't fucking important enough" to matter to his father.

I remarked that this boy inside sounded very angry that important people would not pay attention to his needs and his suffering. I then added that perhaps this boy felt some of these things about me. This moment seemed like an opportunity to speak to Luke's wish that I might rescue him and give him space to air his disappointment that I could not.

Luke nodded, "Yeah, it's like screw everyone, you too."

We sat silent for a couple of minutes; I wondered if the hut door was open. I wanted to see what Luke would do with this tension between us. Would he insist that I come to his aid? Or might he find another way to express his anger? I didn't know.

Luke spoke of how stubborn he felt right then, because he wanted me to know how badly he had been hurt. The defiant child waited to see the adult's reaction. Would I give in, would I ignore him, or would I overpower him?

I mentioned stubbornness is problematic when it shuts down communication about hard feelings that we might want to avoid telling one another. Luke sighed.

He told me he worried I would eventually ignore him when he protested. He thought I would end up acting like his father who always insisted on his own needs. Luke remarked that, at times, he wished he had been fierce toward his father, but he now thought he had weaseled out of more openly confronting and challenging him. "I never really rebelled."

In the months after this exchange, Luke seemed livelier than ever before. His emotional life had more punch to it, and he found himself considering a career change. He told me he didn't want to be "a weasel." He said, "I really don't want you to be disappointed in me. I used to assume you were, but now, I'm hoping you're not."

I found myself feeling a vigorous, passionate boy in Luke the man, and I liked him. I spoke about how I noticed this change in him, and how articulate he could be when he gave himself the chance. I told Luke that I liked what he was showing of himself, a man relating to the boy inside him. The incident of the dog bite followed by his dream helped to open a transformative sequence of images that brought the boy, the weasel, and the dog together along with Luke's father and me. This complicated series of events and images contributed to Luke's being able to break through to the alienated boy inside. The Jungian analyst John Beebe writes that when affect and image are brought together, the result can be a new sense of integrity within the personality when split-off parts become integrated.[57] This healing seemed to occur for Luke.

Hand in the cookie jar

My patient John, discussed in Chapters 1, 3, and 8, continued to surf Internet porn and hookup sites despite trying to stop himself and telling me that he knew it was harming his relationships. John made a mistake at work one day when he left early. He had left his computer on, and when a coworker had to retrieve some documents from his office, she noticed the screen flickering. When she went to shut it off, the screen suddenly sharpened to reveal a pornographic video.

He nearly lost his job. John was distraught and told me what he had done was "stupid beyond belief." He and his wife had separated and were getting a divorce. When she found out about his transgression at work, she apparently told him that she had thought he couldn't sink any lower, but she had been wrong. John did not know how to reply. He recalled that when he was about twelve, his mother had found him with a *Playboy* magazine. She had told him he should know better than to get caught with his hand in the cookie jar. Her remark shamed John about his developing sexuality and masturbation – that his hands led to other shameful pleasures. John begged her to not tell his father, and she agreed, although he suspected that she did not forget and for months held him hostage over this incident. John's experience of his sexuality was deeply mixed with shame, threat of exposure, and punishment.

In Chapter 3, I discussed how he viewed me as a sexual object. His use of me in this way to contain aspects of his sexuality continued during his later treatment when he reported this dream. John said that he *opened the door to my office, which was shining, new and big. Music was playing, and I had a blond streak in my hair like an actor. There were other men and women in the room for a couples group I ran, and he wanted them to leave, but I told him no because I liked working with couples. He started to cry and woke up crying.* John was upset telling me this dream because he felt I might be tired of listening to him. I noticed how in his dream my needs and my pleasure took precedence. I was aware that the dream felt pornographic, along the lines of a scene where someone shows up unexpectedly and is invited to join in. In the dream, John was ambivalent about joining.

I thought about how John's dream represented me – I have no blond in my hair, and I felt the dream suggested a man who was slick and self-centered. I asked John how he understood my appearance in his dream. He blushed and then told me that the porn video found on his work computer had an actor with a blond streak in his hair. When I heard this, I felt uncomfortable at his imagining me in such a role. Considering my feeling, I decided to pursue what connection John might see between that actor and me. This moment was not easy, because I also felt his dream's intrusion into my psyche and this troubled me. Patients have an opportunity, of course, to imagine us in whatever ways they want. This is part of their freedom to contribute to the analytic field. Still, when we suspect that we as analysts and psychotherapists are being used destructively, perversely, and against psychic growth, then we might have to question what is happening – is this analytic couple acting fraudulently or corruptly?

John continued that in the dream I seemed confident and I knew what I wanted. I asked if that impression could have anything to do with the porn actor. He nodded and said, although he knew it was fake, that these actors "embraced their sexuality without hesitation." I thought here about John's shame, and I wondered whether John's dream portrayed him catching me with my hand in the cookie jar. Perhaps his dream implied I had something to feel ashamed of, although apparently, I was not. I encouraged him to say more, noticing my discomfort had lessened. This change in my feeling indicated that John and I could work together on his dream to understand his projections onto me. I felt less like there was a risk the dream would be used defensively to validate a sort of "everyone does it" attitude.

John spoke about his shame over the incident at work. He lamented how embarrassed he felt when he saw the woman again who had discovered the video on his computer. "I had no idea what to say. It was so awkward. I mean, what was she supposed to say? She was polite, but kept her distance. I felt bad for her." I thought it was positive for John to put himself in her shoes – showing empathy for her reaction to his behavior. John explained part of his return to work was a requirement that he attend workshops on gender in the workplace. He found these classes to be surprisingly interesting, and as a result, he said he was trying to limit how much pornography he viewed. He commented on the degrading and sexist aspects of pornography that his viewing tacitly supported. He admitted he would probably keep looking at pornography, but he hoped to do so less. He remarked on how men seem to need visual stimulation as an erotic outlet, whereas he believed women were better at imagining erotic scenarios.

John said he struggled to understand his wife because he found her disapproval "always within arm's reach." He mentioned he found it difficult to not counter her with criticism of his own. Sometimes he felt justified in defending himself by attacking her. He wished they had tried to be less judgmental of each other. He had been in a bookshop recently and bought a copy of Simone de Beauvoir's *The Second Sex*. Although I wondered if he might be over-compensating in manic reparation for his shame and guilt, John did feel different to me, more thoughtful and melancholic. Again, my sense was that he was using the incident at work and his dream about me to learn about himself, as painful as this was.

During these discussions, I asked John if he could compare his experience of me in the room to the blond-streaked version of his dream. He grinned, replying that the dream version was flashy, not how he perceived me during a session. I commented that the dream Robert – he called me by my first name – seemed to have surprised him. He agreed, adding that he thought "it was you on steroids." He clarified that the dream Robert seemed definitely bolder. I wondered what he made of that. John said he wished he were bolder because he believed he held back too much and inhibited his feelings. He gave his relationship with his wife as an example, and he also mentioned his online sexual activities in this regard. Of the latter, he said, "That's a big reason I use those sites, because I wouldn't show myself in the real world." John seemed to be taking stock of how immersion in cyberspace reinforces avoidance of real-life encounters.

In taking his dream further, I remarked that the dream Robert, whom he described as bolder, also rejected John and made him cry – what did that mean to him?

John was quiet while his eyes welled up with tears. He said he doubted I would ever behave like that and openly reject him. In the dream, he felt upset when I wouldn't listen. I reflected he often felt that way in relationships. He paused. He then mentioned that one of his children recently told him to speak up, which made him feel sad because he could see that his children thought of him as not having enough of a presence.

When John said this, I was reminded of his memory of being caught with his hand in the cookie jar, which is a metaphor for sneaking and hiding. Jungian analyst Ellen Siegelman writes, "Much therapeutic work consists of unfreezing the metaphors that have patients in their grip and of relativizing them, showing that their entrenched metaphors represent one way of looking at the world."[58] I remembered John saying he felt held hostage by his mother's discovery, and I thought about how an event such as this one might become frozen in time and turn into a compelling plotline in a personal narrative. I suggested to John that he had learned to hide early in his life so as not to get caught too many times with his hand in the cookie jar. He cried for minutes, and when he spoke, he said his parents relied too much on shaming their children and that he and his siblings were still paying a price. Then, he added he had not yet come to terms with being a twelve-year-old boy caught by his mother looking at *Playboy*. Here, John described his self-alienation from the boy he had been at a pivotal time in his development. Twelve-year-old boys are usually rather excited by their growth, physicality, and nascent sexual awareness.

There was another aspect of John's dream that I asked him about – the couples. John replied that he had learned more about being in a good couple from me than anywhere else. I felt it necessary at the time to comment on his idealizing view of me. He responded, "It's not like I'm saying you have a blond streak."

Special problems

This section looks at especially challenging areas in working with boys and men. Of course, this section could be a book of its own. In Chapter 6, I discussed my patient Jake whose contempt was an ongoing theme and strain. Contempt is one of the negative emotions that most strongly dissolves connections between people. We might use contempt when we want to signal to someone that we are done, no further questions. When we are targeted, we know it by the visceral response in us. It is disturbing, in part because it is intended to disturb, as when Jake replied to many of my comments, "I don't care." Contempt has been found by marriage researchers to be associated with predicting marriage breakups with extremely high accuracy.[59] Contempt is often an attack directed at someone envied, and the contempt tries to obliterate the object's worth. For example, in Chapter 6 where I discuss alienation coming from emotional deprivation in terms of the black rider, I give examples of how this form of alienation can be expressed through contempt.

In my clinical experience, two additional areas merit attention in this context. One is homophobia, and the other is rage. Either of these can be detrimental to a therapeutic alliance, and both can be difficult to address because patients in their grip are breaking a link with the therapist. Whereas homophobia seeks relief through distance and withdrawal, rage engages one against the other to inflict hurt and cause suffering. Both bring intensely negative affects into the analytic field and seem intended to alienate analyst and patient.

Homophobia

The Dictionary of Homophobia states that the word *homophobia* was first defined in 1972 by the psychotherapist George Weinberg as "the fear of being in a closed space with a homosexual," and it entered into other dictionaries in the 1990s as "an extreme aversion to homosexuality and homosexuals."[60] Although this meaning is important, I would like to focus on a variation. This other meaning of homophobia is when boys and men do not want to open up to other males, because doing so feels like it will make them too vulnerable. It is associated with softness, which is experienced as feminizing. An extension of the definition of homophobia along this line is "the disparagement of . . . feminine qualities in men" and is linked to a "hierarchical" construct of gender.[61] Either definition of homophobia, of course, can apply to analysis and psychotherapy, and each can result in avoidance and impasse that undercut a way forward.

The examples that I am thinking of here come from ostensibly tolerant and even socially progressive men who would protest that they might be perceived as anti-gay or homophobic in the first sense. They often express no conscious concern about a male therapist's sexual orientation. However, they have ideas about masculinity that inhibit them from opening up to other men. Frequently, they complain that they have few male friends. Sometimes, they describe themselves with pride as being stoic and hard to read. If they seek therapy with a male therapist, these issues can lead to a position well beyond resistance and more aptly described as a barrier or impasse.

Fred was a thirty-year-old married man who came to me because his wife thought he was coping poorly with his father's terminal illness. Fred was an extraverted, busy professional who told me he had few friends because of job demands. When I asked him who his closest male friend was, Fred replied that this would have been another boy he knew in middle school and no longer had contact with. In college, he dated several young women, and he participated in sports. He thought of himself as outgoing, and he was confused when I asked him more about the friends in his life. I was not sure he saw the contradiction in what he was telling me – that he described himself as a socially eager man lonely in a crowd.

Fred felt his relationship with his wife was generally good, although he acknowledged discomfort when she persisted in wanting to know how he felt about something. "It's like she's trying to pry open a stuck jar lid." I mentioned that perhaps the contents were not yet ready to be exposed, and he laughed, telling me, "Yes, and I guess I enjoy watching her try so hard." I wondered to Fred how psychotherapy would be for him given what he was saying about this jar. Might he come to see me as trying to get at something not yet ready to be shared? He took this question in and then replied he was motivated to understand himself better and recognized that therapy only works when "I have skin in the game." I felt his response was honest, even though I suspected he had implicitly warned me with his story about his wife that I might have to be quite careful in how I approached him.

Fred seemed to want my help. He asked me for a recommendation for a book that might help him to understand his father's illness. He routinely brought up situations from his work and from his relationship with his wife that he wished he had handled differently because he felt he drove others away. We discussed these in some detail, and he identified moments when he became anxious and felt he needed to escape. It seemed like he was making progress, but I noticed something odd about the pattern of our discussions not appearing to matter once Fred walked out of the office. Nothing from our relationship seemed to take hold of him. I ended up feeling that I was working rather hard, but Fred let our efforts slip like water off a duck's back. This sense of a shared experience that then dissipates could fall under the heading of the analytic term "as if" personality, which

Charles Rycroft defines as a "type of schizoid character who behaves as though he had normal emotional responses to situations."[62]

There may have been some truth to viewing Fred this way. I brought up with him my observation of his seeming to want my help, yet also not appearing to find much substantive use in what we discussed. Somewhat expectedly, he became defensive. He told me I was being critical when he was "under so much stress." I noted that it was not my intention to be critical, although I admitted it sounded that way. Instead, I wondered whether I was being helpful to him because it seemed the more I offered in response to his asking, the less he took away. I thought about the jar with its tight lid and his enjoyment of his wife's frustration with it, although, mindful of how it might sound judgmental to mention at this point, I chose not to bring it up.

After a session in which Fred asked me for a referral for his father to get a second opinion on his medical condition, and I gave him names to help with his request, Fred phoned me to say he had decided not to come back. He thanked me and said, "It's just not a good match." I thought long and hard about what he was saying. I phoned him to suggest we meet again to discuss what had happened, but he never responded to my message. I felt somewhat used and discarded like a disposable object. I continued to think about Fred's remark that we were not a good match.

I knew some about Fred's background. He was a second child born seven years after an older sister. His parents separated when he was 3 years old, and he saw little of his father after that. He grew up fairly alone since his mother had to work full-time and had various babysitters attend to him until he was ten. Fred seemed like a lonely man to me, and I felt his genuine need for help, which he did not hide. He might have done better with a female therapist or analyst who could have represented something different to him from what I offered.

In thinking about the relational pattern I describe here, I realized it was similar to what the attachment theorist Beatrice Beebe calls "chase and dodge" behavior.[63] In these interactions, a mother pursues her infant, but he dodges her by pulling away. Beebe finds this pattern is later associated with an insecure and resistant attachment pattern.[64] I mean in no way to infantilize Fred's experience with me; rather, I felt this helped me to understand why I felt our work never steadied and always seemed to be in a state of slipping away. I readily chased Fred, and perhaps that may have been an early countertransference that I remained unconscious of for too long. When I formulated an idea of what seemed to be happening between us, I put it in such a way that Fred felt criticized. My formulation did not help.

I wonder, however, if any formulation that appeared to pry open the lid on the jar would have helped coming from another man. In retrospect, I think Fred unconsciously objected to my gender more than anything else about me. He did not want an estranged father chasing him for a variety of reasons. One of those may have been Fred's reluctance to open up to any man because he felt such deep wounding from his father and he had closed himself off under a shield – or lid – of masculine extraversion. This pattern of avoidance illustrates a relational homophobia that prevents men like Fred from getting close to other men because exposure seems too risky and threatens to uncover vulnerability. A significant father-wound, in such instances, can lead to a resistant boy who does not want to trust anyone like father ever again. In my experience, men and boys like Fred appear in our practices infrequently and typically at the behest of someone close to them, such as a spouse or parent.

Rage

Adam was a man in his mid-thirties who argued a lot with his girlfriend. They could not agree on where their relationship was going. However, the immediate cause of Adam's seeking help was that a long-term friend had recently committed suicide. He had known this woman since childhood, and they had dated briefly in high school before she rejected him for someone else. They later renewed a friendship. She struggled with psychiatric problems and had called Adam the week before she killed herself. He wondered if he had missed something in that call and could have saved her.

Right off, I noticed Adam's irritation and anger were significant. He became irritated with me for making an error on his insurance form. He became angry when I forgot his girlfriend's name. He would often correct me when I asked him a question about something that he believed he had already told me. Sometimes, at the end of his sessions, I felt deflated and small. When I mentioned that he seemed annoyed or angry with me, he looked surprised. "Really? I had no idea. Why would you say that?"

Adam grew up with two younger brothers and his parents in a small city. He described his mother as nurturing but overwhelmed with childcare and her part-time work. He described affection and love toward her, although he expressed that one of his brothers "hogged her attention." Adam portrayed his father as emotionally remote and regimented, and he even wondered if he had a form of undiagnosed autism. He said his father controlled the home with many obsessive rules that he insisted everyone follow. When I remarked this might have been difficult for him as a boy who wanted more freedom, he agreed. "He was a bulldozer." Adam's reply made me think about how I sometimes felt during sessions when he berated me for what seemed to be my breaking a rule. I did not comment on this until a bit later in our work because earlier I had a sense he would have rejected such a comparison outright.

I often attempted to talk with Adam about our interactions, and many of these discussions revolved around exchanges when he became angry with me. This was difficult because he was rather defensive in maintaining that he had expressed no anger to me. Many times, I would describe for Adam what I had seen that made me feel he was angry – his scowl, his curt replies, his raised voice, his glare, his tense posture. Adam gradually took this information in and said his girlfriend often told him something similar. This initial step helped Adam recognize what he was showing to others and to get him somewhat more in touch with a feeling vocabulary. Adam did have the capacity to work this way, lessening his defensiveness and finding more words to articulate his emotional states.

After a year of work, much centered on Adam's grieving his friend's suicide, he decided he wanted a break. He indicated he was not open to discussing this decision, and I felt his opposition to my persisting about it. Two years later, he contacted me because he and his girlfriend were splitting up. He resumed working with me. Adam again seemed to have grief over losing someone important. We talked about his sadness and his fear that he was getting older. I was aware that his anger remained volatile and that he continued to alienate others without understanding why. He described a work situation in which he was sent to the human resources department for his aggressive language with a coworker. Not taking responsibility, he blamed his coworker for seeking revenge by complaining about him.

During this period of our work, Adam came in one day with his insurance claim, which had been denied. He accused me of making a mistake and "fucking it all up." I said that he sounded angry at me and explained that the insurance company might have been at fault. He screamed, "That is fucking stupid! Why is it their mistake? And even if it is, aren't you supposed to take care of it?" He repeated the words "fucking stupid" a couple times more. I felt my own temper rising and my heart beating faster. I felt ambushed and wanted to say something sarcastic, but did not. Instead, I said to Adam that he appeared enraged, that I suspected he was far angrier than he realized, and that he seemed to not see he was running over me with his rage. I said this last part because I remembered him calling his father a bulldozer, and I thought Adam unconsciously identified with his controlling, uncaring father when he felt that his needs were not going to be met.

Adam listened. He calmed down, apologizing for his word choice. He asked, "Was I really that dramatic?" I replied that he became intense very quickly with no room between the words and feeling to pause for consideration. He nodded and commented that he'd not meant to put me down. I remarked that it was not so much that I felt put down; rather, I added, I had felt confused by the abrupt intensity of his anger and I was unable to think clearly in that moment. Adam looked glum.

I reflected on how he now looked sad and encouraged him to tell me what was going through his mind. He said, "This happens a lot. More than I can tell you. I don't even know I'm angry at the time." Adam confirmed that his anger made him feel powerful. Later, we spoke about how in feeling powerful he might also have felt that he could control others like his father. Adam seemed to acknowledge this identification with his father and he felt troubled by it.

When someone directs rage at us, we often respond with a variety of layered feelings. These can be current to the situation yet also a resurfacing of something from the past. Our personal histories manifest in these interactions in complex ways, sometimes clarifying for us what we need to say, sometimes blocking our ability to see what could help. Adam's rage reminded me of times when as a child

I was bullied – which fits in a kind of word play with "bulldozer." My reactions to him were to feel my own rage at not defending myself, my wish to retaliate in revenge, and my desire to assert power over him. Facing a patient's rage, this deep layer of the child in us cannot be ignored, yet he obviously cannot be given free reign. Holding this tension, which is both intrapsychic and interpersonal, is part of an analyst's daily routine. Early on in Adam's treatment, I believe I ignored signs of how intense and unregulated his anger was. In fact, I preferred to call it "anger" rather than "rage," probably to reassure myself.

In the current situation, Adam's rage at me had to be contained before it could be understood. The raw quality of his emotional world is not rare among boys and men, as I hope the preceding chapters have helped to illustrate. Adam's alienation from his inner world was apparent in his disavowal of his rage and in his maintaining that he and his father had virtually nothing in common. How might a therapist or analyst contain such raw emotions? Some of this occurs through encouraging patients to articulate more and more what they are experiencing with us, especially when it is painful.

However, another piece occurs through our paying attention to what is not being said and finding ways to say it. For me, this involves a focus on the analytic field that I described earlier and trying to stay aware of the questions, "Where are we and who are the two of us right now?" It may sound easier than it is. Many theoretical models encompass this process, including those of Jung and Bion. At the same time, theory matters little in the heat of the moment, and I have rarely had a patient come to me because of what theory I represent. Theory is helpful afterward, when we review what has happened and seek to learn from it, and it further supports us in our conversations with colleagues when we obtain consultation for our cases.

Another level to consider in understanding transference and countertransference is that of the patient's important contemporary relationships. For Adam, this primarily concerned him and his girlfriend, as well as the death of his childhood friend. I referred Adam and his girlfriend for couples' therapy, which they tried, and although it eventually led to their separating, they were able to recognize their limitations in meeting one another's needs and to express their loss at that. As I got clearer about Adam's rage, I wondered how his girlfriend had managed when he exploded. He explained that she had told him early in their relationship after one such incident that if he were to repeat it, then she would leave him. He resented her trying to control him with this threat. When Adam had other blowups and she didn't leave, he concluded she was bluffing.

Rage, like contempt, usually undoes the invisible relationship glue connecting us. It is important to consider how we work with such emotional challenges analytically because they affect a person's course of treatment and prognosis. They often are brought into an analytic field when a person wants to discharge rather than contain and reflect. The situation may be workable, or it may not be. Our responses, including our intuitions about a person, frequently tell us more than we sometimes want to know.

Summary of therapeutic concepts

Books with case presentations can be like storybooks that help us to expand our portfolio of narratives that we can use and relate to when we are working in our offices. These stories encompass characters, including ourselves, who are privileged to act on an intimate stage. The creativity coming from the unconscious typically guarantees suspense, surprise, and mystery. Giving the reader a checklist may seem contradictory to this dynamism. That said, I want to summarize the key factors in working with boys and men that deserve repeating here. These come out of the case descriptions in this book, and I offer them as interrogatives to spur further thought.

(1) *What are the patient's primary defenses? How much does he rely on avoidance, denial, and projection? To what extent are dissociative processes evident?* These questions help to evaluate how defensive, walled off, and withdrawn a prospective patient might be. They give an impression of how sealed his house/self is. When access to an inner life is closed off, relationships tend to suffer from superficiality. A transactional attitude to relating can dominate. It is important to test the rigidity of these defenses and to look for instances when there may be other attitudes toward relating that show some depth.

(2) *Can the patient name feelings? Can he describe them?* These questions pertain to the notion of a feeling vocabulary and its usefulness. Without words like these, a story has no dramatic arc. A patient may have to develop this vocabulary through our help in identifying and naming feelings. Noticing subtle shifts in a patient's mood, storyline, and attention can all make present unconscious affects, when we might then ask, "What just happened?" or remark, "You seem different from a minute ago." These kinds of interactions open possibilities for describing feelings and understanding why they are important.

(3) *Can he describe accurately the level and intensity of his feelings?* If not, this may indicate a problem with putting a feeling into the perspective of how much, how big, how strong, and so on. For example, does he go from 0 to 60 mph with little pause? Can he use a simple one-to-ten scale to pinpoint how strongly he feels something? Many boys and men, like my patient Adam, may benefit from feedback about how they appear emotionally to others. They may think they are at a level "3," when what they are showing more closely resembles level "8." Self-perception and the perceptions of others may not match, sometimes pushing others away.

(4) *Can the patient put himself in someone else's shoes? How much empathy can he show for another person?* These questions assess someone's theory of mind and their ability to mentalize. They are associated with a capacity for psychological depth and with emotional intelligence. Considering the research about gender differences in empathy, which I mentioned earlier in

the chapter, may be helpful. A thought exercise of putting yourself in someone's shoes often helps with cognitive empathy. Sensory affective empathy
can usually be reached through careful discussions of significant relationships, including the one between analyst and patient.

(5) *How does the patient respond to the therapeutic frame? What is his rhythm,
and how does he pace himself? How does he feel that I am paid for my work
with him?* These questions help to evaluate attachment patterns that depend
on timing and an exchange of resources. They are important for mutuality
and reciprocity. Problems with these can include egocentricity and self-
absorption – a house/self that devours resources without giving much back.
Feelings about payment can be complex because the analyst is compensated
for a relationship that is, by its very nature, an intimate one; they often harken
back to earlier family dynamics around not only tangible resources, but also
emotional ones.

(6) *How does the patient make use of me? What about me seems to make him
anxious?* These questions invite appreciation of the transference and countertransference. They reinforce our attention on the analytic field to consider
who we are to each other. They remind us of the role of the unconscious and
its complexity. Projections onto the analyst are not static by any means. However, what they mean at a particular moment helps to assess how well we are
working together right now as a pair, as a couple.

(7) *How do we talk to each other? Do we need something to open us up?* These
questions take into consideration that many boys and men find therapy awkward and challenging to their masculinity. Our male patients may prefer safe
warm-up topics, and we may have to be willing to engage this way. Films,
books – both fiction and nonfiction – graphic novels, video games, and sports
can all be subjects that get the story moving. Occasionally, they can be used
defensively to distract or bore us, but even then, their contents often reveal
something important.

(8) *How alienated is the patient? Is he aware of his alienation? How does he see
himself?* These specific questions are, in my opinion, central to working with
boys and men. They underscore a boy's or man's attitude toward his inner
life. When this inner world is undervalued, the resulting distance from self-
experience brings all kinds of troubles, many of them severe, as Chapters 5
and 6 emphasize. Alienation from self typically depletes interpersonal relationships of depth and passion and distorts a person's self-image. Alienation
from self can rob a boy or man from having a sense of purpose, which is frequently what brings them to our offices. They feel adrift, lonely, and cannot
begin to fathom why this is so.

These questions are intended to provide something of a schema for approaching
a house for which invitations are uncertain. The four categories at the beginning
of this chapter offer a conceptualization of what might await a therapist or analyst
on his way inside. Working with boys and men who are alienated requires close

attention to their defenses against relationships and their willingness to broach their inner emotional life. The necessity for therapeutic intervention is often clearer to us and to those who care about them. It is frequently up to us to hold onto this idea while finding out what kind of hurt and wound lies beneath their alienation.

Notes

1 E. Bishop, "Three valentines," in Saskia Hamilton (ed.), *Poems*, pp. 223–5, New York, Farrar, Straus and Giroux, 2011, p. 223. From *Poems* by Elizabeth Bishop published by Chatto & Windus. Reproduced by permission of The Random House Group Ltd. © 2011.
2 Excerpt from "Three valentines" from POEMS by Elizabeth Bishop. Copyright © 2011 by The Alice H. Methfessel Trust. Publisher's Note and copyright © 2011 by Farrar, Straus and Giroux. Reprinted by permission of Farrar, Straus and Giroux.
3 A. Newell, "How many *League of Legends* players are there?" *Dot Esports*, May 13, 2017. Online, available:<dotesports.com/league-of-legends/league-of-legends-number -of-players-14488> (accessed September 6, 2017).
4 See L. Howell, "2016 League of legends worlds pool prize at $5.07m with fan con-tributions," *ESPN*, October 29, 2016. Online, available: <www.espn.com/esports/ story/_/id/17919126/2016-league-legends-worlds-prize-pool-507m-fan-contributions> (accessed September 6, 2017).
5 N. Wingfield, "In e-sports, virtual games draw real crowds and big money," *The New York Times*, August 31, 2014. Online, available:<www.nytimes.com/2014/08/31/technolog y/esports-explosion-brings-opportunity-riches-for-video-gamers.html>.
6 S. L. Calvert, M. Appelbaum, K. A. Dodge, S. Graham, G. C. Nagayama Hall, S. Hamby, L. G. Fasig-Caldwell, M. Citkowicz, D. P. Galloway, and L. V. Hedges, "The American Psychological Association task force assessment of violent video games: Science in service of public interest," *American Psychologist*, 2017, vol. 72, no, 2, pp. 126–43, p. 126. doi:10.1037/a0040413.
7 Ibid., p. 139.
8 J. L. Dieleman, R. Baral, and M. Birger, et al., "U.S. spending on personal health care and public health, 1996–2013," *JAMA*, 2016, vol. 326, no. 24, pp. 2627–46. doi:10.1001/jama.2016.16885.
9 J. Doward, "Men much less likely to seek mental health help than women," *The Guard-ian*, November 5, 2016. Online, available S: <www.theguardian.com/society/2016/ nov/05/men-less-likely-to-get-help—mental-health> (accessed September 7, 2017).
10 K. Weir, "The men America left behind," *Monitor on Psychology*, 2017, vol. 48, no. 2, pp. 32–9, Online, available: <www.apa.org/monitor/2017/02/men-left-behind.aspx>. Quote from page 36.
11 Ibid., p. 39.
12 Y. J. Wong, M. Ringo Ho, S. Wang, and I. S. Keino Miller, "Meta-analyses of the rela-tionship between conformity to masculine norms and mental health-related outcomes," *Journal of Counseling Psychology*, 2017, vol. 64, no. 1, pp. 80–93.
13 Ibid., p. 81.
14 Ibid., p. 88.
15 Ibid.
16 D. Deming, "The growing importance of social skills in the labor market," *National Bureau of Economic Research*, Working paper no. 21473, August 2015, p. 2. See avail-able: <www.nber.org/papers/w21473>.
17 F. Happé, *Autism: An Introduction to Psychological Theory*, Cambridge, MA, Harvard University Press, 1994, p. 38.

18 Deming, "The growing importance of social skills in the labor market," p. 35.
19 M. T. Brady, *The Body in Adolescence: Psychic Isolation and Physical Symptoms*, Abingdon, Routledge, 2016, p. 5.
20 G. J. Taylor and R. M. Bagby, "An overview of the alexithymia construct," in R. Bar-On and J. D. Parker (eds.), *The Handbook of Emotional Intelligence: Theory, Development, Assessment, and Application at Home, School, and in the Workplace*, pp. 40–67. San Francisco, CA, Jossey-Bass, 2000, p. 40.
21 R. Tyminski, "When the therapist must symbolize because the patient cannot: Therapeutic trial by fire," *Journal of Jungian Theory and Practice*, 1999, vol. 1, pp. 27–42.
22 Taylor and Bagby, "An overview of the alexithymia construct," pp. 46–7.
23 A. Schore, "All our sons: The developmental neurobiology and neuroendocrinology of boys at risk," *Infant Mental Health Journal*, 2017, vol. 38, no. 1, pp. 15–52, p. 20. doi:10.1002/imhj.21616.
24 Ibid., pp. 27–8.
25 Ibid., p. 42.
26 Ibid.
27 L. Brizendine, *The Male Brain: A Breakthrough Understanding of How Men and Boys Think*, New York, Harmony Books, 2010, p. 97.
28 D. Verhaagen, *Therapy with Young Men: 16–24 Year Olds in Treatment*, Hove, Routledge, 2010.
29 Ibid., p. 17.
30 M. Kimmel, *Guyland: The Perilous World Where Boys Become Men*, New York, HarperCollins, 2008.
31 Ibid., p. 30.
32 Ibid., pp. 117–8.
33 R. J. Waldinger and M. S. Schulz, "The long reach of nurturing family environments: Links with midlife emotion-regulatory styles and late-life security in intimate relationships," *Psychological Science*, 2016, vol. 27, no. 11, pp. 1443–50. doi:10.1177/0956797616661556.
34 Ibid., p. 1445.
35 Ibid., p. 1448.
36 Ibid., p. 1449.
37 Non-public schools are mostly private, not-for-profit schools that receive public funding to provide educational services for special populations.
38 W. Mischel and E. B. Ebbesen, "Attention in delay of gratification," *Journal of Personality and Social Psychology*, 1970, vol. 16, no. 2, pp. 329–37. Quote from p. 335.
39 W. Mischel, Y. Shoda, and P. K. Peake, "The nature of adolescent competencies predicted by preschool delay of gratification," *Journal of Personality and Social Psychology*, 1998, vol. 54, no 4, pp. 687–96. Quote from p. 692.
40 W. Mischel, O. Ayduk, M. G. Berman, B. J. Casey, I. H. Gotlib, J. Jonides, E. Kross, T. Teslovich, N. L. Wilson, V. Zayas, and Y. Shoda, "'Willpower' over the life span: Decomposing self-regulation," *Social, Cognitive and Affective Neuroscience*, 2011, vol. 6, pp. 252–6. Quote from p. 252.
41 Ibid., p. 253.
42 C. G. Jung, "The psychology of the transference" (1946), *The Practice of Psychotherapy, CW* 16, 1954.
43 Ibid., p. 12, para. 364.
44 Ibid., p. 13, para. 365.
45 Ibid., p. 35, para. 399.
46 J. Cambray, *Synchronicity: Nature & Psyche in an Interconnected Universe*, College Station, TX, Texas A&M University Press, 2009, p. 82.
47 Jung, "The psychology of the transference," p. 35, para. 400.

48 C. G. Jung, *Memories, Dreams, Reflections*, New York, Vintage Books, 1965, p. 143.
49 W. R. Bion, *Learning from Experience*, Lanham, MD, Rowman & Littlefield, 1962.
50 C. G. Jung, *Analytical Psychology: Its Theory and Practice (The Tavistock Lectures)*, New York, Vintage Books, 1968.
51 C. Maier, "Bion and C.G. Jung. How did the container-contained model find its thinker? The fate of a cryptomnesia," *Journal of Analytical Psychology*, 2016, vol. 61, no. 2, pp. 134–54. doi:10.1111/1468-5922.12209.
52 A. Ferro, *The Bi-Personal Field: Experiences in Child Analysis*, London, Routledge, 1999.
53 H. F. Searles, "Oedipal love in the countertransference," *International Journal of Psychoanalysis*, 1959, vol. 40, 180–90.
54 Ibid., p. 180.
55 Ibid., p. 185.
56 Ibid., p. 189.
57 J. Beebe, *Integrity in Depth*, College Station, TX, Texas A&M University Press, 1995, pp. 114–5.
58 E. Y. Siegelman, *Metaphor and Meaning in Psychotherapy*, New York, Guilford Press, 1990, p. 130.
59 J. M. Gottman and R. Levenson, "The timing of divorce: Predicting when a couple will divorce over a 14-year period," *Journal of Marriage and the Family*, 2000, vol. 62, no. 3, pp. 737–45. doi: 10.1111/j.1741-3737.2000.00737.x.
60 L-G. Tin, *The Dictionary of Homophobia: A Global History of Gay & Lesbian Experience*, trans., M. Redburn, with A. Michaud, A., and K. Mathers, Vancouver, Canada, Arsenal Pulp Press, 2008, p. 11.
61 Ibid., p. 12.
62 C. Rycroft, *A Critical Dictionary of Psychoanalysis*, Totowa, NJ, Littlefield, Adams, 1973, p. 9.
63 B. Beebe, "My journey in infant research and psychoanalysis: Microanalysis, a social microscope," *Psychoanalytic Psychology*, 2014, vol. 31, no. 1, pp. 4–25. doi:10.1037/a0035575.
64 Ibid., p. 12.

Chapter 10

Revealing a boy

We two boys together clinging,
One the other never leaving,
Up and down the road going, North and South excursions making,
Power enjoying, elbows stretching, fingers clutching,
Arm'd and fearless, eating, drinking, sleeping, loving. . .

Walt Whitman, "We two boys together clinging"[1]

Anima means soul and should designate
something very wonderful and immortal.

C. G. Jung, "Archetypes of the collective unconscious"[2]

Whitman's poetry reminds me of a kind of close relationship among males that many boys and men only dream about, one with comradery, intimacy, and physical affection. *Chumship* is sometimes defined as a preadolescent friendship between two same-sex friends, boys, for example. However, Whitman refers to young men who have a continued need for intimacy from other young men; they aren't boys on the cusp of their teenage years. And yet, there is a boyish quality in what he describes, a vitality and robustness associated with youthful experiences that one longs for later in life. He alludes to a soulful connection.

Analysts and psychotherapists have differing degrees of comfort with the concept of soul. Jung believed that the word *anima*, as I mentioned in Chapter 1, was a useful term for understanding a person's desire for something larger than himself, beyond his consciousness, giving him a capacity for awe and inspiration. Although skeptics and rationalists among us may dispute the existence of soul, we usually recognize its absence. The OED, for instance, defines *soulless* as referring to a person lacking in "spirit, sensitivity, and other qualities regarded as . . . human."[3] Such a person may further be described as heartless and cold.[4] Someone we think of as soulless frequently disturbs us.

William James, one of America's greatest psychologists, had no trouble writing about soul, religion, and spirituality because he viewed them all as integral parts of human experience.

That unsharable feeling which each one of us has of the pinch of his individual destiny as he privately feels it rolling out on fortune's wheel may be disparaged for its egotism, may be sneered at as unscientific, but it is the one thing that fills up the measure of our concrete actuality, and any would-be existent that should lack such a feeling, or its analogue, would be a piece of reality only half made up.[5]

James explains that experiences of soul come from feelings, in particular, those about our place in the universe and our destiny. Even if some of us choose to believe a random and probabilistic theory of reality, there still will be moments when we have doubts and wonder about alternatives that defy logical explanation. James notes that such a feeling is highly personal and is not easily communicated because it originates in certain self-centeredness. Yet, he finds this feeling to be inescapable. And he tells us that we know when it is missing – we see through it to a lack of important substance; instead, there is a reality that is insufficient at including soulful experience. James expresses kinship with Jung's "something very wonderful," and he also comes close to the poetic meaning of Whitman's "together clinging."

It is risky to conclude a book about male alienation with an appeal to soul. Scientific training was a strong component of my career path. As I review the cases in this book, however, I am struck by the idea of soulful connection that many of my patients yearned for, tried desperately sometimes to locate, and even, some of them, despaired was a cruel hoax. When a thing is noticeable by its absence, we search for ways to find it and to articulate it. Soul belongs to this area of "unsharable" feeling.

A soulless boy or man often interacts with others using what I call a *transactional attitude*. He is concerned primarily with scoring. He is emotionally dry around anything tender, and his internal world can seem sterile and empty. He typically does not even see himself as alienated, although others around him do. He explains his relationships in terms of what he has to give in order to get something greater in return. Surely, this sounds narcissistic, perhaps even schizoid or sociopathic.

One disturbing element of these transactional male relationships is a tendency to see people as commodities. Others are evaluated in terms of potential gains and their apparent worth, and the boy or man using this approach will typically avoid engagement when he believes the cost is too high to him. There are certain commercial values that can be detected as inherent to this kind of mental accounting. Accumulation – of points, money, material goods, prestige, power – is believed to be an end in itself, and a two-dimensional idea of relationships as calculated exchanges prevails. This bleak internal world reminds me of the warnings of consumerism in Erich Fromm's 1976 book *To Have or To Be*.[6] There, he describes unfettered greed and materialism as real challenges to a more soulful way of being in the modern world.

Does the saturation of cyberspace reinforce this transactional attitude? I believe there is cause for concern. The addictive potential of cyberspace is a relatively new phenomenon. We have terms like *social drinking* and *recreational drug use*, but we do not yet have a label for moderate use of the Internet because we usually do not consider it a problem in the same way. Some of the cases described in Chapter 2 and elsewhere in this book seem to indicate that cyberspace contributes to internalizing relationships as mere transactions, which is a huge problem. There is no soul to be found in the dispersed web of the Internet.

Susan McKenzie, a Jungian analyst, has grappled in her writing with Jung's concepts of anima and animus, particularly their gendered implications. She writes, "Jung's anima/animus (A/A) thinking leads us into a trap of linear orderliness, fixed identities . . . a breach in the universality of the collective unconscious. . . . Jung's A/A is a terrible fit for our time."[7] She's right. McKenzie points out that Jung's theory about anima and animus is based on a binary understanding of gender. Contemporary thinking about gender now includes a multidimensional perspective that can stretch and be fluid across what traditionally has been characterized as masculine and feminine.

Fixity in Jung's idea about the anima pertains to his assumption that it must have a feminine aspect in the male unconscious. But why would that always be so? Perhaps, for many men, this would be true – that which represents soul and relatedness would have unconscious feminine qualities. However, it does not follow that this is necessarily true for all men, because that would be, as McKenzie notes, a breach in the collective unconscious that does not really follow logical rules. The unconscious is irrational. To sidestep, therefore, the gender problem of anima, we could instead imagine that the anima occurs as an unconscious representation that might vary for boys and men and does not require a gendered prescription. Perhaps, for some of us, this anima figure might be androgynous. And for others, it might be something masculine that signifies soul and vitality.

I suggest for boys and men who are profoundly alienated, the representation of soul is to be found elsewhere in their psyches – namely, in the figure of a lost and abandoned boy. He may be their anima figure. He may represent soul in the way James discusses it, with "a pinch of individual destiny," and he may also show the same qualities of relatedness that Jung associates with his concept of anima: entanglement, sweet affection, and vulnerability.[8]

The boy in the waiting room I

Nicolas (Chapters 5 and 8) continued to talk about loss in his sessions with me. He frequently returned to memories of his childhood and said he felt that the loss of his father was more significant than he had ever realized. He remarked how he, as an adult, kept his distance from others because he often wondered how long a relationship would last and when it would inevitably end.

He began to speak about how he became a "little man" for his mother after his father left. He described a precocity that enabled him to converse with adults.

It also made him feel responsible for his mother and taking care of her. He had a fantasy that if he were not around for some reason, his mother might be in danger. Although his recollections likely contained separation anxiety, he also spoke about a role reversal: he became the one looking out for her, not her for him. This reversal in a child's development often crowds out his capacity to feel truly free as a child. When I asked Nicolas how he felt telling me these memories, he replied, "Heavy. Just awfully heavy." He expressed the burden of having an inflated sense of responsibility at a time well before he could have ever handled it. He recognized this belief sometimes made him feel guilty that he could not solve his mother's problems, or the problems of anyone he got close to.

When he was waiting one day for his session, Nicolas saw an extraverted seven-year-old boy leaving my office. This boy's mother had not yet arrived, and so he sat down in the waiting area next to Nicolas. He asked Nicolas what he was reading. Nicolas showed him an automobile magazine. The boy continued to ask him questions. What kind of car did he drive? What color was his car? And then, why do you talk to Robert? Nicolas didn't know how to respond and tried to change the subject. The boy told him that he talked to me because he sometimes felt sad. Soon, the boy's mother arrived, and they left.

Nicolas was upset when he sat down. He scowled momentarily but then looked sad himself. I asked what was going through his mind, and he told me about his conversation with the boy in the waiting room. I thought about Nicolas's initial scowl and then his sadness. I asked him what he thought about this conversation with the boy. Nicolas answered that he thought the boy was confident and wondered why he would be in therapy. I inquired whether Nicolas might have an idea about that, and he replied, "Isn't it mostly their parents? I mean, parents really do a number on children, don't they?" He said these comments more as accusations than as questions.

I observed that his conversation with this boy brought to mind ideas about parents intruding into their children's lives in hurtful ways. Nicolas nodded and said he wasn't blaming parents, because he believed they rarely could see how they unintentionally affected their children in a bad way. I remarked that he had been telling me how his father's leaving had a huge effect on his life, imposing a kind of adult responsibility on a boy that would be difficult to carry. Nicolas did not argue this point and accepted my empathy, which was a change for him.

Nicolas said he now saw that he was "walled in" to protect himself from feeling vulnerable with others. He linked this wall to the black box of his Spanish-speaking childhood (see Chapter 5). "I think that box contains my lost dreams, *mis sueños perdidos*." I noticed this was the first time Nicolas had used Spanish in a session with me, and I commented that it felt important to state this because he was getting in touch with a younger part of himself, not pushing him away. I then recalled his scowl and sadness at the beginning of the session and asked what he felt about this boy inside.

Nicolas replied that he was aware of feeling angry because of the boy's role in trying to fix adult problems. He added that the boy didn't have much opportunity to have his own dreams, and that now seemed sad. Connecting in this way with the boy inside and showing him empathy was helpful for Nicolas. Up to this point, he had been alienated from that inner boy, and when I previously drew attention to him, Nicolas had been dismissive, his responses punitive.

Surprisingly, Nicolas then asked me, "How do you switch gears?" He was curious how I might work with a seven-year-old boy and then him. I mentioned that this adult question might be coming from the boy in him, wondering if I could make enough space for them both, perhaps expecting him to be only adult with me. Although he chose not to respond, Nicolas grinned at me.

The "lost dreams," or *sueños perdidos*, in Nicolas's black box of his childhood referenced his boyhood's liveliness, vitality, and willingness to be vulnerable to others. These were deeply connected to the boy inside him, a part of his psyche that I thought of as soulful and desiring to relate to others. Recall that in one of Nicolas's early dreams, discussed in Chapter 5, he tried to shoot a young black boy who would not die: *A young black boy was chasing him with a gun and wanting Nicolas to give him something. Nicolas hit the boy, eventually pulled out a gun, and began shooting the boy who wouldn't die.*

In Chapter 5, I discussed this dream in the context of Nicolas's shadow, a part of his psyche he rejected and was alienated from. Oftentimes, good and valued parts of ourselves can be in this part of the psyche. Jung writes, "It pains our sensibilities to interpret radiant things from the shadow-side and thus in a measure trample them in the sorry dirt of their beginnings."[9] Nicolas needed to reclaim the positive within this boy he wanted to kill. The boy in his dream wanted something from Nicolas, perhaps recognition and acceptance. This dream represented a core conflict in Nicolas between an abandoning adult self – identified with his parents – and a vulnerable young boy walled up somewhere inside a box. The dream's description that he could not die perhaps illustrated that this boy signified Nicolas's soul. As Jung comments, it might be difficult to accept an idea that the soul inhabits a dark region of psyche, yet for many, that can be true.

Alienation and loss of soul

Freud's discussion of the case of Dr. Daniel Paul Schreber makes reference to the term *soul murder*, for example, when he cites Schreber's *Memoirs* in which the latter wrote of "the plot whereby my soul was to be murdered."[10] Leonard Shengold, a psychoanalyst, traces soul murder through literary examples from the 19th century and afterward, and he brings in clinical material to support his definition, which is based on overstimulation of the child that wipes out his ability to have a positive identity: "Soul, or psychic, murder involves trauma from the world outside the mind that is so overwhelming that the mental apparatus is flooded with feeling . . . The child's sense of identity is threatened."[11] Shengold mentions that other research shows that Schreber was abused by parents who crushed his will.[12]

Shengold writes that soul murder is "a crime in which the perpetrator is able to destroy the victim's capacity for feeling joy and love," and he notes it always

Figure 10.1 Lonely Boy Sitting on a Stoop, ca. 1940, Roy Perry (1911–1982)
Source: The Museum of the City of New York/ Art Resource, NY

"implies trauma."[13] He explains that victims of this crime are "left with a continuing burden of murderous rage."[14] Many of the boys and men described in this
book suffered traumatic circumstances in their childhoods that later caused them
to feel alienated from themselves and others. They frequently reported loss of
vitality, purpose, and joy in their lives as well. Boys like TJ and Jake, from Chapter 6, seem to meet this definition of soul murder, and my adult patients John, from
Chapters 1, 3, 8, and 9, and Luke, from Chapters 1, 6, 8, and 9, expressed an inner
desolation that perhaps came close to it.

But John and Luke were aware of experiencing a loss of soul and were desperate to reclaim it. The Jungian analyst Donald Kalsched, in a pair of important
books, writes about the effects of childhood trauma on the psyche and how a
"daimonic" inner figure traps positive life energies, sometimes associated with
the child ego, in a *self-care system*:[15] "The self-care system performs the self-
regulatory and inner/outer mediational functions that, under normal conditions,
are performed by the person's functioning ego."[16] This structure, however, is
largely defensive and self-traumatizing, because it both haunts a person and places

him in circumstances that repeat the original trauma as if he "were *possessed* by some diabolical power or pursued by a malignant fate."[17] Kalsched describes what other psychoanalysts might term *perverse organizations* or internal structures that deplete mental vitality and are self-destructive and anti-growth in their effects.[18] These can be difficult to address in analytic treatment because such a person's defenses are often rigid and long-standing. In Chapter 7, a young man like Tim – with his robot identification – illustrates some of the potentially life-threatening problems inherent to this kind of psychic structure.

The word *alienation* once meant derangement and insanity, and the derived word *alienist* was used for a psychiatrist or psychologist who worked with the insane.[19] Nowadays, *alienation* is more often understood as distance from others and oneself, seclusion, and loneliness. The kinds of alienation that I describe in this book with my patients who were boys and men often are accompanied by a dense barrier to entry into their inner worlds. The four categories that I list in Chapter 9 provide a continuum for how alienated someone might be. This continuum gives a sense for how impenetrable the barrier is and what therapeutic approach may be suited, at least initially, to particular patients.

Shengold's and Kalsched's ideas are useful for conceptualizing what happens to the soul when childhood trauma leads to life-sapping alienation. An addition that I offer is that we ought to consider the function of masculine identifications along with the fate of the boy inside. I believe, like James and Jung, that our experiences of soul can be powerful and numinous and that we usually struggle to find adequate words for describing them. Perhaps this struggle to find the right language is what makes these experiences so tantalizing, not quite graspable, and worthy subjects for art, poetry, and music. If someone – a boy or man in this case – is alienated, I believe he will question at some point whether he has a soul and will feel deeply troubled at not being able to answer this.

Inflexible internal beliefs about masculinity and rigid internal masculine figures, likely reinforcing one another, almost always guarantee that access to an inner world will be difficult. A state of alienation is one result for how these unbending beliefs and stark identification objects work to create barricades to all sorts of relationships. Because of the human psyche's multiplicity, there is no way to systematize either these beliefs or these masculine identifications so we can predict who will suffer greater alienation and who won't. Nonetheless, for many of these boys and men, their questions about soul will frequently be closely associated with the fate of the boy they once were within their psyche. It is as if this boy carries their soul for them. A sense that he is lost and irretrievable can feel apocalyptic.

The boy in the waiting room 2

Ben was a gay man in his early thirties when he sought my help for a panic disorder and began an analytic experience over several years with me. He was the older of two boys. His parents abruptly divorced when he was five years old, as his mother had been secretly involved with another man. She moved to another part of the country, and Ben and his brother grew up with their father. Their father traveled often and entrusted their care to various nannies that he hired until the boys were older. Ben recalled that he barely got a chance to say goodbye to his mother before she left. His father explained her departure by telling Ben that his mother liked peas and he liked corn, as though differences in which vegetables they liked to eat accounted for their split.

When Ben said that he had a "happy childhood" in one of his first sessions, I probably looked surprised because he asked about my reaction. I replied that what he had been describing did not sound happy and that I imagined it would be quite confusing and upsetting for a 5-year-old to lose his mother in this way. Looking sad, he nodded. I wondered why he had thought his childhood was happy.

Ben seemed to have taken in his parents' story about the family and made it his own, even though it mostly contradicted his experiences, memories, and feelings of that time. Gradually, Ben could separate and distinguish his story from theirs, and he found this therapeutic process helpful. He worked hard in his analysis with me, taking risks in being vulnerable in new ways to try to understand why he, almost by default, tended to suppress his own experiences in favor of those of others. It was as if his house had been taken over by squatters whom he had to work at evicting – or at least downsizing into one or two rooms. I don't want to fault Ben's parents completely here. His father and mother did the best they could, and later, Ben would learn there had been many marital conflicts leading up to his mother's decision to leave. Still, Ben had to reclaim his psyche for himself, and this mostly occurred over the first two years of our working together.

After about one year into his analysis, Ben experienced a kind of synchronicity, by which I mean an external event happened that was charged with meaning for Ben even though it came about somewhat randomly. Jung writes, "Synchronicity therefore means the simultaneous occurrence of a certain psychic state with one or more external events which appear as meaningful parallels to the momentary subjective state – and, in certain cases, vice versa."[20] He describes here a field of coincidental meanings that form at the interface between psyche and environment. In such an unanticipated field, a person occasionally discerns significant meanings because of his subjective affective state, even given that the event was completely unpredictable. For instance, once while I was parking my car in the neighborhood where my office was located, a patient rode by on his bike – not noticing me – on his way to our appointment. Somehow the check he was bringing me that day ended up wedged under one of my front tires, and I found it there. This had to have occurred through random luck, but obviously, we both were quite surprised and spent some time discussing how he interpreted this event, as well as what I had thought about it.[21] This incident occurred at a time in his analysis when he was working through his longing for a father figure who might have rescued him from childhood unhappiness.

The event that involved Ben happened in the waiting area outside my office. Before his appointment that day, I finished a session with a five-year-old boy who was seeing me because of temper tantrums. At the end of the boy's appointment, I went with him into the waiting area where his mother and Ben were sitting. I said goodbye to the boy and returned to my office.

Within a minute, I heard the boy screaming and throwing objects. I went out to the waiting area. The boy's mother seemed ill-equipped to handle her son's outbursts; she stood helplessly near the door, as if she wanted to leave without him. I felt the boy might also have recognized she had this feeling, and later, I'd learn that Ben viewed it similarly. I crouched down to the boy's level and held out my hands, asking him to put his hands in mine. He did so, and then I suggested we take three deep breaths together, which he did. I spoke slowly and indicated I wanted him to use his words to tell us why he was upset. I glanced at Ben who was watching mesmerized, but his eyes also looked glassy, as if he might have been panic stricken.

The boy told me, "She's mean, and I didn't want to go." I cued his mother to reply to him, and she spoke about their dinner plans and relatives he would see later that day. He soon calmed down, helped her to clean up the thrown things, and they left without further commotion.

Once in my office, Ben told me he was stunned by what he had seen. He found it difficult to speak about it that session, indicating he felt panicky. Because I knew I would see him again in two days, I spent the session mostly helping him to verbalize his feelings, rather than talking about any meanings or memories. It felt more important to stick close to his affective experience right then. At this point in his work with me, Ben relied on me for finding a way through his anxieties to his other feelings. He would typically take some time to identify them and often was unsure if he could even name them. With slow and steady encouragement, however, he usually could, provided he did not feel pressured. Once Ben felt contained by our relationship, he could tell me what he felt. That day, he eventually said he felt confused and upset.

In the next session, he spoke more freely about what he had seen. He said he felt nervous and unprepared today, although he added "like I'm not telling you something."

I asked him what had been on his mind before he came in.

He paused before telling me that earlier that morning he'd seen a father and son getting into a car. He thought the boy was about five or six. He continued, "For a few seconds, I felt this intense longing, and then I was jealous and envious of their relationship . . . of a loving dad."

I commented that perhaps these feelings had something to do with us. I thought here about a transference that is shaped by desire for contact with a paternal figure. For many gay men, this desire is often defined by painful memories of a father who pulled away from the son, perhaps sensing his son's sexuality developing in a different direction. Such a father may repudiate homosexuality, either consciously or unconsciously, and he may then avoid his son if he believes the son's desire for contact is part of his homosexuality. This rejection is aimed at the perceived difference in the son, and it can have a decisive – negative – impact on the boy's developmental needs for affection from his father.

Ben replied,

> Two days ago, I felt the same things in the lobby when I saw you with that boy. Longing and jealousy. If I could go back in time, I'd have my life in front of me. I might be able to trust people more easily.

He went on to mention that he had walked straight out of a gay bay he had gone into the previous week because he had felt so uncomfortable being among other gay men. He saw this as evidence for his mistrust in approaching a new situation. Ben's internalized homophobia had locked him into self-defeating behaviors around other men, such as avoidance and withdrawal. He had been working on these behaviors during the early phase of his analysis. Going into a gay bar then felt risky to him.

Ben continued to speak movingly about what he recollected from seeing me with the boy in the waiting room. He repeated that I had told the boy "use your words" and encouraged him to say how he felt. He commented, "It really touched me. I wish I'd been told that." Then, after another pause, Ben added in a quiet voice, almost a whisper, "I wish I had you at that age." When I heard this, I felt my heart go out to him, though I did not say anything about my feeling. I thought about his father and words like *irresponsible, narcissistic,* and *playboy* came to my mind. Being a child with such can parent can make the child feel even smaller to himself than he already is.

I asked what Ben recalled about himself at that age. He answered that he was shy and uncommunicative, although he went on to say that when he imagined me talking to him as a boy, he would have "laughed and had fun telling you things." He explained that he had received a different and opposite message to take care of himself and not to burden his father with demands for attention. The nannies tended to focus more on his younger brother, who was a handful behaviorally. Ben learned to shut himself down during these early years. He became compliant, which is a warning sign in child development because the inevitable messy parts of growing up appear not to have room to get played out; these are suppressed at a cost.

As Ben spoke more about this fantasy of an alternate history in which he had my attention – as his analyst for the five-year-old he once was and also as his father – he relaxed visibly. I felt compassion listening to him, and although I wondered about his idealizing me, I didn't feel that fully captured what he was depicting. Instead, I thought about his longing for male contact within these memories of childhood emotional deprivation. Tucked into his longing was a wish to claim a good-enough father, which he felt he'd been denied. Ben had a childhood filled with neglectful circumstances when he had been overlooked. Seeing me interact with the boy in the waiting room seemed to awaken in him a sense that he had also deserved better.

After this session, Ben opened up increasingly to share his inner experience with me. He reported a series of dreams in which he and I were involved in different activities together. Many of these occurred in the house he grew up in, as if he were putting me in his "house" to stake a claim to my attention and paternal care. Many of these dreams also involved his father, who seemed unaware of his boundaries. In the dreams, he often intruded into Ben's space, and Ben would become upset. His father continued to box him in, not just in his dreams. For instance, I asked Ben whether he might tell his father he was angry about something his father had done to him, and Ben said, "No, I can't. He's old now, and it might hurt him. I can't tell him. It feels too late." Ben's father had such power in his psyche that Ben struggled with standing up to him, not only in his dreams but also in reality. Ben's father seemed similar to Luke's father, whom I discuss in Chapter 8, a kind of father who puts himself ahead of his children and has to take center stage. Such a father often emotionally abandons his children even when he remains physically present.

Ben's anger at his father became prominent during this period after the waiting room incident. Seeing me with the boy spurred a growing consciousness of what he felt had been denied him. His anger was useful in separating from his parents' stories of why the family had split up, and it now allowed him to formulate his own story about it. His emerging story also made their neglect clearer to him. He went back and forth about what to do with his anger. "Why push it? If I tell him I'm pissed off, would it make any difference? It won't change his mind."

I commented on Ben's bind between loyalty to his father and mother, and the energy it consumed for him to suppress his own feelings. I also found moments to remark on the feeling of fusion between him and his father. I asked whether his father would really want Ben to be the same as he was?

Ben replied no, adding that his father would appreciate seeing him change. Ben's father had recently told him that he was worried he had passed his own troubles down to Ben.

Ben recalled how upsetting it had been when he came out as gay to his father. His father had told him "it's a phase." Ben felt his disappointment then, and he had tried to show a bit of anger by telling his father, "Whatever." He realized that his father's reaction reinforced his own internal homophobia, which had made him avoidant of other gay men. Ben's homophobia also compounded a feeling that he could not claim an identity apart from his father. To do so felt dangerous, as if one of them might die. But he was now on a path of doing just this.

Several of his dreams about the two of us had a variation on the theme of me calming him down, similar to what he had seen me do with the boy in the waiting room. Often, these dreams recalled times in his childhood when he'd been injured, overlooked, and forgotten. He sometimes worried that his newly emerging story, flush with these recollected memories, was self-centered, as if he did not have a right to author it. However, he could acknowledge that these doubts were mainly rooted in wanting to protect his parents from an emotional truth that belonged to Ben. Many patients struggle with a feeling that they should protect their parents from any questioning of accepted family history that threatens to revise it.

A few months later, Ben reported two significant dreams a week apart. The first occurred after he became aware of more resilience around his anxieties. He was surprised when a typical anxiety-inducing situation that might have escalated for him did not. He noted, "I picked myself up and didn't get blindsided." He recounted that he was now able to observe his behaviors as problems – a change for him – and he commented, for example, that he no longer wanted to isolate himself as much as he had. He said this dream was intense:

> *I came looking for you in a repair shop for cars. The mechanics were your brothers, and they were teasing you. You shoved one of them because he was trying to beat you up. I shouted, What the hell is going on here? There were a couple of boys in your office, your nephews, and they had this terrific boy energy. One of them sat on my knee while you and I talked.*

In his dream, Ben actively sought my help. He remarked that this dream, and others like it, meant, for him, that he was adapting to the idea he could have my help. This insight seemed good. He had worried previously that asking for help was wrong, and that doing so would be an imposition. To amplify Ben's perceptions of me in the dream, I inquired about my brothers, the mechanics. I had in mind that Ben was representing masculinity in a stereotypical way and putting me right in the center of it. He replied that he believed these kinds of men were homophobic. Ben knew that I was gay and had asked me early on in our work about this because he had specifically wanted to work with a gay male therapist.

I asked him to describe what he saw about my dream brothers, and he said they were "30% bigger than you, broad shouldered." He felt there was a reversal of power in the dream because my brothers were threatening me – something Ben felt could happen to him if others knew he was gay. He explained that he was speaking on my behalf by shouting out, "What the hell is going on here?" He added that he did not want to see me get hurt.

I mentioned this thought reminded me of how closely and loyally he protected his father, and perhaps he felt I needed his protection too. I was not sure of this interpretation, however, because I had another idea that Ben was trying to affiliate with me like a gay brother who would stand up against the homophobic brothers. Ben responded that he was concerned I would feel embarrassed that he was trying to help me in the dream. Based on his associations, this dream seemed to be about me as a gay man as much as it was about me as a father figure.

I then asked what he thought about me being teased and threatened by my brothers. He said, "In the dream, it would mean you had these three over-the-top butch brothers. You'd be the smallest, the odd man out, and it would have been a hard life." He continued by explaining that I'd have learned to fight for myself. "I think of you as someone who had to fight to establish yourself, and even today, you are still fighting." I felt curious hearing this, partly because there was some truth in it, although it surprised me that Ben could surmise this. Ben's perception recalls Jung's comment (that I cite in Chapter 9) that analysis is based on a field of mutual unconsciousness – that his unconscious dream life could see into me in a way I had little awareness of.

I wondered what Ben made of the image of me as a fighter. Was I worn, weary, or scarred? I remarked that he imagined me with battle wounds, and he agreed, although he admitted it was "just speculation." In a way, I liked his dream image of me because it was rough at the edges and less idealized. I also wondered what projections were tangled up in it. For example, the idea of being a fighter suggests a person who does not give up, who persists and bounces back. I realized these were all problem areas for Ben, who could collapse and retreat when things did not go his way.

Ben's dream suggested a dilemma that many gay men describe, about struggling to cope with traditional masculine norms that they often feel they do not measure up to. I asked Ben how he imagined a gay boy or young man would have coped in the dream family he described. He replied, "All the stereotypes get confirmed. Gay men are sensitive, fragile, not athletic, terrible car mechanics." Ben indicated that this masculine setting was a place where he felt his own masculine identity needed some "repair." "Is it all right to seek help?" "How does a gay man stand up for himself?" and "What happened to the boy inside me?" – these questions all felt alive and active in his dream.

In the dream, a boy sat on his knee while we talked. This picture is poignant and suggestive of Ben's predicament. He needed to reclaim this boy, and he very much hoped I knew it and could see him. At the time, I felt this dream expressed a transformation of the waiting room incident several months before. Instead of being frozen with fear, Ben was looking for me. Instead of watching me like a bystander deal with a troubled boy, the dream placed my nephew between us, so neither of us would miss him. I was literally related to this boy, and in the language of the unconscious, that made Ben able to relate to him as well (on *his* knee). This placement felt like a move in the right direction of Ben's claiming the boy inside him.

Ben's second dream, just a few days afterward, continued this theme of getting help from me, and it further expressed a variation on what he saw in the waiting room incident. *I was lying* [on the couch] *here talking to you. I realized what was the root of all my anxiety. This recognition caused me to have a seizure, a fit really. It was so forceful it felt like death. You jumped from your chair and grabbed my left wrist. You held it until the fit ended.*

The scene Ben described took place in my office. He was vulnerable and in need of help. He felt he could have died. This near-death feeling may have accurately described how agonized he had felt as an abandoned child left to figure things out on his own. This scene was a reformulation, in my mind, of how he had seen me help the boy in the waiting room months before, except now Ben had assumed the boy's place.

He commented that, in the dream, he trusted me to help him with a feeling he said was "awful." I asked what came to his mind about this feeling, and he replied, "Something super-traumatic . . . when I woke I could still feel the adrenalin rush."

I wondered if Ben could look at that feeling and tell me what he saw now. Visualization of emotional reactions can be a helpful technique with boys and men – although it holds for girls and women too. Visualizing allows something to be first seen and then get described. Therefore, it introduces a mediating step to directly answering, "How did that make you feel?"

Ben closed his eyes and reflected for a bit. Then, he said, "I see my left wrist. It was very specific. My left. My left side. . . . left." He seemed sad at this moment. I remarked that "left" made me think about being left, about someone leaving and not being there for him. He cried a little. We were silent for a while until he said that the dream showed him that "My body has held on to that for so long, being left alone, when she [mother] left me and he [father] couldn't be there for me. He left a lot too." The last comment was a reference to his father's long business trips when Ben had to stay with relatives.

Ben's interpretation about his body holding a traumatic memory felt spot-on to me. The dream may have symbolized his pain, making it more understandable for him. Ben had long had many somatic issues with muscle pains. This dream made an awful feeling accessible, one that connected to Ben's childhood abandonment and neglect. To a young child, such experiences can feel deadly – apocalyptic when the child's world crumbles, and no one appears to take action to help. For Ben, this had meant he had to rely on himself in a way that encapsulated his emotional life and buried it.

He commented that this dream reminded him of a tendency to avoid feelings, although it suggested, too, that he could trust me if he let go of his near-constant attempts to control his feelings. He expressed the risk as a fear that I would leave as well and he would be left alone to die. I mentioned he had already had this experience of his mother leaving and feeling his world come apart. He nodded and continued, "That convulsed my world. Like in the dream too." His voice trailed off, and I asked if he could try to say more about what was going through his mind right then. Ben often struggled at these moments – I suspected he shut down emotionally – and would then change the subject if I did not persist in encouraging him to go more deeply.

He sighed and then replied that in the dream he felt "something awful like death was reaching inside me and pulling my soul out. I'd be like a zombie, just wandering around, no soul, no spark." Ben surprised me with these comments, because I had imagined he might say more about his mother's leaving. Instead, he connected the left boy inside him with a terror of loss of soul. He, too, affirmed that this boy inside carried that for him, and he was frightened that if this boy was unreachable, his soul would be gone. In many ways, Ben felt this had already happened. However, his work in analysis helped him to discover that this boy still lived and did have a spark in him. He was waiting for Ben to claim him.

Ben found his dream to be hopeful. He said, "I didn't die in the dream." He thought that what saved him was our work together and his belief that he had learned to trust me. Although he expressed some idealization of me in this discussion – that I could rescue him as he believed I had the boy having the fit in the waiting room – I was reminded of a psychological dilemma for many children who have been abandoned by a parent. They may develop an internal sense that they cannot rely on anyone. As a result, they may miss out on idealizing childhood figures. This process is both natural and important because idealization is a stepping stone on the road to internalizing figures who inspire and become useful inner resources as children mature.

Trauma is defined, in part, by the circumstance that it is not supposed to happen – it is neither expected nor predictable. When children are exposed to traumatic events, many show surprising resilience. A crucial factor is how do the adults around them respond? Do they pretend nothing has happened, like in Ben's family? Do they rush to cover it up? Or do they engage in some meaningful conversation while communicating that the family can get through hard times? Ben seemed to convey that he had not had an opportunity to sustainably idealize his father or his mother. His childhood wishes were upended when his parents separated so confusingly. His idealization of me seemed, in part, to repair an interrupted developmental process that gave his adult self hope, while reclaiming the lost boy inside.

The fate of the boy in boys and adolescents

I suggest that this internal figure of the boy has much to do with identity that forms throughout male adolescence and into adulthood. Early therapeutic intervention can help many boys in need feel more secure about the boy they are becoming. It is critical for them to develop a more open house/self that tolerates expression of feelings. A risk is their building a boarded-up house, as in category 1 described in Chapter 9, when a boy has a problem even identifying a feeling and realizing it is there. Such a condition seems a sure course moving toward adolescent statements of "I'm broken." Adolescents usually begin to form more conscious understandings of their identities. For some, this process is not smooth when questions about masculinity, sexuality, and emotional expression get tangled in defensive withdrawal and avoidance, as many of the cases in this book illustrate. Often, these young men articulate that their sense of brokenness did not arise in their adolescence, but earlier.

Alex, whom I discussed in Chapter 7, came in for his session and wanted to discuss birth control. He was now nineteen years old. He told me he was confused about whether his girlfriend, who was taking a birth control pill, could become pregnant if "she forgot to take it." He told me he was worried she could because he was not using condoms during sex and she had not taken the pill for several days. I thought it important to provide some factual information to Alex; his concern was legitimate, the short answer to his question being yes.[22]

I realized, in addition, that this was important for us to think about together, so I asked Alex to tell me more about his worry. He said that he could not "cope with her getting pregnant. I'd want her to get an abortion, but what if she didn't want to?" Alex was quite anxious, and I commented that he seemed even more worried now that we were talking about this. He paused to stare out the window. When he turned to look at me, he said, "I don't want children. Never."

Because of Alex's abusive background, I thought I understood some of why he would say this, but I was surprised nonetheless. I asked him to explain, and he related it to what he had suffered as a child. He expressed a fear that bringing a child into such a potentially cruel world was something he did not want to risk himself being a part of as a parent. I wondered if there was anything else in his mind that made him sound so firm about it. Alex gave me a small smile and said, "You know, Rob, I've got this kid inside me, and it takes a hella energy to keep an eye on him."

We spoke some about this kid, and Alex's insight struck me as mature and even wise. Alex thought that his awareness of his inner "kid" required attention and responsibility. He believed that neglect of this part of himself might mean trouble, and he was probably correct. This "kid" had nearly suffered what Shengold or Kalsched might call soul murder, but somehow he survived, and Alex considered it essential to stay in touch with him.

James writes that there are two ways of looking at life: "characteristic of what we call the healthy-minded, who need to be born only once, and of the sick souls, who must be twice born in order to be happy."[23] The healthy-minded adapt and fit in easily; the sick souls, however, traverse a much different terrain of feeling far out of balance and incomplete. These individuals have to engage in a psychological process, in James's view, to find an inner route to some sense of unity, or what Erikson might term *cohesion*. Part of this rebirth, a familiar Jungian concept, for the boys and men that I present in this book frequently involves them finding and then, as Alex put it, "keeping an eye on" the boy inside. For them, this endeavor, which is basically a psychological one, constitutes reclaiming soul and a vital spark.

Social implications

What becomes of a society that allows for the disavowal of this boy inside? Most of this book discusses the individual psychological consequences of alienated states that lead to addictive, destructive, and self-destructive behaviors. We live during extremely alienated times befitting apocalyptic imagery and doomsday predictions. Many social and political analyses of Brexit in the United Kingdom and the election of Donald Trump in the United States refer to alienated voters who have turned against their governing parties. What might these cultural shifts represent at a collective level?

There is, perhaps, an archetypal activation in the collective unconscious from having passed a millennial date that rivets our survival instincts to consider a question of time, namely, how much longer does humankind have? This temporal fascination begets end-of-time scenarios, apocalypse, and final reckoning. I am not a historian by training, but during my college education, I thought about studying art restoration and took art history courses. There occurs within the scope of art history a sense of reaching for the beyond at critical moments in human history.[24] In Chapter 6, I mentioned that Dürer's *Four Horsemen* appeared just before one of these dates (the year 1500). And the decades after 1000 brought on "a growing spirit of religious enthusiasm," with an increase in church building of Romanesque style reaching heavenward.[25]

The social alienation of the years following the year 2000 are linked to economic upheavals coming in the wake of the concentration of wealth among fewer people, automation, and the prominence of cyberspace. Unlike in 1000 or 1500, however, there is no unifying spiritual tradition holding us together as we contemplate these questions: what is next and how much longer? Instead, religious fanatics, primarily young men, now terrorize local populations by driving trucks into crowds, as they have in Berlin, Nice, London, Stockholm, and New York. It is as if we have apocalyptic imagery thrust at us without much solace of soul being preserved for the collective consciousness. Additionally, mass shootings occur so frequently in the United States that we can scarcely keep track of the last one, because they come at a gallop like one of Dürer's horses.

In the United States, this social alienation currently takes a lethal toll through an opioid epidemic. *The Economist* cites a University of Pittsburgh study that predicts prescription opioid deaths of 20,000 annually by 2022 and heroin and fentanyl deaths of over 70,000 by 2025.[26] This ongoing tragedy highlights the desperation of people seeing no future and finding grim answers to the questions, what next and how much longer? As I discuss in Chapter 7, this phenomenon seems to be the territory of Revelation's pale rider bringing death, but it is likewise a territory where there is no soul to be felt or found any more, only despair.

Economic changes since 2000 could be signified metaphorically through Revelation's other riders of the apocalypse: the black horse with its rider's scales measuring greed and injustice, standing for the concentration of wealth along with increasing inequality; the white horse with its rider's crown showing triumph over human limits, representing the march of automation; and the red horse with its rider's sword for war, illustrating the unstoppable advance of cyberspace into all human affairs. These seem like cosmic forces dwarfing us. We feel powerless against them, especially when we see the suffering they can cause. Perhaps a relative loses a job that is now automated; or savings and housing are wiped out, as they were for many in 2007–08; or someone we know is a victim of identity theft. Such incidents, multiplied greatly throughout a society, represent massive waves trampling us like Dürer's horsemen.

A social rebirth of some kind is necessary. I hear in my practice and from colleagues that there is a desire for this renewal in our society among our patients and among our circles of family and friends. The Reformation started 500 years ago, in part to respond to the alienation and stagnation of that time after passing a millennial date (1500). How are we, at a level of community and society, to find relief for our "sick souls" in need of becoming "twice born," to borrow James's language? I expect that this answer will appear from someplace quite unexpected, coming a bit like Martin Luther's ninety-five theses that provoked widespread